Masterpieces of Tapestry

This catalogue has been made possible
through the assistance of
the National Endowment for the Humanities

Masterpieces of Tapestry

From the Fourteenth to the Sixteenth Century

Foreword by Thomas Hoving

Introduction by Francis Salet
Conservateur en Chef, Musée de Cluny, Paris

Catalogue by Geneviève Souchal
Conservateur, Musée de Cluny, Paris

An Exhibition at The Metropolitan Museum of Art

Translated by Richard A. H. Oxby

Designed by Bruno Pfäffli
(Atelier Frutiger & Pfäffli), Paris

Photo-engraving by Les Fils de Victor-Michel, Paris

Type set by Bussière arts graphiques, Paris

Printed by Imprimerie Moderne du Lion, Paris

Sources of photographs :
A.C.L. Brussels
Archives Photographiques, Paris (Joubert, Gourbeix)
The Cleveland Museum of Art
The Detroit Institute of Arts
Bill Finney, Concord, N.H.
Graphic-Photo, Paris
Hermitage Museum, Leningrad
Honolulu Academy of Arts
Frank Kelly, Manchester, N.H.
The Metropolitan Museum of Art
M.H. de Young Memorial Museum, San Francisco
Micro Photo, Lyon
Musée des Arts Décoratifs, Paris
Museo Civico, Padua
Musée de Dijon
Museum of Fine Arts, Boston
Musée Lyonnais des Arts Décoratifs
National Gallery of Art, Washington
Réunion des Musées Nationaux, Paris
Rijksmuseum, Amsterdam
Sörvik, Göteborg
Studio Sallis, Narbonne
The Toledo Museum of Art
Wallerval, Valenciennes
Walters Art Gallery, Baltimore
Worcester Art Museum

French text ©Éditions des Musées Nationaux,
Paris, 1973

Library of Congress Cataloging in Publication Data

Geneviève Souchal,
Masterpieces of tapestry from the fourteenth
to the sixteenth century.

Translation of "Chefs-d'œuvre de la tapisserie
du XIVe au XVIe siècle."
The New York version of an exhibition shown at
the Grand Palais, Paris, Oct. 26, 1973-Jan. 7, 1974.
Includes bibliographies.
1. Tapestry, Gothic-Exhibitions. 2. Tapestry,
Renaissance-Exhibitions. I. New York (City).
Metropolitan Museum of Art. II. Paris.
Grand Palais. III. Title.

NK3005.S6813   746.3'94   73-20007
ISBN 0-87099-086-1

Contents

Foreword

These days, with the impression existing that the great international art exhibition is passé, the present effort may seem something of an anomaly. Certainly it offers all the characteristics of the supposedly doomed species : splendid loans from all over Europe and the United States, impressive quality throughout, interest for scholars and the general public alike, a distinguished catalogue, focus on a specific moment in the history of art, and, finally, the unstated thought that no one is likely ever to see these particular works together again. Despite appearances, however, this exhibition is less a traditional international loan show than it is wholly new endeavor. For it is one of the fruits of a partnership worked out a little over a year ago between the Metropolitan Museum and the Réunion des Musées Nationaux of France, including the Louvre.

The partnership came into being as the result of a deep mutual friendship on the part of the professional staffs of both organizations and the recognition that certain museological activities of vital concern to both — great exhibitions, publications related to them, staffing, and even acquisitions of objects — could no longer be handled solo. From this conviction there came a pooling of resources, funds, and powers of persuasion.

The present exhibition is one of a series of five worked out in the partnership. The others are : *Nineteenth-Century French Drawings from The Metropolitan Museum of Art*, which closed at the Louvre last month and is now on view here; *Italian Renaissance Drawings from the Louvre*, to be shown at the Metropolitan in October; *Impressionism*, which will include some forty-five of the greatest paintings in the style and will be seen at the Louvre in September and here in December; and finally, *French Painting from David to Delacroix*, which is planned to open in Paris in the winter of 1974, followed by showings at the Detroit Institute of Art in the spring of 1975 and the Metropolitan in the summer.

Following its appearance at the Grand Palais in Paris, *Masterpieces of Tapestry* is presented in New York in association with and under the patronage of the National Endowment for the Humanities, and the National Endowment for the Arts, and under the sponsorship of Mr. and Mrs. Ben Heller of New York City. Without the extraordinary aid of the two Endowments and the enlightened generosity of these two art-loving private patrons the exhibition simply would not have been possible here.

As one contemplates such treasures as the enormous tapestry from the *Apocalypse* series at Angers, the incomparable six pieces of the *Lady with the Unicorn* from the Cluny Museum (shown for the first — and probably last — time with The Cloisters' *Hunt of the Unicorn* set), the four wonderful pieces lent us by the Hermitage in Leningrad, the pieces from the Cluny Museum of the *David and Bathsheba* set, and the famed *Winged Stags* from the Cathedral of Rouen, it may be worthwhile to note what tapestries themselves are in the broad perspective of history. As early as art is recorded we are aware of man's urge to transform interior walls from simple, mute surfaces into panoramas of triumph, acts of faith, or modes of decorative splendor. From the walls of Lascaux and Altamira to Thera, to the painted stoas of the Acropolis, to the Clubhouse of the Cnidians at Delphi, where Polygnotos' scenes of the underworld could once be seen, to the palace of the Macedonian kings at Pella, to Pompeii and Herculaneum and Boscoreale, to Bury St. Edmunds and palaces and castles of the Middle Ages — and indeed even into our own day — man has destroyed the bleak immutability of walls with special artifices, tapestries being not the least of these in more recent times. Because of tapestry's imperviousness to cold and damp, it was in a sense northern Europe's answer to the fresco of southern lands.

Tapestries are best seen as we display them here : in somewhat subdued illumination and in superabundance. They then absorb every iota of the light available and grasp every inch of the wall on which they are placed. The wall is driven from our memory as the full expanse of the picture bursts upon us through the planar limits of its space. Among its other achievements, we hope that our exhibition demonstrates this artistic dialectic of destruction and enhancement.

Even with the sponsorship and patronage already mentioned, this exhibition could not have become a reality in New York without the generosity of the many lenders to it. Here we thank them en bloc; the institutions and private lenders who have so graciously let us display their treasures are identified in the individual catalogue headings. Beyond this acknowledgment our special thanks go to our colleagues at the French Ministry of Culture and at the Louvre, for they have done the lion's share of the work : M. Jacques Duhamel, former Minister of Culture; M. Maurice Druon, Minister of Culture; M. Jean Chatelain, Directeur des Musées de France; M. Hubert Landais, Inspecteur Général des Musées, Adjoint au Directeur; M. Francis Salet, Conservateur en chef of the Cluny Museum; Madame Geneviève Souchal, Conservateur of the Cluny Museum, and the Exhibition Department of the Louvre.

T.H.
February 1974

An exhibition such as this one provides an opportunity for us to update our knowledge of medieval tapestry. The study of this subject, unlike that of architecture, sculpture, or painting, is not one that has preoccupied the principal art historians. Yet a great deal of first-class work was done in the 19th and early 20th centuries : Müntz, Guiffrey, Wauters, Pinchart, and others published archival documents and traced the outline of a long and illustrious history, laying solid foundations for a discipline that was new at the time. Nor has it been completely neglected since : studies on the outputs of Arras, Tournai, and Brussels have enriched our knowledge. It must be recognized, however, that since World War I most of the published studies have done no more than traverse old ground, or make doctrine out of what was only working hypothesis — such as the theory of the traveling ateliers on the banks of the Loire for the millefleurs tapestries of the 1500s — or even replace truth with error — as in attributing the Burgundian armorial verdure of the Berne Museum to Charles the Bold when Pinchard in 1865 and Stammler in 1889, who had published all the documents, had accurately recognized on it the device of Philip the Good. Even worse, the history has been distorted by nationalistic prejudice in favor of royal France or the Burgundian Netherlands, and what may be described as a municipal bias — between, for example, Paris and Arras, or Arras, Tournai, and Brussels.

Assertions of this kind make little sense. Except for the often difficult decisions as to whether a work is high-warp or low-warp, only the archival documents, not the study of the works themselves, can inform us about the output of a given production center. This, anyway, is a subject more related to economic history than to art history.

To attribute, by an analysis of style or technique, a given tapestry to Tournai is to imply that there is a recognizable Tournai style or technique. This takes us into very deep water when we consider that there were looms in all the towns of the Burgundian Netherlands and even, no doubt, in certain of the villages (which explains the extraordinary speed with which enormous series were produced in the Middle Ages : they were clearly distributed among large numbers of workers), that the weavers moved freely from one center to another, taking with them their skills and habits, and that the painters and makers of cartoons were no more sedentary than other artists. Tapestry creation did not take place uniquely within the confines of a given city : it was a citizen of Arras, Baudouin de Bailleul, who designed the tapestry of the *Golden Fleece* (now lost) for Philip the Good, who had it woven in Tournai under the supervision of two master artisans established there, after he had approved the sketches or cartoons he had ordered from Bruges. In

1456 the magistrates of Arras protested that the weavers were leaving "to dwell in other cities such as Valenciennes, Tournai, Bergues, and others." The historian may speculate on the reasons for this exodus, but it well illustrates the mobility of the artisans and the consequent diffusion of techniques throughout the Low Countries. It follows that to try to decide where a work was woven is a fairly fruitless and usually pointless task. No specialist tries to assign a 16th-century tapestry to the ateliers of Louvain, which were both active and highly thought of, or to those of Lille, which worked for the Médicis, or of Enghien, Audenarde, Ghent, Malines, Middelburg, or Valenciennes. The Salins *St. Anatole* is known to come from Bruges only because there is a document clearly stating this. As for Brussels, we know the names of some 500 weavers who worked there under Philip the Good, yet formerly only the *Justice of Trajan and Herkinbald* in Berne, with which is associated the illustrious name of Van der Weyden, was reluctantly and after some argument attributed to them. Recent opinion may perhaps have weighed too heavily in favor of this city; but it seems reasonable to suppose that such an abundant production, which must have included storied tapestries, could not have completely disappeared while that of Tournai seems to have been largely preserved.

On the other hand, works have been convincingly attributed to Tournai, and the process continues, largely because numerous purchases are known to have been made there by Duke Philip and Duke Charles from Pasquier Grenier. But it seems that the activities of this important individual have been somewhat misunderstood. It is not certain that Grenier was a tapestry maker, and the title *marchetier* (low-warp weaver?), which he held in 1449, is not precise and may not apply to the rest of his career. He owned considerable property, and when he died he bequeathed cartoons rather than looms or stocks of wool. Pasquier Grenier had clearly become a big-time merchant — he dealt in wine, which in the Netherlands implied import-export activities, as well as in tapestries — and he was capable of generating orders from rich connoisseurs in the princely courts, of organizing, possibly on a large scale, the import of raw materials like wool, silk, gold, and silver, of commissioning and stocking cartoons, and judging from the number of tapestries he supplied, of distributing enormous quantities of work among ateliers that were not all located within the walls of Tournai; he could wait for payment, which was often slow to come in, with the help of bank loans and his own capital; and he could arrange for the export of his goods through the big international ports of Bruges and Antwerp. We know that he delivered to his customers sumptuous storied series like the *Alexander* (1459), the *Passion* (1461), the *Story of Esther* (1462), the *Swan Knight* (also 1462), and the *Trojan War* (1472), and also modest verdures with shepherds, peasants, or woodmen. It is hardly surprising his name appears so often in the documents. However, this does not necessarily mean that he took the slightest part in developing a style.

Much the same probably applies to men like Dine Raponde, Jean Arnolfinfi, and later Richard Danis and the "marchant de tapisseries" Michel Lottin in Bruges, and in Tournai to Philippe Scellier, who at the end of the century supplied cartoons to a weaver in Brussels and another in Audenarde. Such activities clearly contributed to the spreading of a uniform style throughout the Low Countries, and this makes absurd a history of tapestry based on appreciations of style that try to differentiate the manners of the various centers. All the more so since the Northern tapestry weavers spread out all over the Continent. We know that ateliers were started in Italy, and that most of them had a precarious existence. One in Ferrara, however, kept going for more than a century with "Flemings" like Jacomo di Flandria and Pietro di Andrea, and Mille and Rinaldo Grue from Tournai. In Siena, Jacquet, the son of Benoît of Arras, wove more than 40 pieces from 1442 onward, including a *Story of St. Peter* for Pope Nicolas V. Has none of this work survived, limited though it was? Could the Metropolitan Museum's *Annunciation*, in whose architectural elements there seem to be marble inlays in the Cosmati style, have been woven in Italy?

Let us now turn to Arras, whose output preceded that of Tournai, which itself did not appear in any quantity before 1443. The tapestry industry of the Artois district may have owed its origin to its Countess Mahaut at the very beginning of the 14th century — she was making purchases in Arras in 1311 and 1313 — and it was developed by Philip the Bold even before he inherited the province from his brother-in-law Louis de Male. In 1371 Philip distributed 60 sous to "several tapestry-weaver varlets dwelling in Arras" whose ateliers he had visited. This industry acquired a considerable reputation, which has not doubt led to historical error : any early 15th-century tapestry is likely to be described in our time as being from Arras, and experts tend to identify this origin by details such as little clouds in parallel lines and jagged foliage that seems to shiver and vibrate on the surface of the work. But on what are such affirmations actually based? The only documented work, the tapestry in Tournai Cathedral, woven in Arras in 1402, shows few of these details, and in any case, fashion does not take long to generalize such decorative features in a given period. Great as was the output of the Arras ateliers, as proven by many documentary mentions, they were already meeting competition : tapestries had been made in Brussels since the 14th century, and the list of master artisans, guild members, and apprentices registered in that city between 1417 and 1466 is of considerable length. Were the *legwerkers* of Brussels, back in 1404 and 1406, low-warp weavers? Whether or no, their output was abundant, and their tapestries were not necessarily different from those of Arras; some may have been preserved that we are not able to recognize as such. In the collection kept by Jean de Saint-Pol, Duke of Brabant, in his palace at Coudenburg — he lent some in 1415 to his uncle John the Fearless — there must have been some works from Brussels ateliers.

Nor should it be forgotten that the Arras output, though it declined in the middle of the century, did not completely cease even after the town was taken by Louis XI in 1477. For years it continued side by side with the work we attribute to Tournai, and there is no reason why it should have been any different from Tournai work. In 1447 Philip the Good acquired from Guillaume au Vaissel, an Arras merchant, a tapestry of a green arbor with children at school, and to complement this he bought similar pieces in Tournai.

It is nevertheless certain that Tournai overtook Arras, and we may speculate on why Philip the Good took his patronage away from his own fief in Artois to give it to an ecclesiastical principality that, though enclaved in his land, probably did not come under his authority. This is a question for the historians, if they wish to try to answer it. However, the Arras tapestry industry in the time of Philip the Bold was organized in much the same way as was that of Tournai seventy years later. We know now that Hugues Walois and Jean Cosset combined the sale of wine with that of tapestry. When we read in the documents that this Jean Cosset, "valet de chambre" to the Duke of Burgundy, was able to supply one or more tapestries every year for over twenty years, we must conclude that they did not all come from his own ateliers, and that this great merchant farmed out his orders. But he was capable of arranging, on the duke's order, for an atelier to be set up in the château of Hesdin to weave a series of *Twelve Peers of France* on the spot. Did this considerable organization break up under Philip the Good? If so, why? Did the Arras weavers cling to the high-warp technique at a time when low-warp weaving had already long been practised and its advantages over the high-warp were recognized in Brussels and no doubt also at Tournai and elsewhere?

The technical experts have given little attention to problems of manufacture such as this, and have not critically examined enough works; nor have they fully explained or given a satisfactory etymology to the expressions *mar-*

cheteur, tapisserie de marche, à la marche, and *de marcheterie.* Though the word *marche* (step or treadle) seems to appear in numerous documents in opposition to "high-warp", there is doubt that it always means the treadle of the horizontal loom. It is equally doubtful whether Jean Peliche, for example, described as a "marcheteur de Puy en Auvergne", was a low-warp weaver; he seems more likely to have been an intermediary, since in 1449 we find him complaining of having received from Pasquier Grenier certain tapestries that were not "de la fine estoffe que estre doivent" (of the fine stuff they should be). Thus, the appearance in the Northern ateliers of a new weaving process is shrouded in obscurity. To clarify this it would be necessary to collate and examine all the documents that appear to relate to low-warp weaving.

There remain the problems of the Paris ateliers, no doubt the oldest in Western Europe, since they are mentioned as early as 1303. Little progress has been made here; so far, most of the work on the subject amounts to a repetition of what we know of Nicolas Bataille. It seems that this "varlet de chambre" of the Duke of Anjou was personally responsible for the weaving of the Angers *Apocalypse* and of some other tapestries the duke ordered from him, but that he soon became an important merchant, in a position to supply the Court with an incredible number of tapestries that he certainly did not make entirely on his own looms. In a single year, 1395, he supplied five different tapestries to the Duke of Burgundy alone. Furthermore he also sold, in 1393 for example, tapestries described as "d'œuvre d'Arras" (of Arras workmanship). The same is true of Jacques Dourdin, who in 1387-88 was paid for "high-warp cloths made in Arras weave," and of Pierre de Beaumetz who in 1388 supplied Philip the Bold with tapestries measured in Arras *aunes,* as was the *Passion* sold by the Parisian Jean Lubin to the duke in the same year. Documentary mentions of measures in the Arras aune (about 33 1/2 inches) or the Paris aune (about 47 inches) certainly give us important indications as to the origin of a given series; still, careful research must be applied to such questions. It is clear, however, that the famous *Battle of Roosebecke,* completed in five years by the Arras weaver Michel Bernard, was measured in Arras aunes (56 aunes) — since even by the smaller measure it was over 127 feet long, an exceptional length for a single piece. In Paris aunes it would have been more than 216 feet long. But people like Jacques Dourdin, who worked intensively and with impressive regularity from 1386 to 1395, Pierre de Beaumetz, whose only customer was the Duke Philip the Bold, Jean Lubin, and other tapestry weavers in Paris — Simonnet des Champs, Jean Pignie, Guillaume Mulot, and especially Robert Pinçon, who made an *Apocalypse* in 1391 — have almost been forgotten, while Nicolas Bataille, who is lucky enough to have had one of his works survive, is well known.

It has been said that the civil war and then the English occupation in 1420 ruined the Paris tapestry industry, but an end so sudden and definite merits examination; by 1421 there were only two weavers in the capital. In 1423 there were three, including one woman; in 1438, none. Paradoxically, other luxury crafts, that of the goldsmiths, for example, continued to support large numbers of workers. Perhaps John the Fearless, who ruled the city for a time, or Henry V and the Duke of Bedford, who were allies of Philip the Good, deliberately set out to destroy all possibility of competition with the Northern ateliers.

Thus, even with regard to how production of one of the most extraordinary economic and artistic phenomena of the Middle Ages was organized, there remains much for the tapestry historian to search for and, we hope, to find in the documents. But these are not the only, or even the real, problems.

One must speculate on the ultimate purpose of such a copious output. For quite clearly none of the princely homes could find room on its walls for tapestry sets of some ten pieces, each of which was frequently over 16 feet high and 33 feet long. Only the "choir tapestries" of the late 15th century were woven to the dimensions of the sanctuaries they were to occupy. This was not the case, in the 14th century, of the Duke of Anjou's *Apocalypse*, later hung in Angers Cathedral, which in the 19th century could hardly accommodate it, despite the fact that the tapestry was then incomplete. Nor was it the case of the *Story of Gideon*, made for the ceremonies of the Order of the Golden Fleece; the dimensions of the churches where these ceremonies were celebrated in no way matched its 330 feet of length. We know that the tapestry was not hung in Notre-Dame de Bruges for the ceremonies held in 1468. Even less could it have fitted into the small rooms in which the Duke of Anjou presided over the chapter of the Order.

The collections acquired by the kings and princes were simply too large for current use. Philip the Bold left seventy-five tapestries when he died, and even so the inventory was incomplete. His brother Duke John of Berry had twenty-eight at Bourges and Mehun-sur-Yère. Henry VIII of England owned an enormous number. Francis I had more than two hundred tapestries in his store of furnishings at Paris. We know from a famous miniature from the *Très Riches Heures* of the Duke of Berry more or less how these pieces were displayed : folded, wrapped around a chimney breast, perhaps even cut. They were taken from one residence to another, and even on campaign, which is really quite surprising. Charles V, the Holy Roman Emperor, lost the *History of King Clovis,* which he had inherited from his Burgundian ancestors, at the siege of Metz. For what tent or overnight shelter could he have needed a tapestry set whose six pieces must have stretched out over some 200 feet!

Most of these works were left in storage. Philip the Good had a vaulted hall built in his house in Arras "to place and keep safely in for his pleasure his said tapestry". Six guards and twelve servants were assigned to this service, not counting the menders who repaired tapestries damaged by the frequent moves.

Even more than for decorating walls and combating cold, tapestries found use as a medium for capital investment. It was for pressing economic reasons that the Dukes of Burgundy and their Hapsburg successors encouraged tapestry weaving in their Northern states, to replace the cloth manufacture that had been hit by English competition. It was just as much in the interests of these princes to absorb as much as possible of this output, and to make it known to anyone who could be useful. No gift, incidentally, was more prized by people who were not close to the source of this original and sumptuous art: after the disaster of Nicopolis in 1396, Philip the Bold offered tapestries to Bazajet, who replied to his ambassadors that he would "take great pleasure to see high-warp cloths woven at Arras... for cloths in gold and silver the King possessed in fair quantities." Such gifts frequently served diplomatic and political ends. In 1393, the tapestries given to Richard II of England and the Dukes of York, Lancaster, and Gloucester may have had some part in the signature of a Franco-English truce that lasted twenty-eight years, guaranteed by the marriage of Richard to Isabelle of France. Similarly, in 1411 and 1416 John the Fearless sought to ally himself with the English party by gifts of tapestries. When, in 1472, the magistrates of the district of Bruges bought the *Trojan War* from Pasquier Grenier as a gift for their much-feared master, Charles the Bold, there was certainly a political element in their gesture. But frequently, generosity was the only motive for such gifts: it often happened that a prince would order a tapestry for no other reason than to give it to his king. As a gift to Pope Clement VII, who had come from Italy to celebrate the marriage of Prince Henry to Catherine de Médicis, Francis I got out of his store "a great rich piece of tapestry" — the *Last Supper* after Leonardo da Vinci. It is still preserved in the Vatican.

As a medium for investment and a stimulus for economic activity, tapestry was by no means a negligible economic weapon; it was also, along with gold plate, a tangible sign of the rank, wealth, and consequently, power of a prince. Tapestries were regularly hung in the streets (with consequent damage from sun or rain) whenever great festivities united the townspeople around their lord, as for the marriage of Charles the Bold at Bruges in 1468. When Philip the Good returned to Paris in 1461 for the coronation of Louis XI, he sought successfully to dazzle the onlookers, not so much by an exhibition of his rich tapestries as by their very number, for in his house, the hôtel d'Artois, "there was such a multitude of them that he had them hung over one another."

Among the problems that demand the tapestry historian's attention, those of technique deserve to be studied with more care than they formerly received. The timely publication by the staff of the Inventaire Général (an organization set up to classify French works of art) of a "Livret de Prescriptions" fills a gap in our knowledge and supplies invaluable information for the student. No tapestry monograph can be considered authoritative unless it includes a minute examination of the back — which today is usually concealed by a canvas reinforcement. It is there, rather than on the front, that the repairs, alterations, and additions no ancient tapestry is without can be seen. Naturally, we do not claim to have examined this closely the works assembled here. At least we have tried to obtain as many pieces as possible in gold thread, a detail to which much importance was attached in the past : "tapis à or," "rehaussé d'or," or, on the other hand, "sans or" is almost always specified in the accounts and inventories. Few pieces of this kind survive in France. The crime against culture of 1797, which resulted in the burning of most of the royal works to recover the precious metal, deprived that country of its most valuable works, leaving most people under the impression that tapestry was worked purely in wool. However, what is preserved in French museums is mostly routine work. In the texts, many of the orders from the princes stipulate the use of silk and silver or gold thread, which always justified prices very much higher than the average. The *Story of Gideon,* described as "the richest on earth at this time," was woven entirely in gold and silk. Such sumptuous tastes carried on into the 16th century, and it is from this period that date the marvelous gold-thread tapestries that have survived outside France. None remain in France of those belonging to Francis I, but his deeds and inventory show how many pieces enhanced with gold, silver, and silk he had acquired, mostly in Antwerp from Brussels ateliers. We invite the visitor to examine the tapestries shown here with this in mind. Admire the brilliance they derive from the gold and silver threads woven into them. This was even greater at the time of their creation.

The purely artistic problems of the tapestries of the Middle Ages and the Renaissance are mostly in the area of iconography. It is not always easy to identify the subjects. Our catalogue at least includes some new details and rectifications of importance. But there are general questions that have not been dealt with. How and by whom were the subjects chosen? It is clear that the pastoral scenes and verdures were not usually woven to order, but were done in series and stocked to await a purchase. But this was not the case with the great storied series. It is probable that the Duke of Anjou imposed the theme of the *Apocalypse* on Hennequin of Bruges, and that this enormous Angers tapestry series had a determinating influence, for it appears that nothing of the kind had been done before. We are also sure that the choir tapestries of the 1500s were designed to honor the patron of a great church — St. Peter at Beauvais, St. Stephen at Auxerre, Sts. Gervais and Protais at Le Mans; these were specifically planned works. There is sometimes doubt in the case of secular tapestries, though it is known that the *Battle of Roosebecke,* for Philip the Bold, and the *Battle of Liège,* for John the Fearless, were ordered expressly to commemorate recent events. When in 1388 Duke Philip gave his wife, Marguerite of Flanders, a *Life of St. Marguerite,* it is probable that he had it made for her; it was no doubt the same when John the Fearless in 1412 gave a *Handing of Fleurs-de-lys to Clovis* to the Dauphin Louis de Guyenne. But in other cases we may only surmise, and with some caution. Is there a political allusion in the *Story of King Clovis* — the coronation of Clovis as King of France, the defeat of Gondebaud, King of Burgundy, and the renewal of the alliance between the two princes? Was this a gift from Charles VII to Philip the Good after Philip's reacceptance of the Capetian allegiance? Or was it an order from Philip himself to mark his reaffirmed fidelity? It is widely agreed that the *Alexander* of 1459, two pieces of which are preserved in the Palazzo Doria in Rome, was intended to portray the Duke of Burgundy, the Duchess Isabelle, and Charles, the heir to the duchy, under the guises of Philip of Macedon, his wife, and their son Alexander. But Philip the Bold already had a *Clovis,* which he gave to the Duke of Lancaster, and an *Alexander,* which was one of the tapestries sent to Bazajet. Similarly with the *Trojan War* delivered in 1472 : Philip the Bold had bought from Jacques Dourdin a *Hector of Troy,* which he gave to the Grand Master of the Teutonic Order. It seems, then, that most of these historical subjects were traditional from the 14th century on. Indeed, one has only to open the inventories to see that the sovereigns and princes of the Middle Ages all owned the same subjects, sometimes several times over, for example, the *Heroes* and *Heroines, Charlemagne, Legend of the Rose, Seven Virtues and Vices, Story of Fame,* and *Perceval,* to say nothing of the mandatory scenes from the Scriptures — the *Credo, Story of Our Lady, Passion,* and

Apocalypse. One may wonder, therefore, whether an important merchant always waited for a definite order before having a particular storied tapestry woven. Demand was heavy enough that he ran little risk building up stock, and the reputation of someone like Pasquier Grenier was acquired largely because he kept considerable numbers of tapestries ready for sale. We know this was the case in the 16th century : the Antwerp "tapestry exchange" was then a large market where everyone could find what he was looking for. But already in the 14th century there are often clear indications in the accounts, such as "which my Lord caused to be bought," indicating a purchase rather than a special order. Nor should certain significant facts be overlooked. In 1386, for example, for the double marriage of his son John and his daughter Catherine, Philip the Bold had Jacques Dourdin deliver five tapestries, or perhaps even more. Is it credible that this event should have been planned far enough ahead to allow time for them to be woven? The same applies to the pieces for which Jean Cosset received the considerable sum of 2,100 crowns in 1412, on the occasion of the marriage of Antoine, second son of the Duke of Burgundy. One should not generalize, since so many tapestries between the 14th and 16th centuries were obviously made to order. But clearly, many others were woven, not at a prince's command, but on the more or less random initiative of the big dealers. Here lies the explanation of the scale, and especially of the regularity, of tapestry production : how could so many pieces have been delivered year after year if each time the merchants had had to wait for a prince's go-ahead and choice of subject?

Approval was no doubt required on the design, and also on the drawings and cartoons. But in the case of works sold from stock, there is the obvious question of the date of their execution. This was necessarily earlier than the purchase date shown in the accounts, but how many years earlier?

Unless there are clear documentary references, problems of dating are always difficult. Stylistic analysis can only give an indication, often debatable, and its application is always restricted to the drawing and "first edition" of a tapestry. Costume and arms give us only a terminal date, for while no fashion can be portrayed unless it has seen the light of day it may continue to appear in the plastic arts long after it has been abandoned in life. Often heraldry can come to the aid of the researchers — though they rarely pay much attention to it — provided it is borne in mind that coats of arms were often rewoven for a new owner; the case of the Berne tapestries is well known. Some of the heraldic tapestries in this exhibition demonstrate the chronological precision that heraldry can sometimes provide. We shall also see how the horseman of Montacute House was identified by his arms, and how this enabled us to recognize in the documents the Tournai weaver who executed the work. (In this research we have been helped and our conclusions supported by two eminent specialists, Baron Hervé Pinoteau and Jean-Bernard de Vaivre.)

There remains the problem of style itself, since every tapestry is a picture that has been drawn and painted, and can be analyzed in much the same way as a painting. Here our science has made little progress. Much has been written by specialists about where the works were woven, but they have not attempted to probe the secrets of the artists who expressed themselves through the loom. Yet it is these artists and they alone who should command the attention of the art historian.

Alas, we know almost nothing about how the painters and cartoon makers organized their ateliers. Did the great artists of the Middle Ages take part in the execution of the work? We know that Isabeau of Bavaria ordered from Colart de Laon patterns for four rooms of tapestries, and that she did not like them. It seems that the work was often entrusted to specialists; it was they who developed a new, closely worked kind of composition in which it is hard to pick out any detail but which covers a wall admirably. Such a technique was quite different from the current practice in painting. But it is nevertheless possible to assign a role in the Arras ateliers to a great painter: Jacques Daret. He worked with Bauduin de Bailleul, who was described by Jean Lemaire de Belges as a "maker of patterns," and he directed a team of decorators which as early as 1419 was working for John the Fearless, painting large numbers of coats of arms in the abbey of St. Vaast. Because his principal work, the *Story of Gideon,* has been lost, we know nothing of the style of Bauduin de Bailleul. And as for the others, such people as Robert de Monchaux and Jacques Pillet, they are only names to us.

Jan van Roome seems also to have been a decorator, in Brussels, in the early 16th century. Works of all kinds have been attributed to him, but only one is certified as his. He seems to have lent his hand to many techniques, with the exception of major painting.

There were, of course, exceptions. Hennequin of Bruges was a painter and a miniaturist. He is the real creator of the Angers *Apocalypse,* and since his chef d'œuvre is extant it is time for the art historians to take an interest in this eminent artist's style, and to tell us how, by the lyricism of his form, he was able to transfigure the manuscript that directed his inspiration, if not his hand. Perhaps new research will enable us to recognize in certain tapestries the style of such and such a 15th-century master, but as things are today, nothing is sure.

In any case, there are better questions to deal with first. For example, the reuse of cartoons. It sometimes happens that a scene does not lend itself in the way it has been treated to the explanation we would like to give it, or is incomprehensible in the context of the tapestry. In these cases we may perhaps suppose that the cartoon for another subject has been reused without alteration and out of context; it would give us the key to many an iconographical obscurity or disconcerting anachronism.

There are similar problems with the millefleurs tapestries — the pieces in which the whole background is strewn with flowering plants, with no attempt at perspective. Characters are placed here and there more or less at random, sometimes out of scale with one another, and often only vaguely linked in obscure actions. Since they often reappear identically, or almost so, from one work to another, it has been thought that tapestries of this kind were sometimes woven from "prefabricated" cartoons : against a background of flowers repeated indefinitely, the weaver would introduce human silhouettes of little significance, whose patterns he happened to have in stock. However, this practice was probably exceptional, and reserved for modest tapestries without definite subject, like the Cluny Museum's *Courtly Life*. The finest millefleurs tapestries, the Boston *Narcissus* and the Cluny's *Lady with the Unicorn*, for example, are real pictures. Although the figures are portrayed without depth, they center around clearly defined actions.

It remains to note that the reuse of designs explains the memorable suit brought by the painters against the tapestry weavers of Brussels in 1476 : they complained that they had no part in the design of the cartoons, which were drawn by craftsmen who were not members of their guild. This event throws an unusually clear light on the procedures employed in the ateliers. The city magistrate ruled that henceforth the tapestry weavers should confine themselves to designing backgrounds, trees, shrubs, and animals, while the rest of the work was to be done by painters. Consequently, tapestries showing figures that have been reused and are usually of poor quality should not be assigned to Brussels, if we assume that they were done after 1476, when this rule was enforced.

However this may be, the painters' victory in 1476 certainly marks the beginning of an admirable series of storied tapestries that we attribute to Brussels, most woven with gold thread, composed, designed, and painted by artists who knew exactly how to model a face, vary expressions and gestures, show off the luxury of clothing and make it fall in abundant and luxurious folds, and handle tones of light and dark — in short, to work as painters who had learned from the great "Flemish" masters.

If we consider the *Adoration of the Magi* from Sens Cathedral or the Davilier *Virgin,* dated 1485, from the Louvre, it becomes clear that this rebirth of the art of tapestry took place shortly after 1476 and in Brussels, since this city remained pre-eminent thereafter through the 16th century. But we would be wrong to conclude that all was done in Brussels itself during this golden age of tapestry between 1480 and 1520. Many pieces "in the Brussels style" have been preserved; in the documents they appear to have numbered in the thousands, not to mention those that have disappeared without a reference. As earlier in Arras and Tournai, the merchants clearly had to farm out the work to subcontractors, and, in any case, it is hardly likely that centers so recently prosperous and renowned would have had suddenly to close their ateliers. But Brussels established precedence over them, both from the excellence of its design and color and the refinement of its technique.

By means of crowded compositions in which perspective hardly had a place, and scenes with large numbers of characters, many of which served no significant purpose, the cartoonists of this period carefully maintained the individuality of the "woven picture" vis-à-vis the "painted picture," and so remained within the decorative tradition of the 15th century. Their feeling remained Gothic; the Renaissance influence appeared only in the shape and décor of the architecture. The style changed radically when Pope Leo X had the *Acts of the Apostles* woven in Brussels from rich designs commissioned by him from Raphael. It would be wrong to fix this date of 1519 as a milestone in the history of tapestry; however great the enthusiasm of the Roman public for the seven pieces, which were finished and hung in the Sistine Chapel, the work was too new, and indeed too superbly indifferent to the limitations of the weaving technique, to start an immediate stylistic revolution in the Brussels ateliers. Raphael's masterpiece nevertheless helped, along with other factors, to lead tapestry toward a more complete submission to the rules and processes of painting. Many other chefs d'œuvre were to appear further on in this new chapter in the glorious history of tapestry, but it is at this point, with the transition away from the Gothic style, that we come to the end of our exhibition.

F. Salet
October 1973

Only recent or essential publications have been included. Works cited in abbreviated form : J.J. Marquet de Vasselot and Roger-Armand Weigert, *Bibliographie de la tapisserie, des tapis et de la broderie en France,* Paris, A. Colin, 1935. Heinrich Göbel, *Wandteppiche,* Leipzig, Klinkhardt & Biermann, I *Die Niederlande,* 2 vol., 1923, II *Die Romanischen Länder,* 2 vol. 1928.

1
The Apocalypse

Wool
12-15 warp threads
to the inch

Tapestry Museum
Château d'Angers

The last book of the Bible, which predicts the end of time as revealed to St. John by the angel of Christ, was a very popular subject in medieval art, but it was rarely illustrated on anything like the scale of the set of tapestries of which we show the fourth piece, illustrating chapters XI to XIII (verse 7) of the Book of Revelation. The complete set of seven pieces, the first masterpiece of medieval tapestry, is still, after six centuries, one of the art's largest examples.

The scenes of the exhibited piece are in two registers, reading from left to right and top to bottom, with musical angels (damaged) at the top and a flowery meadow at the bottom. On the left, a large seated figure in an open edicule is no doubt one of the guardians of the seven churches of Asia to which St. John addresses the Book. Above, two angels hold up banners, that on the left with the arms of Louis I of Anjou (the arms of France with a border gules); on a plain background are butterflies whose wings bear the same arms or the ermines of Louis's wife, Mary of Brittany. The fourteen scenes are set against alternatively red and blue backgrounds. St. John is in all of them, sometimes participating in the action, sometimes looking on from a kind of watchtower.

Scene 29 of the tapestry (according to the numbering system of R. Planchenault): the angel hands St. John a reed with which to measure the temple of God and the altar (Rev. XI : 1-2). The background is plain, as in all the preceding scenes.

Scene 30 : the two witnesses of God slay their enemies with fire issuing from their mouths, shut the heavens to prevent the rain from falling, and turn the waters into blood (Rev. XI : 3-6). Starting with this scene, the backgrounds are patterned with various scattered motifs.

Scene 31 : the Beast comes up from the bottomless pit to fight and kill the two witnesses (Rev. XI : 7).

Scene 32 : men contemplate the bodies of the two witnesses and rejoice in their death (Rev. XI : 8-10).

Scene 33 : the two witnesses are revived by the Spirit of Life and ascend into heaven, while a part of the city falls in an earthquake, killing seven thousand people (Rev. XI : 11-13).

Scene 34 : the seventh angel sounds the trumpet and the twenty-four elders worship God (Rev. XI : 14-19).

Scene 35 : two angels take up to God the newborn son of the woman clothed with the sun, whom the dragon with seven heads and ten horns wished to devour (Rev. XII : 1-6).

Scene 36 : the dragon, who is Satan, with his angels, is cast down to earth by St. Michael and his angels (Rev. XII : 7-12).

Scene 37 : the woman receives wings to escape from the dragon (Rev. XII : 13-14).

Scene 38 : the earth dries up the flood the dragon has cast out against the woman (Rev. XII : 15-16).

Scene 35

Scene 39 : the dragon fights against the woman's descendants, who keep God's commandments (Rev. XII : 17-18). On the red background are an interlaced L and M, the initials of Louis of Anjou and Mary of Brittany.

Scene 40 : the dragon hands the scepter of power to the Beast with seven heads and ten horns, which has risen up from the sea (Rev. XIII 1-2).

Scene 41 : men kneel before the dragon because he has given power to the Sea Beast (Rev. XIII : 3-4).

Scene 42 : they also prostrate themselves before the Beast, which blasphemes against God and makes war on the saints (Rev. XIII : 4-7).

13 ft. 1 in. × 60 ft. 8 in. (4 m × 18,50 m)

It is not certain whether the scenes that today form the fourth piece of the set originally belonged to it. We know from the ancient inventories that there were seven pieces in the set but by the 19th century it was incomplete and in scattered fragments. Until quite recently all that was known at Angers were four readers facing right, one facing left, and sixty-seven more or less complete scenes, plus a fragment of scene 60, and another, which has since disappeared, of scene 68, and three pieces showing St. John and one an angel, two much restored fragments that are now in Glasgow, and another scene, also restored, that is in San Francisco.

As the figure seven recurs incessantly in Revelation, one could of course suppose that the set as a whole had seven readers and ninety-eight (7 × 14) small scenes, and that the seven pieces were similarly composed with two registers of seven scenes each with inscriptions below that have since disappeared and with a reader on one side, a band of sky with musical angels above, and a band of meadow with scattered flowers below. In most of the pieces the reader would have been on the left, while in at least one, probably the second, he would have been on the right. However, although one can find subjects for ninety-eight scenes both in St. John's text and in the manuscript miniatures that the maker of the cartoons may have used as reference, it has so far proved impossible to insert the missing scenes into those we have, principally because of the rigid alternation of the red and blue backgrounds. Accordingly, it is now thought, for want of a better solution, that the second and third pieces contained only fourteen scenes, which would give a total for the whole work of eighty-four (or 7 × 12) — so we still keep the numerical symbolism.

Scene 36

Scene 42

The Guardian

Despite its defacement, the *Apocalypse* is still the world's largest tapestry series and it is one of the few Gothic works that are today well documented.

The accounts of Louis I, Duke of Anjou, second son of John the Good, King of France, and brother of Charles V, mention the payment on April 7, 1377, of 1,000 francs to the most famous tapestry weaver of the time, Nicolas Bataille, "for the making of two cloths of tapestry of the Story of the Apocalypse which he did for the Duke," and also at the end of January, 1378, of an installment of 50 francs to Hennequin of Bruges, "the king our lord's painter," for the "portraits and patterns he did for the said tapestries of the Story of the Apocalypse" (these were life-size drawings or cartoons). Finally on June 16, 1379, we find an advance to Nicolas Bataille of 300 francs on the 3,000 he was to get for three other pieces of the tapestry to be finished by Christmas. Furthermore, an illuminated *Apocalypse* (Bibliothèque Nationale, French MSS No. 403) that figured in 1373 in the inventory of Charles V's books in the Louvre is noted as missing in the inventory made in 1380, for "the king has lent it to Monsieur d'Anjou for making his beautiful tapestry." We thus know who ordered the work, who made the drawings, and who had it woven and at about what date. There remain, however, several problems.

One might have been able to associate the name of Louis of Anjou with this set since his arms and those of his wife appear on it. It causes no surprise that such a vast weaving should have been ordered by a prince who, with his brothers Charles V, John, Duke of Berry, and Philip the Bold, Duke of Burgundy, were among the most lavish patrons of the Middle Ages. But how to explain the choice of this austere vision of the end of the world on the part of a man who does not seem to have been particularly scrupulous?

The theme of the Apocalypse was a frequent subject of illustration in the Gallo-Roman period and in the miniatures of the 13th and 14th centuries. A large number of manuscripts from this period are extant; some (No. 482 in the Cambrai Library, No. 38 in the Metz Library, one in the seminary at Namur, and the Latin manuscript No. 14410 in the Bibliothèque Nationale, which came from the church of St. Victor in Paris) include compositions very close to those of the tapestries, much more so than those of the manuscript lent by Charles V to his brother. Following a frequent practice in the Middle Ages, Hennequin de Bruges must have used a number of different illuminations as reference; but one only has to look at his scene of St. Michael fighting the dragon to see what a great painter could do with very commonplace scenes, transforming, for instance, the standing angels of the miniatures into a group majestically swooping down from heaven. The static figures of the manuscripts become characters full of life, with varied expressions, with robes abundantly and cleverly draped, and the tiny illustrations of the books are brought up to wall size with an economy of material that lends a monumental simplicity to St. John's grandiose prophesies, set off here and there with piquant details.

The name of Nicolas (or Colin) Bataille appears frequently in the texts between 1373 and 1399, either as a "tapissier et varlet de chambre" of the Duke of Anjou or as a "tapissier et bourgeois de Paris," or again as a "marchant" — the detail "marchant de tappiz sarrazinois" is given once. Bataille delivered to the great men of this time "serges" and high-warp "tapis," which ranged from modest heraldic pieces intended to caparison the royal horses to hangings "à ymages" of great richness, woven in silk and gold. He was clearly one of those courageous businessmen of the time who made a fortune out of high-warp art through his connections with princes. This art was described in a Paris text of 1303 as new, and its considerable development in the course of the last third of the 14th century can no doubt be explained by the traffic of these great merchants with nobles of lavish tastes.

Did the *Apocalypse*, which in 1400 drew cries of admiration from the citizens of Arles at the time of the marriage ceremonies of Louis II of Anjou and Yolande of Aragon, contribute to the extraordinary development of storied tapestries? Until about 1360, in any case, we find only geometric and heraldic designs, and then "bestelettes" (small animals). In 1375, 1376, and 1379 Colin Bataille delivered to Louis I of Anjou several "tappiz à ymages," notably a *Story of Esther* in high-warp weave, the *Complexions*, a *Story of the Passion*, a "great cloth of silk in high-warp work," and a *Life of Our Lady*. Later, Bataille delivered to King Charles VI, his wife Isabeau of Bavaria, and his brother Louis of Orléans a large number of heraldic tapestries, also selling to the latter a *Story of Theseus and the Golden Eagle*, a *Story of Penthesilea*, a *Story of Beuve de Hantonne*, a *Story of the Children of Regnault of Montauban and of the Children of Riseus de Ripemont*, and, for his chapel, a *Tree of Life*. On December 16, 1397, with Jacques Dourdin, another great tapestry specialist, he agreed to a price of 9 livres, 12 sols parisis per *aune* for a sumptuous tapestry "made all in imagery of gold and fine thread of Arras," representing the "jousts that formerly were held at St. Denis" on the occasion of the ennoblement of Louis of Orléans and Louis II of Anjou in May, 1389. This series is mentioned in 1400 as having been delivered, although it measured not less than 285 3/4 square *aunes* (the Paris aune was about 47 inches).

However hard it is for us to understand how such enormous surfaces could be woven so quickly (though the various pieces were certainly woven simultaneously on different looms, and several weavers worked side by side on the same loom), an example like this, which was not unique, would suggest that the *Apocalypse*, of which only five out of the seven pieces appear in the accounts, was made in a similarly short period of time. The style is homogeneous, and the accounts of the Dukes of Anjou are not complete. Moreover Louis I, who died in 1384, inherited the kingdom of Sicily from Joan of Naples in 1380, and in 1382 he had the contested Pope Clement VII invest him as king at Avignon; yet, even if in his deeds no mention is made of this royal title before 1383, it would have been surprising if he had not had the Cross of Jerusalem, the emblem of the kings of Sicily, included on pieces woven at this period alongside his personal emblem, the cross with double horizontal, which appears on the tapestry next to the arms of Anjou. Thus, contrary to the hypothesis that the two last pieces were woven later, there is no reason why the five that we have mention of should not be the last five. The whole of the *Apocalypse* would then have been woven between 1373, the date when the manuscript the king lent his brother was still at the Louvre, and 1379 — unless the 120 livres paid by the duke to "Jehan of Bruges [another name for Hennequin], painter and valet de chambre to the king," in January, 1379, for the "good services he has rendered him in making certain portraitures," the other 50 livres that the artist also received in the same month and in July, and the balance paid to him on March 7, 1381, were also in respect of the *Apocalypse*; this, in any case, would put the completion of the set back only by one year.

Note finally that the sum of 3,000 francs was paid for three of the pieces, or 1,000 francs each. As an inventory in 1563 gives the dimensions of each piece as 5 × 20 aunes (approximately 19 ft. 6 in. × 80 ft.), which was no doubt close to their original size, we may conclude that the square aune was paid for at a rate of about 10 francs, compared to the 3 francs par aune paid to Bataille in 1391 for tapestries with designs of barley sheaves for the bedroom of Valentine Visconti, the wife of Louis of Orléans, brother of Charles VI. The stories of *Penthesilea, Beuve,* and *The Children of Regnault,* for which a total of 1,700 francs was paid in 1396, work out only at about 8 francs per square aune. Though it was only in wool, and consequently less rich than the *Jousts of St. Denis* (which has not survived), the *Apocalypse* was a high-priced work, and we can understand why the citizen of Arles was moved to exclaim : "There is no man who can write down or describe the value, beauty, and nobility of these cloths!"

One of the pieces, bequeathed by Louis I of Anjou to his son Louis II, whose wife Yolande left it to their son King René (died 1480), who in turn instructed in his will that it be given to Angers Cathedral, was kept until May, 1490, by Anne de Beaujeu, Louis XI's eldest daughter. In 1782 the chapter of Angers Cathedral put it on sale, but did not find a purchaser. During the Revolution and afterward it was used to protect orange trees against frost, to stop up holes in walls, to prevent horses from bruising their flanks in stables, and so on. It was sold in 1843 by the Administration des Domaines and bought by a Monsignor Angebault, after which it was pieced together again, restored, and studied. Since 1954 it has been exhibited in the château d'Angers, in a building erected specially for it.

BIBLIOGRAPHY. Hendrick de Marez, *Jan van Brugge,* in *Onze Kunst,* 2 nd. year, 1903[1], p. 153-163, pl. — Marquet de Vasselot-Weigert, *Bibl.,* p. 42-43 and 123-127. — René Planchenault, *L'Apocalypse d'Angers,* Paris, Caisse Nationale des Monuments Historiques, 1966. — Geneviève Souchal, *Les tapisseries de l'Apocalypse d'Angers,* introduction by René Planchenault, (Milan) Hachette-Fabbri-Skira (1969).

2
Presentation of the Infant Jesus in the Temple

Wool
About 12 warp threads to the inch

Musée Royaux d'Art et d'Histoire
Brussels

This scene, which probably formed part of a Life of the Virgin or of Christ, comes from a set of tapestries that may have had a composition similar to that of the Angers *Apocalypse* (No. 1); there were in any case two registers, as there remain at the bottom a part of an angel's wing and the top of an edicule.

In addition to the usual characters (the old man Simeon on the right receiving the infant Jesus from the hands of the Virgin, with St. Joseph behind) there is a young woman who carries a lighted candle and a basket containing, not the two turtledoves mentioned by St. Luke, but the four birds of the Apocryphal Gospel according to Pseudo-Matthew. A recent restoration revealed another candle, implying the presence of another assistant. The vine branches in the background, with their connotation of the blood of Christ, add symbolic meaning to the decoration, as does the foliage in the last pieces of the *Apocalypse*.

4 ft. 5 in. × 9 ft. 3 in. (1,53 m × 2,85 m)

In other respects also — the type of figure, the clouds, colors, and weaving technique — this *Presentation* is similar to the Angers tapestry. It is tempting to think it may be a fragment of the *Life of Our Lady* for which the Duke of Anjou finished paying Nicolas Bataille in 1379. However, we cannot definitely say more than that this tapestry came out of one of the Paris ateliers about 1380, when the style, described as "Franco-Flemish," of the Northern painters, who came in numbers to seek their fortune from French patrons in the time of Charles V and Charles VI, was developing.

Bought in 1894 by the Royal Museums of Art and History, Brussels, from the wife of the Spanish painter Leon y Escosura, who lived in Paris and had exhibited it for the first time in 1876.

BIBLIOGRAPHY. Marthe Crick-Kuntziger, *Musées royaux d'art et d'histoire de Bruxelles, Catalogue des tapisseries (XIVe au XVIIIe siècle),* undated, nº 1, p. 13-15 and pl. 1 — *L'art européen vers 1400,* 8th exhibition under the auspices of the Council of Europe, Vienna, Kunsthistorisches Museum (May 7 1962 - July 31 1962), nº 521, p. 398-399.

3-4
The Heroes

Wool
12-15 warp threads to the inch

The Metropolitan Museum of Art
The Cloisters Collection

From the 14th to the 16th century, the theme of the Heroes was much in favor. Known to have existed already in the 13th century, it was popularized by a poem on the Alexander cycle, the *Vows of the Peacock,* composed about 1312 by Jacques de Longuyen for the Bishop of Liège, Thibaut de Bar. These heroes, models of medieval chivalry, were chosen from the three "laws" : pagan, Jewish, and Christian. There were generally nine of them : Hector, Alexander, and Caesar; Joshua, David, and Judas Maccabeus; and Arthur, Charlemagne, and Godefroy de Bouillon, the conqueror of Jerusalem. From the end of the 14th century on, Bertrand de Guesclin was sometimes added. A collection of heroines is frequently paired with them. Sculpted in stone, painted on walls or in manuscripts, they also appear in stained glass, on pieces of gold plate, on enamels, in engravings, and in tapestries; five of them still figure on modern playing cards, four as kings and Hector as a knave.

We have here, from a set in which the heroes were grouped three by three (four are missing today), one of the pagan heroes, no doubt Hector, and one of the Christians, Artus (or Arthur), the king in the Round Table cycle.

3
Hector

This hero has been variously identified as Hector and Alexander, whose arms have sometimes been confused by the compilers of heraldic records. But Jean-Bernard de Vaivre has shown that the arms we have here, *or a lion gules, arms and tongued argent, seated on a chair purpure and holding a halberd argent with a shaft azure,* were for the people of the end of the 14th century those of Hector of Troy; at this period, Alexander was given two facing lions. Several 15th-century coats of arms and the frescoes in the La Manta castle in Piedmont prove this. But the arms of Hector appear in several variations : in this tapestry the field is gules and the lion holds a sword. The hero is seated on an architectural dais, surrounded by seven small figures, mostly warriors; at the top, in the center, is a woman holding a flower against a background decorated with letters recalling the Y, the meaning of which is obscure, from the scene of the Great Prostitute in the Angers *Apocalypse*.

13 ft. 11 in. × 8 ft. 9 1/2 in. (4,06 m × 2,67 m)

Hector

King Arthur

4
King Arthur

The composition is the same as in the preceding scene, but here the small figures are clerical : cardinals in the upper register and bishops below. King Arthur bears on the tabard he wears over his breastplate and on his standard the arms that are most frequently associated with him : *azure, three crowns or,* the crowns probably being those of his legendary kingdoms : England, Scotland, and Brittany.

14 ft. 1 in. × 9 ft. 10 1/2 in. (4,29 m × 3,01 m)

The presence in the upper register of the piece with the three Hebrew heroes of small banners, three with the royal arms, one with those of the Duchy of Burgundy, and ten with those of John of Berry, the third son of John the Good and brother of Charles V, Louis of Anjou, and Philip the Bold, Duke of Burgundy *(of France, border engrailed gules),* suggests that The Cloisters' tapestries were made for a prince : they were probably woven to the order of, or as a gift for, the Duke of Berry (1340-1416), one of the greatest patrons of the Middle Ages. However, since the set does not figure in the inventory made after his death, it cannot be the set of *Nine Heroes* that is mentioned therein as an Arras work with gold and silver threads.

It has been suggested that The Cloisters' set may have been given away — or perhaps exchanged — by John of Berry before his death, in accordance with the practice of princes of this period to give lavish gifts at the New Year, or for marriages and other great occasions. This theory is supported by the mention, in an inventory for Charles VI in 1422, of a set of *Nine Heroines* that seems to have been analogous to this one, since it included three pieces having "at the top, the arms of Berry, and several small escutcheons." At least for the most part, these also bore the arms of Duke John, since it is stated that at the time of the delivery, in 1432, of two of these tapestries to the Duke of Bedford, regent during the minority of his nephew Henry VI, king of France and England, and also at the time when the third piece was given to "a tapestry-hanger" of the late King Charles VI, there were at the top "the arms of Berry in small escutcheons." Furthermore these documents indicate that in the third piece, devoted to Menalippa, Semiramis, and Lampheto, there figured "several other small figures above these"; the other two, stated to be "very old," had doubtless already lost the figures of this

upper register. This *Heroines* set thus certainly came from John of Berry, and it may well have been the companion of the set in The Cloisters, which does not figure in the inventory of 1422. However, we know that Charles VI had indeed owned tapestries of heroes, since in 1389, and again ten years later, the weaver Jean de Jaudoigne of Paris was paid for repairing them; they were perhaps the pieces that Charles inherited from his father — the "deux tappiz des Neuf Preux" of Charles V's inventory.

It is known that John of Berry had the heroes sculpted on a fireplace in the great hall of his palace in Bourges, and his inventory of 1401 mentions a "nef de table" (a boat-shaped piece of tableware) "stamped with the nine heroes" and his inventory of 1416 twenty "enamels of gold, enameled in light red, of the heroes and heroines, which are above two golden bowls." We know also that there were weavers working for John in 1385, in his Bourges palace, and that he, like his brothers and nephews, was a client of Nicolas Bataille.

The technique of the *Heroes* (weaving style, limited color range) is the same as that of the *Apocalypse,* though it is less fine. Some of the details recur, leading to the supposition that The Cloisters' tapestry was made in the same atelier, or by weavers trained in the same school.

From the stylistic point of view, in any case, there is a clear difference between the work of Hennequin de Bruges (No. 1) and the present work, in which the principal characters have been drawn somewhat carelessly, and the small figures do not always fit happily into their niches. Nor can we assign the work to the great painter and sculptor of the end of the 14th century, André Beauneveu, who in the Psalter of John of Berry portrayed seated figures with much better drawing. James Rorimer and Margaret Freeman have looked for similarities in various works carried out for the duke : deco-

King Arthur, *detail*

rative sculpture, stained glass, manuscripts, and especially his *Petites Heures,* in which there is an Annunciation framed with little figures under niches, and an astrological treatise by Albumasar in which there are stylistic analogies. The book was given to the duke in 1403, and it was produced by the abbot Lubertus, who between 1394 and 1417 had a flourishing atelier for illuminating manuscripts near Bruges. However, for Millard Meiss, the figures of the tapestry reflect the style of the painters to Charles V (1364-1380), which style developed toward the end of the 14th century in northeast France and Flanders. We may add that while some of the figures, the ecclesiastical ones for example, are rather static, others have the animation we find in French manuscripts of the 14th century.

A date of around 1385 has been suggested for reasons of style, because there are no flamboyant elements in the set. In any case, the set can be dated to the last years of the 14th century. As the Duke of Anjou does not figure on a banner (as do Charles VI and Philip the Bold in the piece with the Hebrew heroes), it can be argued that the tapestries were ordered after 1384, the year of his death.

The Arthur *tapestry, without the cardinals, but with the two figures from the* Hebrew Heroes *piece, was sold by J. J. Duveen to M. Chabrières-Arlès, who lent it to the historical exhibition in Lyon in 1877. In 1932 it appeared in the Clarence H. Mackay collection and was bought by the Metropolitan Museum. The other tapestries of the set, sold by the Duveen firm to Baron Arthur Schickler just after the Franco-Prussian War of 1870-71, were hung as curtains, from 1876 onward, in the château of Martinvast near Cherbourg. In 1936 they were in the possession of the New York art dealer Joseph Brummer. A gift from John D. Rockefeller, Jr., in 1947 enabled The Cloisters to buy them, in 91 fragments.*

BIBLIOGRAPHY. James J. Rorimer and Margaret B. Freeman, *The Nine Heroes tapestries at the Cloisters. A picture book,* New York. The Metropolitan Museum of Art, 1953, 24 p., fig. — Millard Meiss, *French painting in the time of Jean de Berry, the late fourteenth century and the patronage of the duke,* (London) Phaidon, 1969, vol. I, p. 58-59 and 365, nº 3, vol. II, fig. 445-446. — J.-B. de Vaivre, *Les armoiries d'Hector de Troie dans la tapisserie des Preux aux Cloisters,* to appear shortly. — *Id. Les trois couronnes des hérauts,* in *Archivum heraldicum,* 1972, nᵒˢ 2-3, p. 30-35; and *Artus, les trois couronnes et les hérauts, ibid.,* 1973, to appear shortly.

5

The Romance of Jourdain de Blaye

Wool

15 warp threads to the inch

Museo Civico, Padua

The subjects of many medieval tapestries were taken from epics. The oldest of this type that we know of illustrates a *chanson de geste* based on a fable of Apollonius of Tyre, written probably in the first half of the 13th century. It then developed in later versions, one of which must be the direct source for this tapestry.

In the original story Fromont is the nephew of the wicked Hardrez, killed by Amis in defense of his brother-in-arms Amiles and Charlemagne's daughter. Fromont wishes to avenge his uncle's death on Girart, the virtuous son of Amis. He goes to Blaye, where the latter lives, and kills him and his wife. He then demands that Renier de Vautamise hand over Girart's child, Jourdain, who is in his care. The faithful vassal substitutes his own child, whom Fromont puts to death. After many adventures, Jourdain succeeds in avenging his parents, and Fromont dies under torture. The story is summarized in the verses at the top left of the tapestry :

Fromons fist renier traveillier
tant que sen fil ala baillier
a morir pour iourdain sauver
sen signeur quas fons vault lever
mais iourdains puis vengance en fist
sus fromont telle qui souffist

(Fromont tormented Renier so much that he handed over his own son to die to save Jourdain, his lord, whom he saw baptized [?], but Jourdain then took sufficient vengeance on Fromont.)

The figure above these verses, with open mouth and raised hands, is no doubt the narrator.

The rest of the tapestry concerns the beginning of the story, continued on other pieces now lost.

Fromont takes ship to Blaye, with soldiers carrying standards that bear his initial. He is probably the figure in the middle of the boat toward the right, a little behind; for, under his pointed helm, he looks like the old man with a beard in the meeting scene on the right.

The group in the boat illustrates the second stanza of four lines :

Regardes de bordiaus fromon
qui par mer va en de dromon
a blaives pour gerat traiir
son neveu sen fait ahair

(See how Fromont goes by sea in a fast ship from Bordeaux to Blaye to betray Girart, his nephew [this relationship differs from the original] whom he hates.)

In the center, the soldiers disembark; one has the letters a and L on his doublet. On the right Fromont, in rich civilian attire, is warmly welcomed by Girart, who is elegantly dressed in a tight doublet with low belt, in the fashion of Charles VI's time (1380-1422), and blue and white hose with soles. Girart's wife and household are on the right in front of his château.

On Fromont's left, a figure bears on the lower part of his garment an inscription of which several letters are partly or wholly concealed : "la belle cha...a."

Above, three quatrains — that on the right incomplete because of the defacement of the side of the tapestry — give the exchange of greetings between the visitor and his host, and Fromont's reply :

Girart, dieve vous croisse bonté
mes ie vous vieng par amisté
veir en blaives vo maison
car mout vous aing, c'est bien raison.
Oncles, bien soiiés vous venus
d'amour sui bien a vous tenus
car noblement me venés vir
honnerer vous doy et servir;
Sire Girart, v...
bien devons fa...
de luy porter...
menés le a bla...

(Girart, may God increase your happiness, but I come to you in friendship to see your house in Blaye, for much I love you, and that is the reason... Uncle, be welcome; I am bound by love to you, for nobly you come to see me, and I must honor and serve you.

10 ft. 8 in. × 12 ft. 5 in. (3,28 m × 3,80 m)

We do not know who was responsible for the cartoon of this expressive work (note, for example, the contrast between Girart's sincere enthusiasm and Fromont's cunning and self-satisfied expression). Whoever he was, at a time when there was little integration of figures into a landscape, this artist was able to plan a whole large panel, with a clear distribution of scenes between a foreground enlivened with animals and strewn with formalized flowers reminiscent of the *Apocalypse* (No. 1), and a background of rounded rocks and hills planted with trees (whose leaves do not as yet show much modeling). Around the panel is a border of festooned clouds very much like those in the *Presentation in the Temple* (No. 2). The tapestry is still close to the works of the 14th century in its treatment, but in its narrative aspect and feeling of space it gives a foretaste of the 15th. The style of the clothes also suggests the last years of the 14th century.

The tapestry was probably woven at Arras, which during the 14th century rivaled Paris and was soon to supplant it. It shows similarities with the only tapestry we can assign to this town with certainty : the *Story of Sts. Piat and Eleuthere,* woven in 1402 by Pierrot Féré for Tournai Cathedral (where it still remains). The inscriptions of our tapestry are in the dialect of Picardy, the region of Arras.

Note, however, that in the general taxation accounts of Flanders, from March 11, 1386, to March 10, 1387, 2,500 livres were paid to "Jehan Dourdin, dwelling in Paris, the same being owed by Monseigneur [Philip the Bold, Duke of Burgundy and Count of Flanders, brother to Charles V, Louis of Anjou, and John of Berry] to him for two tapis sarrasinois worked in gold, after the manner of Arras, of which there was one, the *Story of the Golden Apple,* and the other, the *Romance of Jourdain de Blaya,* as it appears from letters given by Monseigneur the IX of August IIII and VI on these facts." It is certainly not our tapestry that is referred to since there is no gold in it; the "Saracen" work of the tax document was probably a tufted carpet. Was this Jehan Dourdin a relation of Jacques or someone with the same name, or did they get his first name wrong? We know that Jacques Dourdin, one of the best-known tapestry-makers in Paris, shared responsibility with Nicolas Bataille at the end of the century for weaving the lavish *Jousts of St. Denis* (see No. 1), and it appears that he or one of the members of his family had cartoons of the story of Jourdain of Blaye — a rare subject. Furthermore, the *Marriage of Mercury and Philology,* in the Cathedral of Quedlinburg, Germany, made about 1200 in the knotted and cut-stitch technique, shows that designs with figures could perfectly well be reproduced in a carpet, but there was nothing to prevent the same cartoon from being used for a woven tapestry. And what does the expression "after the manner of Arras" mean? That the Paris weavers who normally worked on horizontal looms (low-warp) had here used the Arras vertical loom (high-warp)? That the gold used was special to Arras? Were there other technical peculiarities — the term used can scarcely refer to style — or is this an allusion to the dialect of the verses? We cannot say with any precision what differences there may have been between Paris and Arras works around 1400, but if this piece from Padua was woven, like that of Philip the Bold, "after the Arras manner" it is understandable that it should include verses in the dialect of Picardy, and that there should be similarities between it and the *Story of Sts. Piat and St. Eleuthere.* Paris, at the dawn of the 15th century, was still an important tapestry center — its decline did not begin until a little later — and it may well have woven to order verses in the dialect of a large region as a commentary to the design of a painter whose origin may have been quite different. This is only a hypothesis, but it cannot be excluded, since the pre-eminence of the great weavers seems to have been largely based on the fact that they owned cartoons.

At the beginning of the 19th century this tapestry was at Padua, in a palace occupied by the S. Croce family since at least the end of the 15th century. In 1835, the palace was bought by the municipality, and became a school. The tapestry was used as a carpet for special occasions until 1882. It was then restored and transferred to the Museo Civico.

BIBLIOGRAPHY. Canon Dehaisnes, *Documents et extraits divers concernant l'histoire de l'art dans les Flandres, l'Artois et le Hainaut avant le XVe siècle,* 2 nd. part., Lille, L. Danel, 1886, p. 639. — Roger A. d'Hulst, *Tapisseries flamandes du XIVe au XVIIIe siècle.* Brussels, l'Arcade, 1960, n° 2, p. 7-16 and 296, pl. in b/w and color.

6
The Annunciation

Wool with some metal threads
12-15 warp threads to the inch

The Metropolitan Museum of Art

Seated on the right under an open edicule with partly curved, partly flattened arches and a paved floor decorated with motifs in many colors, Mary looks away from her book, open on a lectern, to listen to the angel Gabriel, who appears at the entry to the building on the left, holding a banner with the words "Ave gracia plena." In the sky, God the Father sends the infant Jesus bearing a cross down toward the Virgin, preceded by the dove of the Holy Spirit. Two baby angels hold a much restored coat of arms, which Erwin Panofsky has suggested is the "cornerstone," the symbol of the Christ to be born. The right-hand part (sinister) is no longer identifiable; the left (dexter) seems to be *gules, a cross fleury or.*

11 ft. 4 in. × 9 ft. 6 in. (3,45 m × 2,90 m)

The design has been compared to that of the *Annunciation* painted at Ypres between 1395 and 1399 by Melchior Broederlam on one wing of an altarpiece intended for the Carthusian monastery of Champmol, and ordered by Philip the Bold, Duke of Burgundy (today in the Musée des Beaux-Arts, Dijon). For James Rorimer, the similarity of composition is such that he regarded this Flemish master as responsible for the cartoon of the tapestry.

We know that Broederlam did supply ideas for tapestries, since in 1390 be did some "little patterns" for tapestries of shepherds and shepherdesses" for Marguerite of Flanders, the wife of Philip the Bold.

There are, however, considerable differences between this *Annunciation* and the Dijon painting. We need not dwell on those in the area of architecture, which is much more developed in the painting, with a greater effect of depth; tapestry weavers of the Middle Ages conceived of their art as a flat decoration, unlike an ordinary picture, that should not give the impression of "making a hole in the wall," and often excluded from their compositions elements that would have introduced too much perspective. This was especially the case in the early 15th century when landscape was only just beginning to appear. The differences in the characters are much more significant. The fiery, contorted gesture of the tapestry Gabriel does not appear in the painting; there, he is more collected — his two wings erect, his hands

holding out his banner at chest level — while the Virgin, also more upright, does not have the tapestry's strange, mannered hand movement to express her surprise.

Rather than through the direct influence of Broederlam, the similarities and differences between the painting and the tapestry are best explained, it seems, by supposing that they had a common model. It was normal to borrow material at a time when there was no such thing as copyright; models and books were regularly used to provide inspiration. This manner of showing the Virgin in the entrance of a building symbolizing the Temple was very common in 13th- and 14th-century Italian painting, which had in turn borrowed it from Byzantine art. Some French and Franco-Flemish artists adopted it in the last quarter of the 14th century, while others placed both the Virgin and Gabriel in an interior — for the French, a church, and for the Flemings, a room in a house. There is nothing surprising in this use of an Italian composition by certain masters. Before the Renaissance of the 16th century, French art was influenced periodically by ancient, Byzantine, and Italian trends, which it in turn passed on to neighboring countries. Especially at the end of the 14th and in the early 15th centuries, French, Flemish, and Italian contributions (noticeable in Broederlam) mingled exquisitely to form a courtly art across Europe, known today as the Gothic International style, whose high point was the masterpiece

painted by the Limbourg brothers, the *Très Riches Heures* of Chantilly, for Duke John of Berry.

The cartoonist for the *Annunciation* clearly belonged to this international movement. According to A. Brandenburg, he was probably Italian because of "the acanthus at the top of the arcade," and the touches of color in the architecture that "seem to recall the Cosmati technique of multi-colored inlays in the marble."

What we can find out about the origin of this tapestry, and where it was woven, does not help us much in identifying its creator. It was probably woven in Arras, the most important center in the first half of the 15th century. The English occupation had dealt a deathblow to the industry in Paris. We find here, at the left, the jagged foliage typical of Arras work. However, in view of the way the weavers worked, filling in their backgrounds with motifs they were accustomed to use, this does not mean that the figures were the work of a local painter. Patrons called on their favorite artists, and there were also cartoon makers who did work for the weaving ateliers. But we know little about how this collaboration was organized, and they may have come from places some distance away. A striking proof of this, a century later, was the weaving of Raphael's *Acts of the Apostles* in Brussels.

This *Annunciation* was found in Spain, but we do not know — the information we have is contradictory — if it had been kept at Gerona or, as is more probable, at Tarragona, and when it arrived there. The coats of arms have also been said to be Spanish, though we do not know what grounds Rorimer had to suggest successively that they were those of the Villanova (there was indeed a Villanova family important in Catalonia in the 14th and 15th centuries) and those of the Escales.

However this may be, the art of northern Spain in the early 15th century, from which this tapestry probably dates, belonged to the Gothic International style, and without drawing any conclusions as to who the cartoonist of the *Annunciation* may have been, we may recall that south of the Pyrénées Italian influences competed with those of the North. For example, the *Resurrection* embroidered on an altar frontal in the church of St. Felix at Gerona resembles another in the Cluny Museum that is one of the most beautiful Arras tapestries of the early 15th century. The art of the Low Countries was especially appreciated by Alfonso V, King of Aragon (1416-1458), one of whose courtiers, Dalmacio de Mur, the first bishop of Gerona and then several times ambassador, bequeathed to his cathedral in Saragossa in 1456 two large tapestries of the *Passion*, woven in Arras.

The Annunciation *appeared in the United States at the exhibition of Gothic art in Chicago (1921) and in that of European tapestry in San Francisco (1922). It was bought in 1924 by Mrs. Harold Irwing Pratt, who lent it to the Metropolitan Museum in 1941, and then gave it to the Museum in 1949 in memory of her husband.*

BIBLIOGRAPHY. Gobel, *Nied,* I, p. 232. — Erwin Panofsky, *The Friedsam Annunciation and the problem of the Ghent Altarpiece,* in *The Art Bulletin,* vol. XVII, 1935, p. 433-473. — James J. Rorimer, *The Metropolitan Museum of Art Mediaeval tapestries, a picture book,* New York, The Metropolitan Museum of Art, 1949, fig. 2; by the same author, *The Annunciation tapestry,* in *The Metropolitan Museum of Art Bulletin,* t. XX, Dec. 1961, p. 145-148. — A. Brandenburg, *C.R.* in *Bulletin Monumental,* t. 128², 1970, p. 172.

7-11
The Trojan War

In the Middle Ages ancient history was a popular subject, and people were by no means ignorant about it even though their knowledge came mostly through collections of legends or other equally unreliable sources. They particularly liked the stories of the Trojan heroes, from whom a number of princes, notably the kings of France, claimed descent. Few themes were so popular for tapestry, and we know of at least five versions of a Tournai work of this kind that must count as one of the most important creations of the last third of the 15th century.

The *Legend of Troy,* a long poem written about 1184 by the Norman cleric Benoît de Sainte-Maure at the request of Eleanor of Aquitaine — or to be precise, the Latin translation of the poem made by Guido of Colonna, a judge at Messina, in 1287, which was in turn retranslated into all the

The second tapestry :
The Rape of Helen
Zamora, Cathedral

45

European languages — inspired, during the 15th century, various mysteries and tales about the destruction of the city. The most important of these was the *Recueil des Histoires de Troie,* which Philip the Good, Duke of Burgundy, had his chaplain Raoul Lefèvre write. He had time to deal only with the first two destructions of the city by Hercules, and about 1467/68, it seems, it became customary to add to his first two books Guido of Colonna's translation of the third. However, according to J.-P. Asselberghs, it was probably the first translation of the *Historia Destructionis Troiae* that the cartoonist used as his inspiration. There was, of course, nothing historical

The sixth tapestry :
Achilles' Tent
Zamora, Cathedral

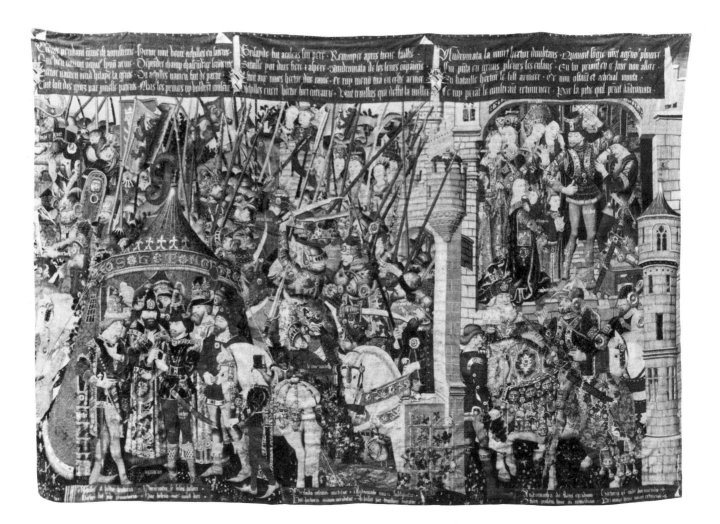

in these accounts, which were not even based on Homer but on the work of two writers of the decadent Roman period, Dictys of Crete and Dares of Phrygia, both of whom claimed to have been present at the siege and made no mention of the part played by the Olympian gods.

The complete set of Troy tapestries originally numbered eleven. We are able to reconstruct the set almost entirely from the surviving pieces, some complete, some not, and from three groups of drawings. Eight of the drawings, in the Louvre, are particularly interesting in that they are examples of the exceedingly rare "small patterns" of the 15th century. Five more of

The eighth tapestry :
The Death of Achilles
Zamora, Cathedral

the drawings, in the Victoria and Albert Museum, were made by the Englishman John Carter after the tapestries that hung until 1800 in the Great Hall of Westminster Palace. The third group of drawings were the work of Victor Sansinetti, a pupil of Ingres, after the set of tapestries that used to be in the courtroom at Issoire, France, and has since disappeared except for fragments. The drawings were published by the historian Jubinal.

The enormous tapestries — in which, most unusually, there are French verses at the top and Latin verses at the bottom — include several scenes, sometimes separated by architectural elements and explained by inscriptions. Sometimes there are so many figures that it is at first difficult to decide who they are. The four tapestries in the Cathedral of Zamora, Spain, lent to the exhibition in Paris but not sent to New York, are the second, sixth, eighth, and eleventh of the set.

The story begins with Antenor's mission from Priam to the Greeks to obtain the return of his sister Hesion, which they refuse. We know the first piece only from two drawings (Louvre and Jubinal). In it Mercury also appears, showing the apple of discord and the three goddess to Paris, who lies sleeping.

The eleventh tapestry :
The Fall of Troy
Zamora, Cathedral

7
Fragment from the Second Tapestry
(the Rape of Helen) :
Soldiers in Paris' Company

Wool and silk
12-13 warp threads
to the inch

The Museum of Fine Arts,
Boston

This fragment showing heads of soldiers comes from the second piece of the set, which also survives complete as the first of the Zamora tapestries. The first of three subjects in the complete tapestry is that of Priam charging his son Paris to succeed where Antenor failed and bring back his aunt, Hesion. Occupying half of the Zamora tapestry in the center is a composition showing ships off the island of Cythera and Paris carrying off Menelaus' wife, Helen, from in front of the Temple of Venus; the soldiers whose heads make up the present fragment are coming up from behind the hill on which the temple stands. Finally, Helen is shown being received by Priam and his court, again accompanied by soldiers.

Of this second piece we have, besides the complete Zamora weaving and the present fragment, a drawing by John Carter after the lost Westminster set.

This fragment, never before published, formerly belonged to Joseph Lindon Smith of Boston, who placed it on loan to the Museum of Fine Arts, Boston, in 1934. He gave the tapestry to the Museum in 1942.

In the third piece, which we can almost entirely reconstruct, thanks to one of the Westminster drawings and a tapestry in the Burrell collection in Glasgow, Menelaus is shown lamenting, Achilles consults the Delphic oracle, Patroclus questions the soothsayer Calchas, the Greeks attack the port of Tenedon, Ulysses and Diomedes come to discuss the return of Helen with Priam, and Achilles prepares to kill King Teutras in Mysia.

The fourth piece, which we know in part only from one of the Louvre drawings and one in the Victoria and Albert Museum, shows the landing of the Greeks before Troy and the first battle.

The fifth tapestry is also known only from drawings in the Louvre and in London; it showed the fourth of the twenty-three battles said to have taken place beneath the walls of Troy. On the right, the Trojan heroes are being congratulated by their women.   J.L.S.

263/4 in. × 21 1/2 in. (68 cm × 52,1 cm)

8
The Sagittary Fighting the Greeks :
Hector and Achilles at Achilles' Tent :
the Arming of Hector

These three pieces belong to the sixth member of the set. As preserved at Zamora, the sixth has lost its left quarter — the scene in the largest of our three pieces. Here, during the fifth battle, Diomedes is on the left; to the right is the greater portion of the following scene in which, in front of Achilles' tent, Hector suggests single combat to the Greek heroes. This

*Hector and Achilles
at Achille's Tent*

*The Sagittary
fighting the Greeks*

*The Arming
of Hector*

scene appears also in the Issoire drawings. (The verses in French of the stanza are sewn into the center of the seventh piece in the Burrell collection, Glasgow.) In the small fragment, a remnant of the master set woven for Charles the Bold, which was later at Issoire, we see the heads and upper bodies of Agamemnon, Achilles, and Hector. Next to this scene in the complete tapestry comes the eighth battle; one of the Jubinal drawings also shows it.

Our third piece contains the scene of Hector being armed for battle in women's presence, despite the pleas of Andromache and his sons; below, Hector leaves for the fight and meets his father, Priam. It may be that this fragment comes from the tapestry of which the other three-quarters are known from the Issoire drawings. The same scene appears in one of the small patterns in the Louvre.

J.L.S.

14 ft. 5 in. × 13 ft. 3 in. (4,40 m × 4,04 m)

31 in. × 45 in. (788 cm × 114 cm)

15 ft. 7 1/2 in. × 8 ft. 9 1/2 in. (4,76 m × 2,67 m)

The scene with the Sagittary was formerly owned by Raoul Heilbronner, Paris, and then by P. W. French and Company, New York. It was purchased by the Metropolitan Museum from the dealer Ruiz y Ruiz in 1952. The fragment with the heads is from one of the tapestries originally in the possession of the Besse family, who lived in the Château d'Aulhac. At the time of the Revolution the tapestries were taken to the Palace of Justice in Issoire. The fragment was purchased from the dealer Niclausse in 1955. The piece with the arming of Hector belonged to F. G. Roybet and then to Jean Dollfus, both in Paris, afterward to Clarence H. Mackay, New York. The Metropolitan Museum purchased it from the Mackay estate in 1939.

9

The Sagittary Fighting the Greeks

Wool and silk

Worcester Art Museum

This fragment comes from another, probably later, weaving of the sixth tapestry. It represents the same Sagittary fighting Diomedes and the Greeks as is seen in the largest of the Metropolitan's pieces. There is a trace of this fifth battle on the left of the Zamora piece, and since we also know the same battle from a drawing of the Issoire pieces and from a fragment of a French inscription that goes with the center of the seventh piece in the Burrell collection in Glasgow, we know that there were at least four weavings of this tapestry.

J.L.S.

11 ft. 9 in. × 6 ft. 5 in. (3,58 m × 2,42 m)

The next to last private owner of this piece was Otto Kahn, from whom Mrs. Aldus Chapin Higgins of Worcester, Massachussets, purchased it a number of years ago. It was a gift to the Worcester Art Museum from Mrs. Higgins' estate in 1970.

The Sagittary fighting the Greeks

*Palamedes killing Deiphobus and killed by Paris;
Calchas urging the discouraged Greeks,
including Achilles, to fight on*

10

Palamedes Killing Deiphobus and Killed by Paris; Calchas Urging the Discouraged Greeks, including Achilles, to Fight On

Wool and silk

Worcester Art Museum

The seventh piece was devoted to the tenth battle, in which Hector is killed, and to the celebration of the anniversary of his death, during which Achilles falls in love with Polyxena; it also showed Achilles' fruitless efforts to persuade the Greek leaders to abandon the siege, and, after their refusal, the twelfth battle. We have no record of Hector's death except an incomplete stanza with the Louvre drawings, but we know the rest of the tapestry from this fragment, part of a tapestry in the Burrell collection, Glasgow, and one of the small patterns in the Louvre. J.L.S.

11 ft. 6 in. × 6 ft. 1 in. (3,50 m × 2,42 m)

This fragment has the same recent history as its companion piece from the sixth tapestry (No. 9).

The eighth tapestry, preserved at Zamora, deals with the eighteenth, nineteenth, and twentieth battles. In the eighteenth battle, Paris fights Menelaus and Philomenis fights Agamemnon, to whose aid Telemon comes, while Archilogus overcomes "Brinus de Guvells." During the nineteenth, Achilles slays Troilus, son of Priam and Hecuba and brother of Polyxena, and he drags off the dead man tied to his horse's tail. Next, Paris and his men shower arrows on Achilles, whom Hecuba has lured into the temple of Apollo with a false promise of Polyxena's hand in marriage, in order to avenge Troilus. Achilles' left heel, his only vulnerable point, is pierced; the Greek hero has come without armor and he dies in spite of having put up a defense that leaves the ground littered with bodies. During the twentieth battle, Ajax kills Paris and is himself pierced by an arrow.

Besides the Zamora tapestry, one of the Louvre drawings is of this piece.

The ninth piece showed the entry of Penthesilea, queen of the Amazons, leading her maiden warriors. Having admired Hector, she came to help the Trojans. In a tapestry in the Victoria and Albert Museum and in one of the Louvre drawings we see her arrival in Troy, her fight with Ajax and Telemon after overpowering Diomedes in the twenty-first battle, and her upsetting Pyrrhus with a lance thrust in the twenty-second battle, after a scene in which the boy has received his arms from his father.

11
Ulysses and Diomedes Discuss Peace with Priam

Wool and silk

Museum of Fine Arts, Montreal

The subject matter of the tenth tapestry is the twenty-third battle, including the combat between Pyrrhus and Penthesilea, who dies after having wounded her enemy. Untimately, Antenor and Aeneus betray Troy, whose fall is predicted by evil omens. This fragment showing the last scene, plus another, almost complete tapestry in the Palacio Liria in Madrid, a drawing in the Louvre, a drawing in London, and three drawings from Jubinal, provide all we know of the tenth piece. J.L.S.

13 ft. 5 in. × 6 ft. 5 in. (4,09 m × 2,42 m)

The present fragment, like No. 8 was part of the master set woven for Charles the Bold, formerly at the Château d'Aulhac. In modern times it was in the collection of Count Schouvaloff, St. Petersburg, and that of Countess Benckendorff, Berlin. Before it entered the collection of the Montreal museum it was owned by Duveen Brothers, New York.

Of the eleventh and last piece, as with the eighth, only a drawing in the Louvre has survived besides the tapestry in Zamora. It shows the first stage of the fall of Troy with the pretended departure of the Greeks, who have recovered Helen. Next, the Greeks pour into the city through the breach made by the Trojans in order to bring in the great horse. In the slaughter that follows, Pyrrhus slays Priam after the latter has taken refuge in the temple of Apollo. Then Polixena, entrusted by her mother Hecuba to Antenor, is handed over by this traitor to the Greeks. Pyrrhus holds Polixena responsible for the death of his father and beheads her on Achilles' tomb. "Talamonis Ajax" seizes the old queen and Cassandra, both of whom had taken refuge in the temple of Athena. The Greeks demolish the city and begin to re-embark.

At the beginning of the 20th century the arms of Guzman, Enriquez, and Toledo, those of the sixth count of Alba and Aliste (who gave the tapestries of the Cathedral of Zamora at the beginning of the 17th century) covered the shields at the tops of the Zamora pieces, in which are depicted the arms of Don Inigo López de Mendoza, second count of Tendilla and first marquis of Mondéjar (1435-1515). However, the Zamora tapestries were not made for López de Mendoza, since his arms, though woven on the original warp threads, include a red that is slightly different from that used elsewhere in the pieces. Manuel Gómez-Moreno has suggested that these were part of the "tapestries, brocades, silks, and other things," loaded on twelve beasts of burden, that King Ferdinand I of Naples sent to Pope Innocent VIII in 1486 after their reconciliation, to thank him for his mediation in the peace negotiations the Catholic King Ferdinand of Aragon had sent his servant to conduct. The Troy tapestries would in this case have belonged to the King of Naples before López de Mendoza had his arms added to them. Unfortunately, none of his inventories have survived, but J.-P. Asselberghs has found a copy of his will, in which, following a common practice in Spain at the time, he ordered his property to be sold "to pay for the provisions of his will." Perhaps it was in this sale that the count of Alba and Aliste acquired the tapestries.

Ferdinand of Naples would thus have owned a *Story of Troy* in 1486, like so many of the great kings and patrons of his time. Charles the Bold, Duke of Burgundy, had one, given to him before September 1, 1472, by the city and district of Bruges; Mathias Corvin, King of Hungary (died 1490), had another; Henry VII of England told the keeper of his private seal on March 13, 1488, that he had just bought from Jean Grenier, tapestry maker in Tournai, eleven pieces of "th' istorye of Troy"; and, finally, King Charles VIII of France had at Amboise in May, 1494, a "Story of Troy containing eleven great pieces," from which he had the arms removed and replaced by his emblem, the sun (an incomplete ninth piece from this set is in the Victoria and Albert Museum). This alteration shows that the present pieces were not woven for King Charles.

Asselberghs thought that the Naples-Zamora set might be one of the oldest versions of the set after that of Charles the Bold, which seems to be the first. But the accounts of the city of Bruges say that the set was given "to our respected lord and prince at his instant prayer and desire" — which formula seems to signify that the duke knew about the tapestries and was keen to own then, having seen them, in the course of manufacture or completed. Nicole Reynaud thinks that an earlier version may have been made for Dunois, the bastard of Orleans (died 1468), one of Charles VII's great captains; for he had, among his tapestries, "XIII patterns of Troy." If the present set was not made for him, it may have been for another French seigneur, such as Charles of France, brother of Louis XI.

This theory also fits better with the origin of the models. The eight Louvre drawings are accompanied by eight stanzas in tiny, neat, Gothic script decorated with a kind of filigree used aroubd 1460-1475. These drawings are certainly not reduced copies but *petits patrons* intended to be enlarged to the size of the final cartoons. As Asselberghs has noted, there are differences between the drawings and the tapestries. In the sixth piece (No. 10), for example, Andromache has two children, whereas she has only one in the drawing. Such changes may be taken as "artistic license" on the part of the enlarger. The Louvre drawings have recently been attributed by Nicole Reynaud, who is writing a thesis on the subject, to the brothers Conrad and Henri de Vulcop, painters to Charles VII, his wife Marie of Anjou, and his second son Charles de France, brother of Louis XI. The same style and even some of the exact motifs recur in a group of illuminated manuscripts, one of which was certainly done by the Vulcop brothers for Charles.

At the same time, we know that Henry VII's tapestry was bought from Jean Grenier of Tournai and that a year and a half earlier, on September 22, 1486, this English king granted his protection to "Paschal" and "John" Grenier, merchants from Tournai in France, and gave them permission to import tapestries into his domain. Without any doubt it is the leading Tournai tapestry merchant, Pasquier Grenier, and one of his four sons, that are referred to. Perhaps this order and the first weaving were done for a French noble (Dunois, Charles de France, or another) around 1467 — taking into account the time required to weave these eleven enormous pieces — and, according to Nicole Reynaud, it might be this very set that came into Charles VIII's possession; in any case, the fact that the emblem had been replaced proves that the work is too early to have been made for him. Pasquier Grenier certainly kept a number of ateliers working for him; he could thus have had more than one set woven simultaneously. But the Zamora set is most probably a repeat, made for someone who wanted to follow the fashion. It was woven, in any case, earlier than 1486.

It is also important to know that it comes from Tournai. Tapestry manufacture there was subject to regulation as early as 1398, for around the middle of the 15th century, the period when Philip the Good, Duke of Burgundy, ordered the sumptuous *Gideon* series from two of its master weavers to serve as a setting for the Order of the Golden Fleece ceremonies, this city supplanted Arras. But we hardly ever know from which center surviving works came, and only three can be definitely assigned to Tournai : this *Trojan War*, the Bourges *Story of St. Ursin*, and a millefleurs tapestry with the arms of Jean de Daillon (No. 47) — which, incidentally, was identified as from Tournai only during the preparation of this exhibition. The Zamora pieces, with others, are thus a landmark in the history of tapestry.

It is hardly less rare an event that we can put names to the designers, and it is unique for this period that we can compare the *petits patrons* with the completed works. Lastly, the series is a salient example of the taste of the period. To us, the enormous surfaces seem sometimes confused, but the complexity is perfectly in keeping with the function of tapestry as a continuous wall covering. The animation of the drawing is marvelous, the contrast in the faces (the brutality of the soldiers, the grace of some of the women) is hardly to be equaled.

This style of presentation continued to the end of the 15th century; we shall meet it again with all its typical features of composition, architecture, and characterization in another great series of the last third of the 15th century, the *Vengeance of Our Lord* (Nᵒˢ 12-14).

BIBLIOGRAPHY. A. Gómez Martinez and B. Chillón Sampedro, *Los tapices de la catedral de Zamora*, Zamora, Tip. de San José, 1925, p. 21-31, 63-86, 113-120 and pl. — Jean-Paul Asselberghs, *La tapisserie tournaisienne au XVᵉ siècle*, Tournai, 1967, p. 7-11 and 17-19, pl. p. 43-45; by the same author, *Charles VIII's Trojan War Tapestry*, in *Victoria and Albert Museum Yearbook*, 1969, p. 80-84, fig.; and *Les tapisseries tournaisiennes de la Guerre de Troie*, in *Artes Belgicae*, Brussels, Musées royaux d'art et d'histoire, 1972, p. 5-94, fig. (quotation from *Revue belge d'archéologie et d'histoire de l'art*, t. XXIX, 1970). — Geneviève Souchal, *Charles VIII et la tenture de la Guerre de Troie, ibid.*, p. 95-99. — Nicole Reynaud, article to appear in *Revue de l'Art*, 1973.

Note : The catalogue section inclusive of Nos. 7-11 was prepared from a text by Geneviève Souchal. The reworking of the text and the additions of descriptive material on each of the tapestries exhibited here is due to J.L. Schrader, Associate Curator, The Cloisters.

12-14
The Vengeance of Our Lord

This set is thought to have been inspired by the *Jewish Antiquities* of Flavius Josephus and especially by the apocryphal *Acta Pilati;* its immediate source was probably one of the literary texts of the 15th century that dealt with the Savior's "vengeance." This story, mingled with legend according to medieval tastes, was already known from a verse chronicle of the 12th century and had been dramatized, in the 15th, by Eustache Marcadé (died 1440), who made it the conclusion of his great *Mystery of the Passion.* Later it was spread out over four *journées* (day-length dramas) with 22,000 lines and 177 characters under the name of *The Mystery of the Vengeance of Our Lord,* and was printed for the first time in Paris in 1491 by Antoine Vérard. It was apparently staged at Amiens in 1446, at Abbeville in 1458 and 1463, and at Lille in 1484. The dramas could thus have inspired a tapestry; we know from Emile Mâle's work that the religious theater had a strong influence on artistic subject matters at the end of the Middle Ages. However, the same story occurs in *The Golden Legend* and in a romance entitled *The Destruction of Jerusalem,* published in 1491 by Jehan Trepperel; shorter and somewhat different, these versions cannot have been the source for the tapestry, but it shows that the theme was known widely enough to have been so used.

The story, which spreads over several decades, is that of the punishment of the Jews for the murder of Jesus, at the demand of Justice. The emperor

Tiberius, who had heard of Jesus' miracles and of the cure of Vespasian's leprosy by Veronica's veil, blames Pilate for having caused the death of so great a prophet. Pilate tries in vain to pass the blame but is brought to justice and commits suicide in his cell. Then come the reigns of Claudius and Nero. Nero gives orders for his statue to be set up in the Temple; the Jews rebel and Vespasian is sent with his son Titus to pacify Judaea. After being proclaimed emperor he returns to Rome, leaving Titus to starve out Jerusalem and seize it amid scenes of carnage.

An inventory of the French King Charles V of 1364 mentions two "tapis" of Vespasian, which no doubt formed part of a *Vengeance of Our Lord.* We know of at least three sets of this story, all quite different. One, two pieces of which are in the Tournai Museum and one in the Metropolitan, is similar to the Caesar tapestry in Berne; of the second, a single fragment, *Pilate and the Messenger,* is in the Österreichisches Museum für Angewandte Kunst in Vienna; and of the third set, several pieces survive, three of which are exhibited.

12
Nero Sends Vespasian and Titus to Judaea

Wool and silk
15 warp threads to the inch

Musée Lyonnais
des Arts Décoratifs

This is indeed Nero, but no attention has been paid to ancient dress. Nero, whose name is repeated twice, on his sleeve and between the medallions on which is the two-headed eagle, is dressed as a medieval sovereign, and his imperial crown is closed and high like a miter. Surrounded by numerous courtiers, he instructs "Vespasianus" and Titus, who kneel before him, to subdue Judaea. To the right, before the city wall, the soldiers take their leave; in the foreground "Vespasianus" prepares to mount his horse. Above, Titus and his companions leave through a fortified gate to embark on a ship that is already full of soldiers.

At the top are two banners with traces of inscriptions : *Vespasuen et le vaillant Titus qui noblement entreprinrent le fais; d'autres citez pour le grant renommee au devant d'eux les clefz on aporta.*

The letters on the two archways, Titus' scabbard, the borders of garments, and parts of harnesses, seem to be purely ornamental.

12 ft. 5 in. × 15 ft. 5 in. (3,80 m × 4,70 m)

detail

valpaliaus

Nero sends Vespasian and Titus to Judea

13
The Coronation of Vespasian

Wool and silk
About 12 warp
threads to the inch

The château of Saumur
Collection of the Church of
Notre-Dame de Nantilly

After subduing Judaea, Vespasian had only Jerusalem to take when Nero and Galba died (69 A.D.). While Otho and Vitellius quarreled Vespasian had himself proclaimed emperor by the Eastern army. Here he is crowned by two mitered figures, in the presence of his son Titus and a crowd of armed men.

10 ft. 2 in. × 10 ft. (3,52 m × 3,05 m)

14
The Siege of Jerusalem

Wool and silk
About 12 warp threads
to the inch

The château of Saumur
Collection of the Church
of Notre-Dame de Nantilly

Two other Saumur tapestries showing battle scenes have been considered until now to belong to this series, but Nicole Reynaud thinks their style is different and that they consequently belong to another set. In this piece, Titus is launching his final assault on the city. Its abbreviated name (Jhrlm) appears on the left above the gate being forced by Titus' soldiers. A replica of this tapestry, taller and narrower, and with Latin inscriptions at the bottom, is in the Bargello Museum, Florence.

9 ft. 4 in. × 17 ft. 11 in. (2,85 m × 5,65 m)

Less well known than the *Trojan War* (see Nos. 7-11), *The Vengeance of Our Lord* is so strikingly close to it in style and technique that it may be attributed to the same artists and weaving center.

There is exactly the same crowding as in the *Troy* set, and also the same way of isolating certain scenes by the use of identical architectural forms (low open archways flanked by smaller arches, gates set between crenelated towers, flattened tops to the towers, etc.); the figures are also the same, with their pointed elbows, their frequently bent knees, their faces with long noses and beards jutting at an angle from their chins. The *Vengeance* drawings were thus certainly by the same artists, or in other words, as Nicole Reynaud has pointed out, by the Vulcop brothers, painters to the French royal family. Perhaps the same cartoonist enlarged the drawings for the two sets.

The date of the drawing seems to be the same as that for the *Troy* set, or 1465-1475, the decade when the Vulcops were at the height of their activity. The artists seem to have disappeared before 1479.

The weaving may have been a little later, but it is also identical with that of the *Troy* tapestry — the only work apart from the Bourges *Life of St. Ursin* that we can so far attribute to Tournai with absolute certainty. *The Vengeance of Our Lord*

was thus clearly also woven at Tournai, and may well form part of the output of Pasquier Grenier and his sons. No doubt they did not have them woven directly in their own ateliers. Pasquier Grenier seems to have rapidly evolved into an entrepreneur and merchant, and when he died in 1493 it is "patterns" that are mentioned in his will and which he distributed among his sons. Most of his activity probably consisted of ordering cartoons, which he had woven in various different ateliers, and which remained his property. At the time, Tournai was, according to Commynes, "a fine and very strong city," "neutral" and living in "full liberty," but "very well disposed to the king." It is not surprising that Pasquier Grenier, who did a great deal of business in France, should have looked for other artists than those of the Low Countries and should have turned to the painters to Charles VII and his family. This is a point of some importance in that it would explain why some years later cartoons by the disciple of these artists who drew the *Trojan War* and the *Vengeance of Our Lord,* namely, the master of the *Hunt of the Unicorn* (Nos. 19-25), should also have found his way north.

The Lyon tapestry was bought in 1896 from Don Pedro Ruiz in Vitoria, Spain. The Saumur pieces have been in the church of Notre-Dame de Nantilly since an unknown date.

BIBLIOGRAPHY. Roger-A. d'Hulst, *Tapisseries flamandes du XIVᵉ au XVIIIᵉ siècle*, Brussels, l'Arcade, 1960, n° 9, p. 71-76, col. illus. — J.-P. Asselberghs, *La tapisserie tournaisienne au XVᵉ siècle*, Tournai, 1967, p. 12, 15, 16, 37-38 and pl. 30-32. — Nicole Reynaud, to appear shortly in *Revue de l'Art*, 1973.

15
The Crucifixion of St. Peter

Wool and silk
15-20 warp threads
to the inch

Beauvais Cathedral

This is the ninth piece we know of to day from a set of the *Life of St. Peter,* based on the New Testament and legend. It illustrates his martyrdom, as medieval piety saw it : St. Peter had asked to be affixed to the cross upside down, but the people were furious and wanted to free him and kill instead his persecutor, Nero, shown here on the left with a laurel crown. However, the apostle interceded for him, and God opened the eyes of the sorrowing onlookers : they saw angels with crowns of roses and lilies, and St. Peter took a book and read from it aloud. Seeing that the faithful perceived his glory, he recommended them to God once more and for the last time, and gave up the ghost. It is this event we see here, since the apostle has his eyes shut and two angels are carrying his soul up to God, while two others hold the book and the crown.

The scene is summed up in the inscription at the top : "How Saint Peter was bound to the cross with his feet toward heaven, the angels bringing him a crown of roses and lilies and a book from which he read that which he said to the people."

In the background are small banners with the word "Peace."

To the right are two shields : the upper one has the arms of the bishops of Beauvais, *or, a cross gules, accompanied by four keys of the same in pale;* the lower bears those of the tapestry's donor, Guillaume de Hellande, *quartered, in the first and last argent a bend gules charged with three hammers or* (Helland) *and in*

the second and third, or, a cross gules, accompanied by sixteen eagles azure (Montmorency), *with an inescutcheon gules semé with trefoils or, two addorsed fish* [bars] *of the same* (Nesle-Offémont). The complete tapestries of the set have these shields in all four corners; we therefore know that the left side is missing here, with perhaps one or two scenes, the other pieces having different numbers of scenes.

At the bottom is an added floral band.

8ft. 2in. × 4ft. 10in. (2,50 m × 1,50 m)

We know by the inscription, which has now disappeared, on this last piece, and by the inventory of the Beauvais Cathedral treasure made in 1464, that this tapestry was given by Bishop Guillaume de Hellande and that it was woven in 1460. Son of Robert, lord of Hellande en Caux, and of Jeanne de Montmorency, who was herself the daughter of Jean de Montmorency, lord of Beausault and of Breteuil en Beauvaisis, and of Isabeau de Nesle, Guillaume was archdeacon of the church of Rheims and later bishop of Beauvais, where he was consecrated on August 24, 1444, the year of the truce between the kings of France and England. He would have regarded this long-awaited suspension of hostilities as a particular blessing on his bishopric, whence the word "Peace" sewn into a tapestry that may have been "a public monument to his joy." Although this is certainly possible, this word is more likely to have been the bishop's personal device, since it appears on other belongings of his in the 1464 inventory, for instance a bench cover, two pieces for the episcopal throne, and five cushions in vermilion tapestry strewn with foliage.

As the date 1460 was once present on this last piece, it is probable that this was the year when the set was finished; furthermore, in a codicil added to his will in 1460 or 1461, Guillaume states that he has given *The Life of St. Peter* to his cathedral.

Opinions are divided as to whether the set was woven at Arras or Tournai. It is more interesting to speculate on where it belongs from the point of view of style. The tapestries' monumental character, the stiff figures with grave, impassive expressions, and the heavy folds of the clothes all recur in a group of tapestries of the third quarter of the 15th century, today usually attributed to Tournai, including especially the *Justice of Trojan and Herkinbald* in Berne, the *Story of Clovis* in Rheims, and the *Swan Knight* in Cracow and Vienna. Maybe this is a work of a painter like Baudouin de Bailleul in Arras, who ran ateliers making cartoons for weavers. This is more likely than that it is linked with a set of paintings illustrating the *Life and Passion of St. Peter*, done by Henri de Beaumetiel after drawings by Robert Campin for the chapel of St. Peter in Tournai, and which are mentioned as early as 1438. The closest analogy is with a *Crucifixion of St. Peter* on the left wing of a mid-15th century altarpiece in the Metropolitan Museum, which Charles Sterling attributes to a painter of the Picardy school who was strongly influenced by Rogier van der Weyden. The tapestry nearest to these pieces in style seems to be a little-known work in the Isabella Stewart Gardner Museum in Boston, the *Destruction of the House of Ahab*.

The St. Peter set was kept complete in Beauvais Cathedral until 1793, when it was dispersed. Several pieces were given back to the Cathedral in 1884 by the General Council of the Oise département; others found their way into private collections and are now in the United States or in Paris.

BIBLIOGRAPHY. Charles Sterling, *The Metropolitan Museum of Art. A catalogue of French paintings, XV-XVIII centuries*, Cambridge, Harvard University Press, 1958, p. 1-7, illus. — Jean-Paul Asselberghs, *La tapisserie tournaisienne au XVe siècle*, Tournai, 1967, p. 12-16. — Adolph Cavallo, *Tapestries of Europe and of Colonial Peru in the Museum of Fine Arts, Boston*, Boston, Museum of Fine Arts (1968), n° 3, t. I, p. 51-55, t. II, pl. 3 (col.), 3a abd 3b.

16
Horsemen

Wool and silk
18 warp threads
to the inch

Walters Art Gallery,
Baltimore

These five horsemen in short robes, except the royal one on the right, who is richly attired and wears a hat with a closed crown, are obviously part of a larger tapestry.

12 ft. 4 in. × 5 ft. 2 in. (3,61 m × 1,70 m)

This superb piece has not been exhibited before. It is similar to a tapestry in the church of Notre Dame at Nantilly, Saumur, which shows noblemen riding with ladies. There are the same rather stiff figures, wearing similar damask robes with the relatively simple motifs of the middle of the 15th century, making the same characteristic gestures with their hands — forefinger pointed and the thumb separated from the other fingers — and especially with the same faces — strongly marked features, small, full mouths, heavy eyelids — in three-quarter view.

We shall meet the same type again (Nos. 28-30). The vigor and sincerity of these works, which were probably woven at Arras or Tournai, place them among the most successful examples of mid-15th century French decorative art.

Such a date is suggested not only by the style of the horsemen, but also by the fashion of their clothes. The king still wears the long sovereign's robe, while his companions, whose shaped hoods recall those in the Chatsworth *Hunts* (Victoria and Albert Museum), have the short robe with triangular pleats of the middle of the 15th century, and their hair is cut at ear level in a way that was in fashion from about 1410 to 1465.

Bought by Henry B. Walters, at an unknown date, from the collector Raoul Heilbronner.

17
Charlemagne

Wool
12-15 warp threads
to the inch

Musée des Beaux-Arts,
Dijon

In this piece, which is mutilated on all four sides, Charlemagne is shown not as he so often is, as a hero (see Nos. 3-4), but as a church-builder. He wears a large hat with the imperial crown, and over his armor an emblazoned tabard, *per pale of the eagle of the Empire and of the fleurs-de-lys of France* — arms that were attributed to him in the 13th century by Adenet le Roi in his *Enfances Ogier*. Behind him are courtiers, including the archbishop "Turpin," and masons who are occupied in building the church, wielding trowel and spirit level and bringing stones. J.-P. Asselberghs has recently suggested that this scene comes from a Story of Charlemagne inspired by the legend attributed to Turpin. Closely related tapestries, based on the same legend, portraying scenes of the *Battle of Roncevaux*, are in the Victoria and Albert Museum, at Tournai, in the Bargello Museum, and in the Musée du Cinquantenaire, Brussels.

8 ft. 5 in. × 4 ft. 9 in. (2,55 m × 1,45 m)

The inscriptions on the *Battle of Roncevaux* tapestries show forms used in the Tournai dialect, so one may suppose that the Charlemagne tapestry was woven in this city. There is a similar crowding of characters in numerous other tapestries attributed to Tournai. But we cannot tell whether the cartoons were done in a specialized atelier, such as that of Baudouin de Bailleul in Arras, or drawn by a painter like those for the *Trojan War* (Nos. 7-11).

The tapestry was probably woven during the reign of Louis XI (1461-1483), early in which the very high bonnets worn here by several characters appeared.

Sold at Sotheby's, London, May 11, 1962. Acquired in 1964 by the Musée des Beaux-Arts.

BIBLIOGRAPHY. Louis-Carolus Barré, *Contribution à l'étude de la légende carolingienne. Les armes de Charlemagne dans l'héraldique et l'iconographie médiévale*, in *Mémorial du voyage en Rhénanie de la Société nationale des antiquaires de France*, Paris, 1953, p. 289-308, 11 illus. — P. Quarré, *Musée des Beaux-Arts de Dijon. Nouvelles acquisitions* in *La Revue du Louvre et des musées de France*, 1964, p. 249-250, illus. — *Charlemagne, œuvre, rayonnement et survivances* (Exhibition catalogue), Aix-la-Chapelle, 1965, n° 758, p. 527 and pl. VIII. — J.-P. Asselberghs, *La tapisserie tournaisienne au XVe siècle*. Tournai, 1967, p. 16 and 25-26, n° and pl. 10.

detail

18-24
The Hunt of the Unicorn

Wool, silk,
and metal thread
13-21 warp threads
to the inch

The Metropolitan
Museum of Art,
The Cloisters Collection

While the *Lady with the Unicorn* (Nos 37-42) takes its name perhaps unjustifiably from an animal that plays only a secondary role in the series, this admirable set, which rivals the Cluny set in beauty, is devoted to the pursuit and capture of the unicorn. According to the medieval bestiaries, treatises more concerned with symbolism and morality than zoology, the unicorn, a cloven-footed horse with a goat's beard and a long fluted horn, was so wild and swift that no one could take him by chasing. In order to capture him, a maiden had to be left in the forest, and the untamable beast would come and go to sleep with his head on her lap; the hunters could then seize him. This miraculous capture was considered to symbolize the incarnation of Christ in the womb of the Virgin Mary, and tapestries showed the capture associated with the Annunciation.

These seven tapestries do not form a homogeneous set. It has long been recognized that the *Start of the Hunt* and the *Unicorn in Captivity* are different in style from the other five pieces, but also, from the point of view of subject matter, they fit together poorly : the *Unicorn in Captivity* does not easily follow the last piece in the main group, in which the animal appears to be dead, while the *Start of the Hunt* does not suggest a particular kind of hunt. These two tapestries were no doubt bought by or given to the person who ordered the other five, since they also bear his monogram; but they come from another set, and the fact that they are together today is due to chance, to an early owner's penchant for the theme, or because a certain wall surface had to be covered.

18
The Unicorn at the Fountain

First series, 1

Hunters surround a fountain from which flows a stream with wild animals on either side, including a hyena, an animal rarely shown except in the bestiaries. The unicorn places his horn in the water to purify it, his horn

having been thought to possess this power. A monogram composed of an A and an uncial E back to front, linked with a girdle, is woven into the center and the four corners.

12 ft. 1 in. × 12 ft. 5 in. (3,68 m × 3,78 m)

19
The Unicorn Tries to Escape

First series, 2

The hunters attack the animal with lances. A monogram F-R woven at the top more finely than the rest (20-22 threads to the inch) is certainly a later addition.

12 ft. 1 in. × 14 ft. (3,68 m × 4,27 m)

20
The Unicorn Defends Himself

First series, 3

The animal defends himself by charging, and disembowels one of the dogs with his horn.

12 ft. 1 in. × 13 ft. 2 in. (3,68 m × 4,01 m)

21
The Capture of the Unicorn

First series, 4

The piece consists of two fragments that were probably cut to cover double doors. Here we see the moment when the unicorn has come to put his front hooves in the maiden's lap. There remain only an arm and a hand delicately clasping the animal's neck. To the left, a female attendant signals to the hunters, who have today disappeared; only a horn-blower appears amongst the foliage.

6 ft. 8 in. × 4 ft. 4 in. (2,03 m × 1,31 m)

22
The Death of the Unicorn

First series, 5

Pierced by spears (top left), the unicorn lies with closed eyes across a horse that has brought him to the château entrance, where he is offered to a noble couple.

12 ft. 1 in. × 12 ft. 9 in. (3,68 m × 3,89 m)

23
The Start of the Hunt

Second series, 1

Pierced by spears (top left), the unicorn lies (center) with closed eyes across a horse that has brought him to the château entrance, where he is offered to a noble couple.

12 ft. 1 in. × 10 ft. 4 in. (3,68 m × 3,15 m)

24
The Unicorn in Captivity

Second series, 2

Against a millefleurs background, the unicorn lies in an enclosure, fastened by a chain to a pomegranate tree.

12 ft. 1 in. × 9 ft. 9 in. (3,68 m × 2,97 m)

As noted above, there are clear differences between the first and second series. Only the second are true millefleurs tapestries — that is, pieces in which the figures are placed against a field of juxtaposed flowers that occupies the entire background. In the five pieces of the first series, although the foliage element is important, the action takes place in a real landscape with a flower-bordered stream at the bottom, a forest above, and at the top, châteaux silhouetted against a sky. (Much of the detail at the tops has disappeared, the tapestries having been cut along their upper edges to the shape of the trees.) Furthermore, the foliage treatment is not the same in the two tapestries of the second series, and the blue of the backgrounds differs from the blue of the "classical" millefleurs tapestries (Nos. 32, 33, 35, for example). Turning to the monograms, the drawing of the A-E is thinner in the second series, much more harmonious in the first, with the horizontal of the A decorated with a kind of upside-down fleur-de-lys, and the riser of the E notched halfway up (this detail is missing in the monogram of the fragments, no doubt due to an oversight by the cartoonist). Lastly, the style of the figures is different in the two series, perhaps most notably in the *Start of the Hunt,* where the differences from one figure to another may result from the use of unrelated models. The drawing of the figures in the first series is generally of much higher quality.

James Rorimer concluded from these differences that the two millefleurs tapestries were made much later than the others. He saw in the five of the first series an allusion to the marriage of Anne of Brittany to Louis XII, which took place on January 8, 1499, and thought that the millefleurs tapestries were added when François d'Angoulême — possibly the young man in the center of the *Start of the Hunt* — married Claude of France in 1514. The whole work would then have been given by the new king to his godfather, François de la Rochefoucauld, and the F and R sewn into the top of the

Unicorn Tries to Escape would be the latter's initials (unless they stood for Francis I — *Franciscus Rex*). Rorimer based this hypothesis on the fact that Anne of Brittany owned a large collection of tapestries, that a manuscript in the Pierpont Morgan Library made for her about 1496 is decorated with the letters A, N, and E, that she used the emblem of the girdle and even founded an order named after it, that she loved flowers and wore clothes and jewels similar to those of the lady in No. 22, and lastly that the colors of the nobleman who offers her his arm are those of Louis XII and the features of the royal couple have something in common with those of the pair to whom the unicorn is brought. A further argument for him was the presence on the dogs' collars of ornaments resembling fleurs-de-lys and the inscription OFANC RE, xhich he interpreted as O FRANCORUM REX.

These arguments are not convincing. The resemblances are questionable, the costumes those of the time; and all contemporary monarchs owned tapestries. There were countless examples of letters joined by a girdle at the end of the Middle Ages. Furthermore, such monograms never seem to use the first and last letters of a first name, and we know of no other work with this emblem that belonged to Anne of Brittany. Such joined letters are usually the initials of a couple's first names, or sometimes those of a first name and a surname; or, like the two facing E's that Philip the Good, Duke of Burgundy, used at the end of his reign, or the two back-to-back E's that the last marshal of Saint-Pol and his daughter Jacqueline of Luxembourg used (see No. 49), they appear (obscurely to us today) as the distinctive sign of a person or sometimes of a family. Doubtless there were coats of arms in the sky at the top of the tapestries, which may explain why they were so carefully cut away, probably at the time of the Revolution. Our present knowledge, then, does not allow us to say for whom these tapestries were made. Without doubt, it was someone of high rank, since the beauty and richness of the pieces are exceptional.

Firstly, the material is of rare sumptuousness : fine wool, numerous metallic threads, silk in even greater abundance and in infinitely more varied shades than in, for example, the *Lady with the Unicorn* (Nos. 37-42). The colors, especially, are of unsurpassed brilliance : on the plants, deep blues and greens set off with yellow and white highlights, sparkling red on the garments and fruit, a host of light tones, and especially the lavish use of a color that was rare at the time, a fiery orange that appears both on the hose of several of the hunters and, with unprecedented daring, on one of the dogs in the *Start of the Hunt*. The workmanship is also of an extraordinary perfection, at least in the five pieces of the first series, that of the *Death of the Unicorn*, which is a little finer in weave than the others, being the best of all. The fabrics — damasks, velvets, moirés — are treated with remarkable virtuosity, and the faces are modeled in delicate and varied tones, with pink on the cheeks and red on the lips. There is nothing to match, in other tapestries of the time, the subtle shading of the ground, where there is a clear impression of thick grass and flowers growing in abundance.

The drawing, too, is exceptionally fine, except perhaps in the *Start of the Hunt*, where the head of one of the figures, too large, is certainly by a second artist. One might object that the compositions are still entirely Gothic, showing nothing of the balanced arrangements of the Renaissance, but these scenes, with their very high horizons and figures placed over one another in the midst of thick vegetation, admirably fulfill tapestry's role of wall decoration. The detail is unrivaled, whether in the plants, which are drawn in such a lifelike way that almost all have been identified, or in the animals, of which we hardly know which most to admire : the unicorn, enticed or wounded, the pheasant admiring its reflection in the waters of the fountain, the stag serenely dreaming on the banks of the stream, the innumerable dogs, the birds (partridge, woodcock, heron, ducks), or the squirrel hidden in the hazel tree, on the left of the *Death of the Unicorn*.

The characters — a mixture of graceful figures, blond youths, slender women with mannered gestures, and servants with nutcracker jaws and gloomy expressions, leaning forward with knees and elbows bent — have not yet been studied in their most important aspect : their style. Their small patterns — which may have been enlarged to full size by another painter — are probably by an artist, today unknown, whose hand may also be seen in engravings of books printed in Paris in the last twenty years of the 15th century and in the early 16th, who also inspired several stained-glass windows, particularly in Paris and in Normandy, and who no doubt also made miniatures. The line of his engravings is discernible in the illuminations of a tiny *Book of Hours* belonging to Anne of Brittany, which was done after 1491 and is now in the Bibliothèque Nationale.

Nicole Reynaud, who is writing a thesis on the painters of Charles VII and his family (see Nos. 7-13), thinks that this artist, in whose work one may be surprised to find figures in some ways similar to those in the *Trojan War*, otherwise so different (see Nos. 7-11), was the pupil of the masters she is studying. She attributes the Louvre's Troy drawings to this man, who must have inherited a stock of models from which he borrowed his hatchet-faced figures with bent knees; these appear in his work alongside more genial and static characters that were probably more in accord with his own temperament.

The designer of the *Hunt of the Unicorn* no doubt played an important part in French art at the end of the 15th century. It has not yet been adequately assessed; the task has been made more difficult by the disappearance of so many paintings and historical Paris buildings. He probably worked both for royalty and the tapestry ateliers, whether directly by supplying cartoons or indirectly through engravings that were enlarged or transposed by others.

Which ateliers? For the date of these tapestries, the end of the 15th century, this is almost impossible to say. We know of various centers, the most important of which at the time were Tournai and Brussels, and we have information on a number of weavers, and on the works they made, yet we can only rarely match them up with the tapestries that have been preserved. We do not really know where the unicorn tapestries were woven. It does appear that they were done in low-warp, which was the only technique at the time that could reproduce such detailed cartoons. Brussels weavers used it, but Tournai also had, side by side with its high-warp weavers, "marcheteurs" who worked in low-warp. There were other centers as well. The odds are perhaps in favor of Brussels, which seems to have been responsible for the most lavish works of this period. Certain details tend to support this : the treatment of the moirés and damasks, for instance, and especially of the foliage, in which an abundance of pale green, yellow, and cream silk catches the light.

The fact that the *Hunt of the Unicorn* was probably woven in low-warp technique is not without importance. The difference imparted to it by this form of weaving compared with tapestries like the *Lady with the Unicorn* (Nos. 37-42), which were most likely woven on high-warp looms, its fineness, and its use of rich materials and subtle colors, have so far blinded us to similarities that appear if we consider only the drawing of the figures. The unicorn ensnared by the maiden (No. 21) is the mirror image of the one whose neck the Lady caresses in *Sight* (No. 37). The attendant who delivers him — her face with noseline extended into the

pure arch of her eyebrows, her dark hood turned back over a gold-worked ribbon, her large fine hands, her slim, arched back, flat-chested body in a tight red-velvet dress, her belt ending in a pendant and her W-neckline with a golden chain — is the sister of the women in *Hearing* (No. 38). The rose hedge is identical with that in *Taste* (No. 40), several of the dogs in the *Start of the Hunt* are like those in the other set, and the civet in the *Unicorn at the Fountain,* an animal rarely shown, comes up again in *Taste.* The lack of male figures in the *Lady with the Unicorn* prevents us from carrying the comparison further; however, there are undeniable similarities in the drawing, the difficulty being to discount the differences due not only to the weaving and the colors but also to the influence on the work of the cartoonists, whose job was to bring the sketches up to weaving size, and who were probably not the same.

The Cloisters' tapestries are mentioned in 1728 in an inventory of the château of Verteuil at Charente, which belonged to the La Rochefoucauld family. At the time of the Revolution, the People's Society of Ruffec, nearby, urged that of Verteuil to destroy any tapestries with royal arms, and it was no doubt at this time that the upper parts were removed, since they must have carried coats of arms. The tapestries escaped destruction and were bought back in the 19th century by a La Rochefoucauld and stayed at Verteuil. Soon after 1920 they were bought by John D. Rockefeller, Jr. who gave them to The Cloisters in 1937 and 1938.

BIBLIOGRAPHY. Marquet de Vasselot and Weigert, *op. cit.,* p. 62, 151, 189 and 229. — James J. Rorimer, *The Unicorn Tapestries at the Cloisters,* The Metropolitan Museum of Art (1962), 40 p., 35 flg., cov. ill. by the same author; *The Metropolitan Museum of Art, The Cloisters, The building and the collection of medieval art in Fort Tryon Park,* New York, 3rd ed., 1963, p. 162-175, fig. — E.J. Alexander and Carol H. Woodward, *The flora of the Unicorn Tapestries* (article in the *Journal of the New York Botanical Garden,* May-June 1941), 1967, 29 p., fig. — Julien Coffinet, *Arachné ou l'art de la tapisserie,* Paris, Bibliothèque des Arts (1971), p. 202-203 and 205; pl. 201 and 203. — Geneviève Souchal, *Le cartonnier de la Chasse à la licorne,* to appear in *Revue de l'art.*

The Unicorn in Captivity, *detail*

25
Noble Couple

Wool
12-15 warp threads
to the inch

The Metropolitan Museum of Art

Two inventories, one of 1416, the other of 1422, describe a subject similar to that of this piece; it shows, as was frequent in the 15th century, a lord and a lady holding a falcon (see No. 36), but here, the lord is stirring the water of a little basin with a stick, and in the background there are two woodmen, a running child, and a small figure holding a branch. Of a similar style must have been John of Berry's great backing-piece in gold thread "in the middle of which is a queen holding a sparrow hawk and two ladies around, one pouring water into a basin and the other beating the water"; and Charles VI owned a work "made *à la marche* [in low warp], on a green background, with figures of children and others, little birds and

detail

foliage, and in the middle a fountain and a lady stirring the water with a little stick." This action may be explained by the advice of King Modus in one of the most famous books on hunting of the Middle Ages : a newly caught bird will not bathe, and one must splash the water so that, attracted by the sound, it will do so.

Notice the woman's splendid headdress, the large chain that the lord wears across his sleeve, and the bells hanging from his belt, and also from the cross-belt of the little figure on the right; such bells were very fashionable in the second half of the 14th and in the 15th century, on collars, belts, scarves, and other pieces of clothing.

10 ft. 2 in. × 9 ft. 9 in. (3,10 m × 2,97 m)

This exquisitely colored tapestry, much restored, is interesting in that it shows that the convention of placing figures on a blue hillock set against a red background with "torn-off" branches — the "vermilion field" on the old documents — existed well before the making of the *Lady with the Unicorn* (Nos. 37-42), the best-known example of the conception.

Our tapestry must be dated around 1420-1430, though it has been considered much later because of the shoes *à la poulaine* worn by the man, the costume style, the type of face, and the weaving itself. These arguments are not persuasive. Shoes were pointed from the end of the 14th century, and the type of cloak and the two-horned headdress of the lady went out of fashion about 1425. The style of the work is not of the mid-century; rather, it is reminiscent of the *Offering of the Heart* in the Cluny Museum, which can hardly be later than 1510-1415. The sketchily treated flowers on the hillock are closer to the rudimentary plants of the 14th century (compare No. 1) and of the first half of the 15th than to the naturalistic bouquets that appeared in the second half of the century. Furthermore, though cartoons were reused for a considerable period of time, we have proof that out-of-fashion costumes were often brought up to date (see Nos. 55-56). Another example of this updating is No. 28, which reuses the model for the present work with some modifications : the falcon is reversed, the lady's costume is cut low at the neck, and the head is different — more inclined and with a headdress that seems a little different from the present one.

A drawing in Dresden depicting a joust on water, a seated couple, and lords and ladies with a mirror, is considered by Jacques Dupont to have close analogies with the *Très Riches Heures* of the Duke of Berry, to be a Paris work of about 1410, and to be the earliest surviving sketch for a tapestry. Though the men in this drawing wear either cloaks or short robes and the extravagant hoods found in the *Hunts* from Chatsworth, all of which remained in fashion for some time, the women have the high-belted costumes with small collars and wide sleeves we see here, and one of them has the same kind of two-horned headdress.

All of this, together with the precious hand gestures, suggests a French work not far from the mannerism of the courtly period, a basic characteristic of the International Gothic style of the beginning of the 15th century, but admirably rounded out by the realism of the period that followed. It is probable that this *Noble Couple* was woven in the center that was then so famous that tapestry itself was called after it in several languages (English, *arras*, Italian, *arrazi*; Spanish, *paño de ras*). The English occupation seems to have dealt a death-blow to the Paris tapestry weavers, since only two appear on the tax roll imposed by the King of England on the burghers of the city in 1422. We therefore suggest that the present work, along with the two following, was produced in Arras.

From the collection of Frank Jay Gould, Paris, who gave it to the Metropolitan Museum in 1946; now exhibited at The Cloisters.

BIBLIOGRAPHY. Jacques Dupont, *French school (about 1410)*, in *Old Masters Drawing...*, vol. IX, n° 35, Dec. 1934, p. 51-52 and pl. 51. — *2,000 Years of tapestry weaving. A loan exhibition, Wadsworth Atheneum, Hartford, December 7, 1951 to January 27, 1952, The Baltimore Museum of Art, February 27, 1952 to March 25, 1952*, n° 72, p. 35 and pl. VII.

26
Noble Couple

Wool, with some silk
(probably due to restoration)
12-15 warp threads
to the inch

The Metropolitan Museum of Art

"The French are a noble nation; they are wise, very versed and delicate in all matters touching the art of living, courtesy, and nobility. They are elegant in their apparel and magnificent in their equipment; they are dressed according to their own fashion." So wrote Gutierre Díaz de Gámez, who came to France in 1405, in the account of his journeys he made to his master, the Spanish nobleman Pero Niño. There is surely something of this elegance of the first years of the 15th century — of the royal court, of that of the Dukes of Anjou, Berry, and Burgundy — in this scene which, despite a great deal of restoration, remains one of the most gracious records

we have of the life of the lavish patrons of the age. Despite the Hundred Years War, they were able to amass fabulous treasures; in the famous manuscripts of John of Berry and in works like this they have left us a reflection of their luxury and refinement.

8 ft. 7 in. × 7 ft. 8 in. (2,60 m × 2,34 m)

Probably woven in Arras about 1420, this elegant work was made on the same cartoon, reversed, as No. 25, perhaps a few years earlier. It is narrower, and does not include the little character with bells on his costume, and the red background does not show at all in the lower corners. It is interesting to see how cartoons were used again with small differences. This was facilitated in the high-warp process by the fact that the cartoon could be held up over the warp.

This work was owned by the Bacri brothers of Paris about 1912. It was given to the Metropolitan Museum by Mr. and Mrs. Frederick B. Pratt in 1935.

27
Lady Holding a Falcon

Wool
12-15 warp threads
to the inch

The Metropolitan Museum of Art

This lady in a garment lined with ermine, sitting on a blue hillock with a falcon on her wrist, was woven almost to the same cartoon as No. 25, she is thus, except for her head, also the mirror image of the lady in No. 26. Here, the trees planted on the hillock take up much less of the background, leaving more space for the "torn-off" branches, among which play small rabbits, the drawing of which is the same as in the *Lady with the Unicorn* (Nos. 37-42) of half a century later.

8 ft. 6 in. × 5 ft. 7 in. (2,59 m × 1,70 m)

We again observe how the weavers worked, altering cartoons to suit their convenience. Here, the lady's headdress, with hairnet, padding, and hanging fabric, suggests a later date than the two-pointed headdresses of Nos. 25 and 26. We can therefore date this charming work — although it has been much restored — at around 1435-1440.

Same history and bibliography as for No. 26.

28-30
Lords and Ladies

These pieces, known as the *Rose Offering,* are magnificently authoritative despite their restoration.

28
Four Lords and Four Ladies

Wool, silk,
and metal thread
12-15 warp threads
to the inch

The Metropolitan Museum of Art

The figures are set out in two registers, against red, white, and green stripes, and are not linked in any action. Sumptuously attired, they have a bored look and seem to be keeping themselves in countenance by holding a rose or fingering something on their belts.

12 ft. 6 in. × 8 ft. 9 in. (3,81 m × 2,67 m)

29
Three Lords and Two Ladies

Here the figures appear, lost in their dreams, against stripes patterned with rose trees that emerge from a hillock.

10 ft. 2 in. × 8 ft. 3 in. (3,10 m × 2,51 m)

30
Two Lords and one Lady

There are only three figures on this piece. It is slightly different from the others in that the rose trees are much bigger. At the bottom on the left is a monkey holding a kitten.

9 ft. 7 in. × 10 ft. 11 3/4 in. (3,33 m × 3,84 m)

These tapestries used to be considered an illustration of the rose-offering custom, according to which, in the spring, the peers of France presented roses to the Parlement. Taking another view, Stella Rubenstein has suggested a connection with the French king Charles VII (1422-1461), whose colors were white, red, and green, and one of whose emblems was the rose tree. The royal connection is the more likely, for the tapestries are sumptuous, with metal threads not only in the clothes and jewelry but also, most unusually, in the leaves, buds, and open rose hearts.

Some have considered these pieces to be examples of French art of the period between the painters to the Duke of Berry and Fouquet, or even based on paintings by Fouquet. M. Rosenthal has linked them with the engravings of an *Exercitum super Pater Noster,* which he believes were made in the Low Countries around 1430, and with engravings by the Master of the Garden of Love. Lilli Freschel, on the other hand, compares the lord on the right of No. 30 with the figures of the German Playing Card Master and suggests that they have a common source : a Van Eyck portrait of Duke Philip of Brabant.

It would be quite in keeping with the customs of the time

for the figures in these tapestries to be based on popular personalities. Nevertheless, the artist who drew these awkward figures has given them a vigorous personal character and made them different from any others. They have an unforgettable presence, placed as they are against the background for no other reason than to decorate it with their striking simplicity. These characters are an easily recognizable type, with their style of drawing, their attitudes, and especially their faces — so characteristic with prominent eyelids, fixed expression, curved mouths, and small rounded chins. We meet them again in two roughly contemporary tapestries, the *Horsemen* of Baltimore (No. 16) and of Saumur, in which the characters wear similar costume, cut from the same cloths.

These pieces have usually been dated around 1435-1440, but they are perhaps later by a few years, since such details as the dark locks on the women's foreheads do not seem much in evidence before 1450. There was, incidentally, such misery in the period before the truce of 1444 that even though luxury went side by side with direst poverty, the purchase of such a tapestry is more easily explicable a little later, when Charles VII had recovered the whole of his kingdom and France was emerging from the effects of the Hundred Years War.

Formerly in the collection of Sigismond Bardac, Paris; purchased by the Metropolitan Museum in 1909.

31
The Winged Stags

Wool and silk
12 warp threads
to the inch

Musée Départemental des
Antiquités de la Seine-Maritime,
Rouen

Three winged stags, around whom float elegant banners with partially restored inscriptions, appear against a flowered landscape. The one in the center is lying in an enclosure and holds a red standard sprinkled with suns, showing a St. Michael fighting the dragon, and these lines :

C'est. estandart / est. une enseigne
Qui. aloial françois enseigne
De jamais ne la bandonner.
S'il ne veult son / bonheur [honneur?] donner.
(This standard is a sign that tells each loyal Frenchman never to abandon it, if he does not wish to give up his honor.)

In the foreground, two lions are accosted to the shield of the kings of France, *azure three fleurs-de-lys or.* To the right, the second stag, which has around its neck a crown to which are attached the royal arms, prepares to step into the enclosure. On its banner are the lines :

Si. nobles n a / dessoubz les cieulx
Je ne. pourroye / porter. mieulx.

(So noble there are not beneath the skies... I could not carry better.)

To the left, the tapestry is mutilated; there remains only the fore part of a third stag, similar to the second, with these lines on its banner :

Armes. porte. tres glorieuses. [beginning of badly restored word]
Et. sur. toutes victorieuses.
(I carry very glorious arms, victorious over all others.)

11 ft. 5 in. × 12 ft. 6 in. (3,47 m × 3,80 m)

This poetical and magnificently vigorous work has been attributed by Paul Martin to Charles VII (1422-1461), who had taken over as one of his devices the winged stag of his grandfather Charles V, as well as the sun of his father Charles VI He used the rose tree as his personal device (No. 30), and also bore standards with images of St. Michael. The terms "glorious" and "victorious" fit him well in view of his reconquest of France from the English.

However, C. Ducourtial and I. du Pasquier follow E. Picot in linking this work with the founding of the Order of

St. Michael by Louis XI on August 1, 1469. They see in the two lions of the foreground two leopards that they think personify Charles of France, the king's brother, and so date the tapestry before the birth of the Dauphin, the future Charles VIII, on June 30, 1470.

This theory does not stand up, since in this case the royal arms would be surrounded by the collar of the order; we know of no exception to this rule from 1469 on. In any case, the winged stag is an emblem that was used by kings of France from Charles V on. They support, rampant, the arms of France on the Munich Boccaccio miniature, which is attributed to Fouquet and shows the "Lit de Justice" of Vendôme that condemned the Duke of Alençon in 1458. Again, at the beginning of the 16th century, a translation of the *Chronicles of France* of Robert Gaguin, printed in 1515, contains an engraving in which St. Denis and St. Rémy appear on either side of the royal arms, which are surrounded by the ribbon of St. Michael and already topped by the closed crown, while below there is an inscription carried by two winged stags, erect on their hind legs, with crowns around their necks.

Martin and Jean-Bernard de Vaivre have shown that the standard on our tapestry is that of Charles VII "in crimson vermilion satin with a Saint Michael in the field... powdered all over with golden suns," as the chronicler Alain Chartier describes it, corroborated by other sources. However, there are similar references in the accounts of Louis XI, at least in 1464.

The verses on the banners can hardly be interpreted otherwise than as an allusion to the victories of Charles VII at the end of the Hundred Years War : the battle of Formigny (1450) and of the reconquest of Normandy, and the battle of Castillon (1453), and the reconquest of Guienne. Do the two lions outside the enclosure, symbolizing the kingdom, represent the leopards of England (in heraldry, the animals are very similar)? The implication would be that the work was ordered by royalty. But the shield on the enclosure in the center of the composition is buckler-shaped, which would be quite unusual for a king of France. We should not exclude the possibility that the tapestry was woven for a "loyal Frenchman" — a nobleman who wished to demonstrate his loyalty to the king.

We should look for its date not in the years between 1450 and 1461, as Martin would have it, from the type of armor worn by St. Michael — this could have been archaicized — but between 1450 and 1461, and in any case, if we accept the Louis XI hypothesis, before 1469.

From the point of view of style, the stags are much better drawn than the lions and the landscape that surrounds them; they appear to have been done by a French painter of Fouquet's circle.

From the collection of Gaston Bissieu. Acquired by the Musée Départemental des Antiquités de la Seine-Maritime in 1892.

BIBLIOGRAPHY. Paul Martin, *La tapisserie royale des « Cerfs-volants »*, in *Bulletin Monumental*, t. CV, 1947, p. 197-208, pl., fig. — V^e *centenaire de la création à Amboise de l'ordre de saint Michel. De l'ordre de saint Michel à la Légion d'honneur, Exposition, 7 juin-20 juillet* [1970], *Hôtel de Ville d'Amboise*, catalogue by C. Ducourtial and J. du Pasquier, n° 12, p. 30-31. — J.-B. de Vaivre, *Les cerfs ailés et la tapisserie de Rouen*, to appear shortly.

32
Semiramis

Wool and silk
About 15 warp threads
to the inch

Honolulu Academy of Arts

This attractive tapestry, with three women against a classical millefleurs background, probably comes from a *Heroines* set. The figure in the center, wearing a rich surcoat over a more or less fanciful breastplate, is turned toward a messenger armed with a long arrow, and is combing her hair. On the left, a servant holds up a mirror. Above is an inscription in alexandrines :

Je fus Sémiramis Royne de babilone.
barbariens conquis Ydois et suriens.
jusques en septentrion alé et mis mon trosne
et sy occis le roy des ethiopiens.

(I was Semiramis, Queen of Babylon. I conquered barbarian Indians and Syrians. I went up into the North and set my throne there, and slew the king of the Ethiopians.)

Semiramis was indeed one of the nine *Heroines* that from the 14th century on were paired with the *Heroes* (see Nos. 3-4). Curiously, they include no heroine from the Bible — though Judith would seem tailor-made for this — but only legendary characters, including several Amazons : Hyppolyta, Menalippa, Lampheto, and Penthesilea, the Amazon, queen, who appears on a millefleurs tapestry in Angers.

Queen of Assyria and Babylon, Semiramis was daughter of a mortal and a goddess. She was exposed by her mother in the desert, and there fed by doves before being found by a shepherd. She married first the governor of Syria and then King Ninus himself, whom she later had assassinated. She became mistress of the Assyrian empire and reconquered Media, Persia, Armenia, and Arabia, and subjected Egypt, Lybia, a part of Ethiopia, and Asia as far as the Indus River. The Hanging Gardens of Babylon, one of the wonders of the world, were attributed to her. After she had reigned for forty-two years, her son contested her throne, and she disappeared into heaven in the shape of a dove.

Her beauty was as famous as her courage. According to the Latin historian Valerius Maximus, she had only to appear half-naked and with hair disheveled, when a rebellion broke out while she was dressing, for all to be settled. It is probably this scene that is shown here.

8 ft. 3 in. × 8 ft. 5 in. (2,52 m × 2,55 m)

From the point of view of style, these elongated figures with tiny heads are similar to those of the *Lady with the Unicorn* (Nos. 37-42), with the exception of a certain awkwardness in the central character. No doubt the weaving center was the same, but not the cartoon maker. He was probably an artist of the still little-known French circle of the end of the 15th century.

The costumes, from what knowledge we have, confirm this end-of-the-century dating. The messenger-girl still wears, on her high, clear forehead, the little ring of dark cloth that was fashionable in the middle of the 15th century and became rarer after 1480; but perhaps the artist was trying to indicate that the characters were from the past. The servant's dress, however, already has sleeves cut back to show a chemise underneath. Semiramis, on the other hand, wears an open surcoat that at the time had become no more than ceremonial dress, as worn, for example, by Anne de Beaujeu, sister of King Charles VIII, on the triptych by the masters of Moulins.

From the Manzi collection, sold in 1919. Bought by Leon Schinasi from Duveen of New York. Donated in 1946 to the Honolulu Academy of Arts by the Charles M. and Anna C. Cooke Trust.

BIBLIOGRAPHY. *Semiramis. A Gothic Floral Tapestry in the Honolulu Academy of Arts*, in *The Art Quarterly*, vol. IX, 1946, p. 176 and 181, fig. — Helen Comstock, *A Tournai Floral Tapestry for Hawaii*, in *The Connoisseur*, t. 119, n° 504, June 1947, p. 107-108, fig.

33
Narcissus

Wool and silk
14-18 warp threads
to the inch

Museum of Fine Arts,
Boston

The lyricism of this millefleurs tapestry would be difficult to equal. On a background strewn with small animals, an elegant young man bends over his reflection in the waters of a fountain; this would be enough to identify him without the inscription "Narcisus" on his thigh.

This tapestry probably belongs to a series with mythical characters, of which several millefleurs examples exist : a *Hercules*, for instance, in the Musée des Arts Décoratifs, Paris, attributed by Ella Siple to the same designer and atelier, but which despite analogies of style and weaving technique probably does not come from the same set, as the weaving is less fine and the scale of the figures is different. *Narcissus* is life size, while the *Hercules* is nearly seven feet tall, as are the *Jupiter* and *Neptune* in the Detroit Institute of Arts. However, it is clear that the *Narcissus* and *Hercules* must have come from the same weaving center.

9 ft. 3 in. × 10 ft. 3 in. (2,82 m × 3,11 m)

detail

94

Rarely have clumps of flowering plants (pinks, columbines, daisies, marigolds), animals (civets, rabbits), or birds been treated as accurately and attractively as in this tapestry. Notice the differences from the flora and fauna of the *Hunt of the Unicorn* (Nos. 18-24), even though the quality is exceptional in both cases. Ella Siple considers the grace of Narcissus "Botticellian" and wonders how Florentine influence could have come in here. Once more (see Nos. 18-24 and 32), we must point out how little we know of French art circles of the end of the 15th century (from which this tapestry probably comes), though they probably included Italian and Flemish elements.

From the collection of de Talgonet, Château de Rozay, and Lady Baillie, Leeds Castle. Bought in 1968 from Wildenstein and Company, New York, by the Museum of Fine Arts.

BIBLIOGRAPHY. Ella Siple, *French Gothic Tapestries of about 1500*, in *Burlington Magazine*, vol. LIII, Sept. 1928, p. 145-146, pl. — *When Tapestries were in Flower, Museum of Fine Arts, Boston*, December 19, 1972, through March 4, 1973, nᵒ 7.

34
Hopscotch Game and Fruit Picking

Wool and silk
About 14 warp threads
to the inch

Musée du Louvre

After scenes of aristocratic life, pastoral subjects (which had appeared in tapestry in the 14th century) were favorites for millefleurs pieces. This one belongs to a group of three; the others are entitled *Working with Wool* and *Dancing*. Here, a peasant brings a hopscotch game to a couple while, on the right, a woman catches in her skirt pears shaken from a tree full of birds by a young man wielding a crook. As usual in millefleurs tapestries, animals are scattered over the background. A dormouse, on the left, has climbed into one of the trees, multilated when the tapestry was shortened.

Of the two coats of arms at the top, one is *or, a lion azure, under a chief gules* (Bohier); the other is *per pale, dexter,* with the preceding arms and *sinister, azure, a bend compony or and gules, a star or in chief* (Briçonnet).

7 ft. 2 in. × 12 ft. 7 in. (2,25 m × 3,95 m)

The set thus belonged to Thomas Bohier and his wife Catherine, née Briçonnet, both of powerful families that occupied important positions, for instance in the *Chambre des Comptes,* at the end of the 15th and the beginning of the 16th centuries. One Briçonnet even became archbishop of Rheims, and later Chancellor of France; another was a cardinal. Thomas Bohier (died 1524) was Général des Finances and one of the leading personalities during the reigns of Charles VIII, Louis XII, and François I; around 1513-1515 he began the building of the château of Chenonceaux, and his wife (died 1526) took an active part in supervising the works.

According to Pierre Verlet, we cannot tell whether the tapestries were ordered at this time, but it is possible to suggest a date as late as 1520 for their manufacture. However, the arms seem to have been rewoven, and since the style suggests a slightly earlier date we may be right in thinking that these pieces were made about 1510 and that Thomas Bohier and Catherine Briçonnet did not have them made, but bought them finished and had their arms added.

In making this choice, they showed the taste of their class (Jean le Viste also belonged to it, as we see in Nos. 37-42) for works that were full of freshness and charm, and less solemn that the great Brussels tapestries of the period; they also certainly cost less. They are a reminder of pleasant life in the French countryside, at a time happily free from civil or foreign wars.

At the beginning of the 20th century this work was in the château of the Duke de la Trémoïlle at Serrant (Maine-et-Loire). With two other pieces of the set it was acquired by the Larcade family, who gave it to the Louvre in 1945.

BIBLIOGRAPHY; Pierre Verlet, *Les tapisseries de la donation Larcade*, in *Revue des Arts*, 1951, n° I, p. 24-30, fig.

35
Concert at the Fountain

Wool and silk
12 warp threads
to the inch

Musée des Gobelins, Paris

We know of three other *Concerts* with millefleurs backgrounds : one at Angers, one in the Cluny Museum, and another in Pittsburgh; the principal figures in the last two are identical. All three have fewer figures than the present work, which, according to A.P. de Mirimonde, is probably an allegory of love. There is a lute-player, a woman playing a viol, another who is filling a bowl with water while she holds back a young man by the skirt of his coat, a little girl playing, a clown, and a young falconer — all around a lady who plays an organ placed on the curbstone of a fountain.

9 ft. 11 in. × 12 ft. 6 in. (3 m × 3,80 m)

This evocative picture of the aristocratic pleasures of the early 16th century, in rich colors, clearly belongs, from its admirably executed background of plants and the style of its figures, to the classical millefleurs group (Nos. 37-42). The lady at the organ, in particular, is treated in the same spirit as the one in the Angers *Concert,* and the slightly tortuous movement of the young man on the right recalls the attitudes of some of the characters in Nos. 63-66.

The way in which the figures are disposed is typical of millefleurs tapestries, in which the subject is super-imposed, without any regard for composition, on a back-ground of plants that has no depth. Often the characters do not look at one another, and they could well be replaced by others without any effect on the coherence of the work. This is the case here; it is perfectly possible to imagine the group on the right separated from the rest, and the other subsidiary figures could have been disposed differently. The scale of the figures is also not consistent. It is easy to guess how the weavers worked : they had a library of models in various sizes which they distributed, sometimes skillfully, sometimes awkwardly, on the backgrounds of flowers and birds that were their stock in trade. This method suggests a weaving center where recourse to cartoon makers was minimal.

Furthermore, this was an article of standard production with no gold or silver thread, and so relatively inexpensive — the kind of work that noblemen or rich burghers would buy to decorate their châteaux with, as an agreeable reminder of the way they passed their time. These inexpensive materials, the brilliant colors used, and the charm of the figures and flowers enabled the creators of these tapestries to make them very attractive works.

In the 19th century No. 35 was in the château of Saverne, where it had been brought by one of the four Rohans who were bishops of Strasbourg in the 18th century. This bears out the tradition that it comes from the château du Verger and was ordered, like the Angers Lady at the Organ, by Pierre de Rohan, Marshal of Gié (died 1513), father of the Charles de Rohan who owned the Angels Carrying the Instruments of the Passion (Nos. 43-45). Acquired in 1889 by the Musée des Gobelins.

BIBLIOGRAPHY. Joseph Destrée, *Deux idylles, Tapisseries de l'époque de Charles VI, (1380-1422),* in *Annales de la Société royale d'archéologie de Bruxelles,* t. XXVI[1,2], 1912, p. 141-147, fig. — William H. Forsyth, *The Noblest of Sports : Falconry in the Middle Ages,* in *The Metropolitan Museum of Art Bulletin,* May 1944, p. 253-259, fig.

36
Nobleman Presenting a Heron to a Lady

Wool and silk
About 12 warp threads
to the inch

The Metropolitan Museum
of Art

Many medieval tapestries depict a noble couple with a falcon; for instance, the *Offering of the Heart* in the Cluny Museum, a millefleurs tapestry in the Robert Lehman Collection, now in the Metropolitan Museum, and the tapestries in the Metropolitan with pink backgrounds (Nos. 28-29). In this one, which has been extensively restored and is little known, the nobleman kneels to present a heron to the lady, who pushes the falcon away from it.

7ft. 8in. × 10ft. 11in. (2,34 m × 3,33 m)

The interest in this work is chiefly in the fact it is one of the rare millefleurs tapestries with a pink background — the *Lady with the Unicorn* (Nos. 37-42) being the best-known example. The documents, which also mention tapestries with yellow and white backgrounds (virtually no trace of which remains), are proof that verdures with a vermilion ground were not exceptional, but the toll of the centuries has been such that few survive : the six Cluny pieces, a *Departure for the Hunt* in the Art Institute of Chicago, a *Standing Nobleman* — very close to the noble couple we have here — in the Walters Art Gallery in Baltimore, and lastly a *Bishop of Astorga* in Philadelphia and the two pieces from the former Martin Le Roy collection.

As is always the case in this group of tapestries, the flowers and shrubs on the hillock where the characters are placed (here it is green, not dark blue) are "planted," whereas on the pink background the branches are torn off from their stems; this may be a transposition of the bunches of greenery that were sometimes pinned on wall tapestries as a temporary decoration.

The flowers here include roses, columbines, pinks, daisies, and pansies. Seeming marvelously true to life, they are typical of the classical millefleurs decoration, in which the figures' surroundings combine an authentic countryside atmosphere with an air of unreality.

We have dealt elsewhere with the origin of these works (see Nos. 37-42). Here again the style is French, and we may compare the treatment of the faces, which have been vigorously modeled by the cartoonists and weavers, with those of the characters in choir tapestries like the Angers *Life of St. John the Baptist.*

We have here a whole collection of works that clearly form a group stylistically and are quite different from Flemish paintings, even if they have borrowed certain of the painters' details, such as the dresses with heavy broken folds. Judging by the costumes, this piece can be dated early in the 16th century.

Lent to the Metropolitan Museum for many years by Andrew W. Mellon, the tapestry was given to the Museum in 1964 by Mrs. Mellon Bruce.

BIBLIOGRAPHY. Joseph Breck, *The Tapestry Exhibition* (New York, 1928), in *Bulletin of the Metropolitan Museum of Art, New York,* vol. XXIII, 1928, p. 184, fig. p. 180. — William H. Forsyth, *The Noblest of Sports : Falconry in the Middle Ages,* in *The Metropolitan Museum of Art Bulletin,* May 1944, p. 258, fig. p. 257.

37-42
The Lady with the Unicorn

Wool and silk
About 15 warp threads
to the inch

Musée de Cluny, Paris

Against a faded red background scattered with small animals and flowering branches torn off from their trunks, we see a deep blue "island" planted with sprays of blossoms and four kinds of tree (oak, holly, pine, orange), among which frolic other small animals. On the island are a lion and a unicorn and either one or two women (varying through the set) engaged in aristocratic pastimes.

We have already seen (No. 36) how this pink background, the "vermilion" field of the documents, was common in the Middle Ages, though few tapestries of this type have survived. It is therefore not the background that makes the *Lady with the Unicorn* series unique, even though the color harmony here is close to perfection, but rather the beauty of the design, the quality of the workmanship (though this is less rich and fine than in many other pieces — the *Hunt of the Unicorn,* for example), and lastly the lyricism of the figures; all these have a magical appeal that places the set among the principal tapestry masterpieces of all time. This very quality has led to farfetched interpretations of the unicorn's presence, and to the reading of

profound mysteries into the occupations of the lady and her maid. In fact, the unicorn was considered an almost ordinary animal in the Middle Ages, and except in two of the pieces in which its role is privileged compared with that of the lion (Nos. 37 and 40) its chief function here, as so often, is to act with the latter as a supporter of arms. These six tapestries are not primarily heraldic in significance, despite the recurrence of banners, streamers, shields, and mantles *gules, a bend azure charged with three crescents.* These arms have nothing to do, despite a long belief, with Prince Zizim, conqueror of Constantinople and ill-starred rival of his brother Bazajet, who was held prisoner for some time in the château of Bourganef, near Boussac (whence the set of tapestries comes) at the end of the 15th century. The arms are those of a well-known family of lawyers, the Le Vistes. As for the dreamily graceful figures, we must discard the hypothesis that they illustrate a medieval romance, or that, as George Sand believed, they are portraits of a woman whom Zizim loved; neither do the have, as has been more recently suggested, Marian or Catharinan symbolism. It is more likely that five of the pieces have a mundane subject : the *senses.* The sixth may be either an offering in homage; or, more probably, a leftover from another set of the same nature; records from the 19th century, unfortunately lacking in detail, show that there were other pieces in the château de Boussac than the six we now know.

37
Sight

Here, only the lion acts as an arms supporter; while the Lady, who is seated, holds up a mirror to the unicorn, which has placed its front hooves on her lap. The allegory of a sense is here confused with the legend, so popular at the time, of the unicorn's capture by a maiden.

10 ft. 2 in. × 10 ft. 10 in. (3,10 m × 3,30 m)

38
Hearing

The Lady is playing a small organ, while a girl works the bellows.

12 ft. 2 in. × 9 ft. 6 in. (3,70 m × 2,90 m)

39
Smell

The Lady is decorating a chaplet with flowers from a bowl held by her maid. Note the little monkey smelling a rose — a detail that underlines the symbolism of the work.

11 ft. 11 in. × 10 ft. 7 in. (3,67 m × 3,22 m)

40
Taste

A parakeet perches on the Lady's gloved left hand, and her little dog lies on the train of her dress; she takes a sugared almond from a box held out by her companion. Once more, the sense in question is emphasized by the monkey, which is putting something into its mouth. There is a palisade of roses at the back of the hillock.

12 ft. 4 in. × 15 ft. 1 in. (3,75 m × 4,60 m)

Taste, *detail*

41
Touch

In this piece, it is the Lady who is holding the banner; with her left hand, she touches the unicorn's horn, no doubt as a reminder of its marvelous property of detecting poison in food. Such horns — or at least the objects people in the Middle Ages thought were unicorn's horns — were held in great value; in reality they were the tusks of the narwhal.

12 ft. 4 in. × 11 ft. 9 in. (3,15 m × 3,58 m)

42
The Choosing of the Jewels

Although like the others in composition, style, colors, and weaving technique, this tapestry differs in that behind the figures one sees a tent of rich blue cloth sprinkled with tear-shaped decorations in gold, and bearing the inscription "A mon seul désir" followed by an indistinct letter. The lion and unicorn hold open the flaps of the tent, in front of which is the

Lady, with her favorite dog beside her, choosing a necklace from a coffret that her maid holds for her. This piece was interpreted as a kind of dedication at the time when the whole set was thought to be a gift from Jean de Chabannes, lord of Vandenesse and younger brother of the Maréchal de la Palisse, to his fiancée Claude Le Viste; the last letter of the inscription was then taken to be a J, for Jehan. This theory has now been abandoned, since the date it implies, 1510-1513, is too late for the style of the work and the fashion of the dress. What we have here is probably an illustration of the kind of elegant occupation of which there were other examples on the pieces that have disappeared : for instance, George Sand describes one in which the maid is holding out to the Lady a golden ewer and bowl. Other millefleurs tapestries show similar scenes, the Cluny Museum's *Courtly Life*, for example, and we know that the Le Viste family owned more tapestries like this; for in the château of Montaigu-le-Blain, in the Bourbonnais, at the time of the division in 1595 of the property of Jean de Chabannes' great-niece Eléonore, there were tapestries that have since been lost with a red background and arms with three crescents and unicorns together with little animals or sibyls; these pieces must have been akin to the Cluny tapestries and inherited from Claude Le Viste.

12 ft. 4 in. × 14 ft. 10 in. (3,80 m × 4,64 m)

Claude Le Viste probably inherited the tapestries that were at Montaigu-le-Blin in 1595 from her father. Only the three crescents are mentioned; the arms were certainly the same as those on the *Lady with the Unicorn*. Now, Jean IV Le Viste, Claude's father, who was a counselor in Parlement, president of the Cour des Aides in 1489, lord of Arcy and other places, and who died in 1500 leaving only daughters, was a person of sufficient importance to own a large number of these tapestries; they recorded the heraldic pride of one of the most powerful Lyon families at the end of the Middle Ages, one which sent several of its members, including Jean IV, to Paris to occupy important government positions. After him, a number of these tapestries must have been passed on to Claude, who had no children from her marriages to Geoffroy de Balzac and later Jean de Chabannes. Her tapestries must have been divided between the Chabannes, inheritors on her husband's side (those at Montaigu-le-Blin), and Jeanne Le Viste, daughter of her first cousin, to whom she bequeathed her property. Henri Martin has researched out a pattern of marriages and successions that would explain how the

Lady with the Unicorn could have passed down from this Jeanne Le Viste, wife of Jean Robertet (the nephew of the famous Florimond), to the Roche-Aymon family, two members of which became linked in 1660 with the owners of Boussac; they probably brought the tapestries to the château, where they remained until 1882.

Even if the tapestries did come to Boussac in this way, we must ask ourselves whether they could not have been ordered by direct ancestors of Jeanne Le Viste; if not by her father, Antoine, who was president of the Paris Parlement and died in 1534 (the most important man in the dynasty), at least by her grandfather, Aubert (died 1493), who was *rapporteur* and *correcteur* in the Chancellery and one of Louis XI's political aides, and was in particular used by him against his cousin Jacques d'Armagnac, Duke of Nemours, who was beheaded in 1477.

All in all, the probabilities are in favor of Jean, who had his arms placed all over the Arcy château, and whose will stipulated that the chapel of the lords of Vindecy, "in which his arms shall be laid," was to be rebuilt and should include

"a beautiful window, in which shall be placed an image of Our Lady... and also... on one side in the same window, the image of Master Saint Jehan, who shall present his person to the same image of Our Lady, attired in the manner of a knight, in armor, on which shall be his arms." Jean Le Viste's desire to be remembered by his armorial bearing is thus obvious. Furthermore, the letter that follows the inscription "A mon seul désir" may well be a J followed by an abbreviation sign, and would thus be a signature to a phrase that, far from being words written in gallant homage to a fiancée, is much more likely to be Jean Le Viste's personal device; this, incidentally, fits in much better with what we may guess about this individual — that he was a man concerned above all with his own success, who proudly recalled in his will the visit Louis XI made to him in 1482, on his return from a pilgrimage to Saint-Claude.

We would date the Cluny tapestries in the last twenty years of the 15th century, at the height of Jean IV's career, because of analogies with a *Penelope* in the Museum of Fine Arts, Boston, a remnant of a set of *Famous Women* woven for Cardinal Ferry de Clugny, bishop of Tournai, between 1480 and 1483. Marthe Crick-Kuntziger has also compared the *Lady with the Unicorn* with a beautiful tapestry of *Perseus* (private collection) that bears the arms of Charles Guillard (1456-1537) and his wife Jeanne de Wignacourt, which she dates about 1490. There is no doubt that the style of these slim, elegant figures is of the end of the 15th century, as is that of their costumes, in which the slashed sleeves that were so fashionable in the 16th hardly appear.

The similarities with the *Penelope*, however, stop at parallels in weaving technique and subject details (hair styles and costume, small lions on the chair posts, flowering branches).

On the other hand, the Cluny set is much closer to the *Hunt of the Unicorn* (Nos. 18-24) than appears at first sight. There are differences in the weaving and the materials (the *Hunt* is certainly low-warp and contains metal threads, of which there are none in the *Lady*, as well as more silk and brighter and more varied colors). The unicorn in the *Capture* (No. 21) is almost identical with the one *in Sight* (No. 37), and the servant girl who points it out to the hunter is of the same type as the figures in the *Lady* set : tall, with straight, slightly inclined, flat-chested bodies in tight dresses with W- or trapezium-shaped necklines, fine hands, and faces with small, round chins. The designer of the Cluny set has always been considered as French, so there is no need to search in the Moulins court or at Brussels, especially, for a candidate. He was one of those artists who illustrated books printed in Paris at the end of the 15th century and whose work Jean IV and Aubert Le Viste, who lived there, certainly knew.

There remains the problem of where the series was woven. Much as been written about this — more than it deserves, as it is only one of the questions that remain for the tapestry historians to resolve.

For a long time, the *Lady with the Unicorn* and all the finest millefleurs pieces were attributed to ateliers known as those "of the banks of the Loire," because their style is French, and because many bear the arms of nobles who lived in the Loire area, where the Court was often in residence. As the documents make no mention of any regular tapestry-weaving activity in the district, the hypothesis of itinerant ateliers was put forward. Recently, however, Sophie Schneebalg has recalled the existence of large numbers of weavers working in Brussels in the 15th century, whose work is more or less unknown; she reminds us of the agreement in 1476 between the painters and weavers of the city, that granted the latter the right to draw for themselves the plants and animals in their verdures. Noting that the only mille-fleurs tapestry of which we have a payment record, that in the Berne Historical Museum, which bears the arms of Philip the Good, Duke of Burgundy, was woven by the Brussels weaver Jean de Haze, she attributes the most beautiful works of this kind to that city.

It is certain that millefleurs tapestries — verdures, as they were called then — were woven there, but it does not follow that all should be assigned to Brussels.

If we look closely, we can find differences between the "classical" millefleurs pieces like the *Lady with the Unicorn*, in which the bouquets are treated freely and with taste and are never the same, and the millefleurs tapestries of Philip the Good, in which the bouquets, despite their beauty, are woven with a rather mechanical precision, and all the floral décor on the right is a mirror image of that on the left. This implies that there was a detailed cartoon that was copied twice, which in turn implies low-warp weaving, because with this technique the colored cartoon placed under the warp provides the weaver with a strict guide. In high-warp, on the other hand, the cartoon is transferred onto the warp with tracing paper, or at any rate this is the practice today; in the Middle Ages such paper probably did not exist and the transfer was much less accurate. The weaver could only transpose onto his warp, probably using cloth, the main lines of the figures, and the design of the plants was up to him entirely, and he varied them according to his fancy. The classical millefleurs — the *Lady with the Unicorn*, the Cluny Museum's *Courtly Life*, the *Semiramis* (No. 32), the *Narcissus* (No. 33), and others — are woven like this; consequently, they were not woven in Brussels, where the *legwerkers* apparently worked only in low-warp. If indeed such millefleurs tapestries were woven in Brussels, one would expect to find many in the countries to which Brussels exported, and where many of her other works survive. But almost all the beautiful mille-fleurs tapestries we know of are in France or come from there.

Where, then, were the *Lady* set and comparable pieces woven? We know too little about activity in Paris at the time, except that the merchants were there, to say definitely that Paris was the source. Crick-Kuntziger suggested Bruges for the *Famous Women* of Cardinal Ferry de Clugny, because he took refuge there when the troops of Louis XI turned him out of his see at Tournai; but were was nothing to stop weavers continuing to work for an absent bishop, and the *Story of St. Anathoille of Salins* at the beginning of the 16th century has rather different characters. How about Tournai, from which city apparently came tapestries that were very close to some of the millefleurs pieces? Nor should we forget that Arras began to be active again after it had been laid waste by Louis XI, following the siege of 1477. For the time being, since we cannot be sure, it is probably more sensible to leave this problem and content ourselves with grouping together works of similar style and execution, in the hope that later discoveries will give us the basis for a definite conclusion.

Purchased with the château in 1833 from Countess Ribeyreix, née Carbonnières, by the Town Council of Boussac, Creuse, France, which sold it to the Cluny Museum in 1882.

BIBLIOGRAPHY. A. and C.M. Fleury, *Le château d'Arcy (Saône-et-Loire) et ses seigneurs*, Mâcon, Protat, 1917, p. 57-65 and 191-200. — Marquet de Vasselot et Weigert, *op. cit.*, p. 62-63 and 199. — Henry Martin, *La dame à la licorne*, in *Mémoires de la Soc. nat. des Antiq. de France*, t. LXXVIII, 1920, p. 137-168, fig. — Phyllis Ackermann, *The Lady and the Unicorn*, in *Burlington Magazine*, t. LXVI, Jan. 1935, p. 35-36. — Marthe Crick-Kuntziger, *Un chef-d'œuvre inconnu du Maître de la «Dame à la licorne»*, in *Revue belge d'archéologie et d'Histoire de l'art*, t. XXIII, 1954, 18 p., 7 fig. — Pierre Verlet and Francis Salet, *La dame à la licorne*, Paris, Braun (1960), 47 p., fig. — René Fédou, *Les hommes de loi lyonnais à la fin du Moyen Age*, Paris, les Belles-Lettres, 1964, p. 347-348. — Maurice Dayras, *Réflexions sur les origines de la tenture de la «Dame à la licorne»*, in *Actes du 88e Congrès national des Sociétés savantes, Clermont-Ferrand, 1963, section d'archéologie*, Paris, Imprimerie Nationale, 1965, p. 311-344, 4 fig. — Maria Lanckorónska, *Wandteppiche für eine Fürstin. Die historische Persönlichkeit der «Dame mit dem Einhorn»*, Frankfurt-on-Main, H. Scheffler (1965), 80 p., 6 pl., 32 fig. (com. by F. Salet, in *Bulletin Monumental*, t. CXXII, 1964, p. 418-420). — Sophie Schneebalg-Perelman, *«La dame à la licorne» a été tissée à Bruxelles*, in *Gazette des Beaux-Arts*, n° 1186, Nov. 1967, p. 253-278, 20 fig. — *A propos de la Dame à la licorne*, in *Gazette des Beaux-Arts*, n° 1201, Feb., 1969, p. 127-128. — Geneviève Souchal, *A Tapestry masterpiece*, in *Auction*, vol. III, n° 2, Oct. 1969, p. 38-42, fig.; and *Le Musée de Cluny*, Paris, Ed. des Musées nationaux, 1972, p. 88-98.

43-45
Angels Bearing the Instruments of the Passion

Wool and silk
15 warp threads
to the inch

Tapestry Museum,
Château d'Angers

Though the column of Christ's flagellation, the crown of thorns, the cross, the nails, the sponge dipped in gall, and the lance that pierced his side were already subjects for illustration in the 13th century, it was from the 14th to the 17th that the theme of the Angels Bearing the Instruments of the Passion became popular; it found its finest expression in the second half of the 15th and early 16th centuries, especially in Anjou.

The reason for this, perhaps, was that, as is related by an author of regional *Chronicles* published in 1529, King René, grandson of Duke Louis I of Anjou, had composed "several beautiful sayings of the Passion of Our Lord," and these were transcribed in the chapel of the Franciscan friars of Angers, which he built and where he left orders for the tomb of his heart to be placed. These eight stanzas have disappeared, but a scholar of the

Ancien Régime kept a copy of the text, and they are almost all reproduced in the paintings in the chapel of the château de Pimpéan at Grézillé, Maine-et-Loire, or in the present set of tapestries. Here, they are completed by other eight-line verses, for ceremonies other than those of the Franciscans. Their importance is obvious in the tapestries, where they have clearly been treated as the principal subject — laid out in the middle on wide banners; the role of the angels, each of whom carries an instrument, is reduced to that of presenters of the text.

There are seven stanzas and angels against a millefleurs background sprinkled with small animals, with, at the top, two kinds of shields and crosses *pattés of argent and gules.* One of the quartered shields, surrounded by the collar of the order of St. Michael, is *in the first, gules, an escarbuncle of chains or* (Navarre), *in the second, argent, a serpent azure crowned or devouring a child issuant gules* (Duchy of Milan), *in the third, gules, nine voided lozenges or placed three by three, a label with four lappets argent* (Rohan), *and in the fourth, of France, a bend compony argent and gules* (Evreux). The other shield, surrounded by a tressure, is *per pale, dexter,* with the preceding arms, and *sinister, argent, a fesse gules, a border azure.* A millefleurs strip bearing the same crosses and arms is sewn across the bottom of the three pieces.

On two of them — one has two stanzas and figures, the other three — the angels are turned to the right. Only one, with two angels, shows them turned to the left. As the crown of thorns, the nails, and the Holy Face are missing from the instruments, though they are present in the Angers Franciscan chapel and at Pimpéan, we may deduce that the set contained a fourth piece with three angels facing left, with the tapestries so arranged that they faced each other two by two, with their angels turned toward the altar.

43
Three Angels Facing Right

The angel on the left holds the purse with Judas' thirty pieces of silver and the end of the banner which, unlike the others, carries verses of sixteen feet instead of eight in the form of two parallel stanzas, the caesura of every odd verse rhyming with that of the following even verse :

"O homme quy la pomme priz   La pire que jamès prist hom
Regarde cy le povre priz   Et la cruelle mesprison
De Judas qui par trahison   Vendit au Juifz Jhesus crist

detail

Par envie et contre raison
Judas sy fut moult diligent
Car pour trente denier d'argent
Hélas il en fit grant marché
Le sauveur en fut derraché

Ainsy que on le voit par escript.
De vendre son bon maistre et sire
Le livra pour le faire occire.
Le mauvaiz traiste delloial.
Et battu sur son chief roial».

(O man, who took the apple, the worst that ever man took, see here the wretched price and the cruel scorn of Judas, who through treachery sold Jesus Christ to the Jews, by envy and against reason, as is told in the scripture. Judas was most diligent to sell his good master and lord, for for thirty pieces of silver he delivered him to be killed. Alas, the evil traitor made great business of it. The Savior was thus struck down and beaten on his royal head.)

The angel in the center holds the lance with which the centurion Longinus pierced the side of Christ after his death on the cross. According to the *Golden Legend*, "having his sight obscured by illness and old age, he rubbed his eyes with the blood of Our Lord which flowed down his lance," and "immediately saw better," and was converted.

"Longis aveugle chevalier
Fut a la mort du redempteur
Et pour plus fort le travailler
Affin qu'il n'eust jamès retour
D'une lance jusques au cueur
Luy frappa sy cruellement
Que y ne demoura liqueur
En tout son corps aucunement."

(Longinus the blind knight was at the death of the Redeemer and to torture him the more so that he should never come back to life he smote him with a lance to the heart so cruelly that there remained no liquor more in all his body.)

The angel on the right supports with his arm the column of flagellation and carries two whips and rods.

"Regarde en pitié et voy comme
Benignement par la doulceur
Tres dure angoisse por toy homme
Voulut souffrir ton createur
En ceste atache a grant douleur
Ou son benoist corps longuemen
Si quoy ne peult dire greigneur [plus grand]
Endura non pareil torment."

(Look in pity and see how kindly and sweetly thy creator was willing to suffer very dire anguish for thee, O man, fastened thus with great pain, where his blessed body endured unequaled torment, than which none can be greater.)

5 ft. 11 in. $\times$ 22 ft. 8 in. (1,80 m $\times$ 6,90 m)

44
Two Angels Looking to the Left

The first, a cloth over his arms, carries a plate on which is the ewer for the washing of the hands.

"L'innocent fourré de malice
Pilate en veult lavé ses mains.
De paour de perdre son office
Juga le sauveur des humains

Combien qu'il seust que mal faisoit
De livré l'aigneau pur et monde.
Ambicion tant luy plaisoit
Que mal en est en l'autr monde."

(Pilate wished to wash his hands of the innocent man accused of malice. For fear of losing his office he judged the Savior of the human race, however evil he knew it was to deliver the pure and clean lamb. Ambition so pleased him that he suffers for it in the other world.)

The angel on the right bears the cross, in the shape of a Greek T.

"Voy la digne croix precieuse
Ou Jhesus moult piteusement
Souffrit peine très angoisseuse
Pour toy garder de dampnement.
Or advise, homme, humblement
Et considere, je te pry,
Que tu dois bien devotement
Servir cil qui lors te serir*." [* *for :* servi]

(See the noble precious cross where Jesus most piteously suffered in great agony to guard thee from damnation. So take heed, O man, humbly, and consider, I pray thee, that thou must devotedly serve him who then served thee.)

5 ft. 11 in. × 15 ft. 3 in. (1,80 m × 4,65 m)

45
Two Angels Facing Right

The angel on the right holds the vessel of vinegar mixed with gall and the stick tipped with a sponge.

"Lieve des yeulz, regarde icy
Homme pecheur, et te souviengne
Que cruellement sans mercy
Ceste esponge dame* fiel plaine [*for :* d'amer]
Fut par la cruaulté in humaine
Mise a la bouche du Roy celeste
Puis de la lance plaie villaine
Fut faicte a son doulz costé destre."

(Lift up thine eyes and see here, O sinful man, and remember how cruelly without mercy this bitter sponge filled with gall was with inhuman cruelty placed in the mouth of the celestial King and then with the lance a fearful wound was made in his sweet right side.)

The angel on the right has the shroud.

"Voy le suaire ou ton sauveur
Fut ensevely doulcement
Voy son sang, sa digne sueur
Voy les fouets des quez las tant
Fut battu si tres aprement

Que sang sailloit a abondance.
Pense que corporellement
Receupt ce pour ta delivrance.»

(See the shroud in which thy Savior was gently buried; see his blood, his noble sweat, see the whips with which he was so roughly scourged that the blood flowed abundantly. Think that he suffered this in his body for thy deliverance.)

5 ft. 11 in. × 12 ft. 5 in. (1,80 m × 4,70 m)

It is with great simplicity and unexpected success that the artist of this exceptionally beautiful work (one of the rare religious millefleurs tapestries we know) has resolved the problem of integrating these long inscriptions into a decorative surface. The plants and animals, which are particularly fine, link the set to the classical millefleurs group (see Nos. 37-42); among these, it is one of the most admirable, with its angels, large wings spread and with sad expressions, kneeling in their albs half-covered with dalmatics or brillant copes.

It has been known for more than a hundred years that this set came from the priory that Pierre de Rohan, Marshal of Gié, one of the most important noblemen of the time of Louis XI and Charles VIII, had built near his château du Verger, Maine-et-Loire, at the end of the 15th century, and which was occupied by the monks of Sainte-Croix de la Bretonnerie, whose emblem (white and red crosses) appears on it. At the beginning of the present century, Canon Urseau identified the arms as being those, not of Pierre de Rohan himself, but of his eldest son Charles, high steward of France, and of his second wife Jeanne de San Severino; the tapestries were thus later than this marriage, which R. Planchenault has indicated took place on June 2, 1512.

Assuming that the tressure surrounding the parted shield is a sign of widowhood, they were dated after the death of Charles de Rohan on May 6, 1528; which seems late for their type and style. In fact, as was said in the 19th century by Barbier de Montault, the tressure may have another meaning, which would make it possible to bring the date of this series back to that of the marriage to Jeanne de San Severino, and this fits much better. According to A. Brandenburg, a document of August 25, 1515, quoted by Father Anselm, makes it possible to pinpoint the date even closer; it bears a seal of Charles de Rohan in which there is no label in the third quarter of the shield; this heraldic "charge" would thus have been an heir's "difference," which would disappear on the death of his father Pierre de Rohan on April 22, 1513. The set would thus be dated between June, 1512, and April, 1513.

Louis de Farcy thought he recognized The Angels Bearing the Instruments of the Passion *in an inventory of the du Verger priory drawn up on August 20, 1790 : "A set of tapestries showing the passion above choir balustrades in silk and wool, of about 16 aunes... Sold by auction to Monsieur Thiberge on August 2, 1971, this work was then described as in eight pieces." This figure, the title given to the set, and the length indicated, which does not correspond either to that of the three pieces that have been preserved or to that of the whole if there had been a fourth piece similar to the first, have led R. Planchenault to reject this identification. Thus we do not know when the set left the priory. The chapter of Angers Cathedral was given or bought it before 1858. Monseigneur Chappoulie, bishop of the diocese, has placed it with the other old cathedral tapestries in the château museum.*

BIBLIOGRAPHY. Louis de Farcy, *Monographie de la cathédrale d'Angers, le mobilier,* Angers, Josselin, 1901, p. 129-133. — Ch. Urseau, *L'Anjou aux Primitifs français,* in *Revue de l'Anjou,* (new series), t. XLIX, 1904, p. 17. — R. Planchenault, *Sur quelques tapisseries de la cathédrale d'Angers,* in *Les Cahiers de Pincé et des Musées de la ville,* Angers, (new series), nᵒ 22, 1954, p. 1-6, fig.; and *Petites notes sur les tapisseries d'Angers,* Caisse nationale des Monuments et des Sites (1967), (no page number). — A. Brandenburg; to appear in *Bulletin Monumental,* 1973.

46
The Lamb of God

Wool
A little more than
10 warp threads
to the inch

Hôtel-Dieu, Beaune

The Lamb appears against a blue background scattered with alternate keys and towers in front of the Instruments of the Passion, with the moon and sun on either side. Below is a coat of arms *per pale, dexter, azure, three keys or, sinister, a tower or.*

In the Middle Ages, tapestries that identified their owner and advertised his success through heraldry were common, but there was an immense

variety in the ways the arms and motifs taken from them were disposed. We have here an overall pattern formed of the keys of Nicolas Rolin, Chancellor of Burgundy from 1422 to 1462, and the tower of his second wife, Guigone de Salins. And the Instruments of the Passion, as we saw in connection with the Angers *Angels* (Nos. 43-45) was a popular subject in the 15th century.

4ft. 3 in. × 10ft. 2 in. (1,30 m × 3,10 m)

This tapestry belongs to a set in which the pieces with red background scattered with shields, turtledoves, and the word SEULLE alternating with stars and monograms of the letters N G are much better known. There still remain thirty of the thirty-one mentioned in 1501 as being used to decorate "on solemn feasts" the sickbeds "in the great chamber of the poor," as well as two others with similar backgrounds, one with a St. Anthony in the center, which were intended to adorn "the thrones standing at the sides of the altar." The piece we have here, and also another with the Pascal Lamb, is recognizable in the 1501 inventory: "Item, two other tapestries with arms as above, with which the pulpit and sometimes the altar are decorated."

We do not where the set was made. Up to now it has been thought that it was given by Chancellor Rolin to the Hôtel-Dieu at Beaune, which he founded by a deed dated August 4, 1443; the deed invokes the aid of St. Anthony the abbot and promises "to furnish it with all... utensils and necessary objects" and "to supply the chapel with vestments, books, chalice, and other ornaments," all within the period of four to five years in which he hoped to complete the building. In fact the chapel was consecrated on December 31, 1451 and the house for the poor was opened the next day. It has therefore been thought that the tapestries were made, if not between 1443 and 1452, at least before the death of the Chancellor on January 18, 1462.

Nevertheless, it is more likely that the tapestries were a gift from his wife, Guigone de Salins. For the arms that appear all over this piece are not those of her husband, but her own, parted, in accordance with the rules governing the arms borne by women, with the three keys of Rolin *dexter,* and the tower of the Salins *sinister;* we see them again on the famous composite picture in the chapel, in which Rogier van der Weyden painted the Last Judgment with the portraits of the donors.

The wife of the Chancellor Rolin could have made this gift to the Hôtel-Dieu, in which she also took a great interest, either before her husband's death, or, as is more likely, afterward — that is, between January, 1462, and December 24, 1470, when she herself died. For when she was widowed she came to live in Beaune, and although the directors of the Hôtel-Dieu were backed in refusing her authority until it was restored by the Paris Parlement in 1468, she never ceased to be interested in the foundation, and after the Parlement's decree she moved in and was ultimately buried there. In 1462 and 1463 she gave the Hôtel-Dieu fifteen "queues" of wine and four hundred gold crowns; in 1467 she canceled a debt of another four hundred crowns she had lent; and on February 10, 1466, she gave a sumptuous cross in gold and six silver cups "with sundry other things and pieces of furniture already placed by me in the hands of the governor, mistress, and sisters of the said Hostel-Dieu," as the deed states.

There is another element that points to the period between 1462 and 1470 : it is the word SEULLE on the tapestries with red background. This is not the motto of the Chancellor, as was assumed when pavement stones inscribed with it, surrounding the initials N G, were found in his house in Dijon. It is Guigone's, and not, as has also been said, the symbol of a lamenting widowhood, but her personal device, which she must have used throughout her marriage, like the "Tant que je vive" that the Duchess of Burgundy used at the same period. The proof of this is to be found on Nicolas Rolin's tombstone : there can be seen the two mottoes : "Deum time" (Fear God), which was the Chancellor's, and "Seule," which can only refer to his wife. There is nothing strange in the mistress of the house being evoked on a heraldic paving stone; there were probably other paved rooms with "Deum time" in honor of Nicolas. In any case the presence of the single word "Guigone," accompanied by the turtledove, the symbol of faithful love and no doubt her personal emblem, on most of the Beaune tapestries, would seem to confirm this hypothesis.

After Nicolas Rolin, had provided the Hôtel-Dieu with the necessities, his widow was concerned with adding decoration, and perhaps also with affirming her disputed status as patroness, by a gift of tapestries on which there was an obsessive repetition of her personal mark. If we accept this hypothesis, we can date their design and manufacture still more closely : they would have been ordered when, after the Chancellor's death, Guigone's authority was rejected by the Hôtel-Dieu, and finished within two or three years. By 1465/66 they were perhaps already in the Hôtel-Dieu.

BIBLIOGRAPHY. J. Guiffrey, *Les tapisseries de l'hôpital de Beaune,* in *Bulletin archéologique du Comité des Travaux historiques et scientifiques,* Paris, 1880, p. 89. — J.-P. Asselberghs, *Tapisseries héraldiques et de la vie quotidienne,* Tournai, 1970, n⁰ 1, fig. 1.

47
Millefleurs Tapestry with Horseman and Arms of Jean de Daillon

Wool and silk
12-15 warp threads to the inch
Montacute House, Yeovil,
Somerset, England

(The National Trust)

For some time it was believed that the warrior of this tapestry, mounted on a horse whose rich caparison bears the letters I-E linked by a knotted cord, and holding a banner decorated with what is probably a wolf together with the same I-E, might be one of the *Nine Heroes.* However, none of the heroes in this tradition seem to have possessed an emblem like this. It is more probable that we have here a knight bearing his standard. Pierre de Rohan, Marshal of Gié (see Nos. 43-45), was depicted in five different ways on the tapestries in his château du Verger : fully armed, carrying a standard, carrying a pennant, as a general, and as Marshal of France. The horseman here is thus probably the person whose arms are woven into the top left-hand corner : *quarterly, in the first and last, azure, a cross engrailed argent; in the second and third, gules, fretty or, a canton argent charged with a crescent sable; and as an inshield, gules, six escutcheons or.* These arms are those of one of the best-known members of the Daillon family, Jean I, and of him alone, since his sons, according to J.B. de Vaivre, bore different arms.

The tapestry has been shortened at the top and at the sides in the course of a restoration, during which the end of the banner and the horse's right leg were altered.

11 ft. 10 in. × 9 ft. 2 in. (3,60 m × 2,80 m)

Jean de Daillon came from a minor noble family, the origins of which are obscure. According to Commynes, who talks about him several times in his *Mémoires,* he was "nourished in his youth" with Louis XI, "whom he knew right well how to please." He held high positions in the King's service, except for a period when he was in disgrace. He was as resourceful as he was devoted to his own interests, and managed to get himself made Lord of Lude. Knowing that his master "gave readily something to him who first brought him news of great import," he contrived to be the one who informed the King of "the discomfiture of the Duke of Burgundy" at Nancy in 1477. His name also appears linked with large sums of money in the accounts of Louis XI's time, and he was one of the few at the King's bedside when he was seriously ill in 1480. He died before the King, however, probably at the end of 1481.

In 1474 he was Governor of Dauphiné province; following the fall of Arras in 1477, he was appointed the King's Lieutenant for the city. From this "he made great profit" : "twenty thousand crowns and two martens' skins." De Vaivre has suggested that he may at that time have bought or been given "a tapestry depicting him in armor," which would make the Montacute tapestry "an example of Arras work after the fall of the Duchy of Burgundy." Obviously, Jean de Daillon could have had work for him some of the weavers of a town that was shortly to lose everything, even its name, as its inhabitants were driven out by Louis XI. But it is more tempting to connect the present piece with an entry in the archives of Tournai dated April 1, 1481 : "To Wuillaume Desreumaulx, tapestry weaver, who had agreed with Monsieur du Lude, Governor of the Dauphiné, to make for him a tapestry of verdure for a room, the said tapestry being a gift and present made to the said gentleman by the city, in recognition of divers past favors and acts of friendship he has made to the aforesaid city... on the price of the which agreement, it has been ordered to be paid to the said Wuilleme to advance and expedite the work of the said tapestry the sum of LXX livres." Another payment to Desreumaulx shows that the tapestry given to "the Lord of Lude... which he has had made and woven of silk in several and divers pieces, in accordance with the said device" measured no less than 457 square aunes. Therefore it was a set of several pieces. A third mention shows that "it was made in several and divers workshops" and that "the stuffs used in the work had been inspected, so as to know that they were true and suitable." Lastly, on December 3, 1482, letters sent by Jean de Daillon's widow asked that "the tapestry formerly made to be presented to Monseigneur du Lude, now defunct, be delivered to Pasquier Grenier, for her and her children"; and on April 8, 1483, the city councilors of Tournai recorded its "delivery made to Monseigneur the bishop of Sees, the brother of Madame the widow of the late Monseigneur du Lude." Everything fits in : the term "verdure," which at this date was used to mean what we now call millefleurs tapestries to distinguish them from the later verdures, or landscape tapestries; the presence of silk; the date, which corresponds with that of the armor worn by the horseman; and lastly what we know of the character of this individual "who was greatly attached to his own profit," and had declared to Commynes that he expected to "become Governor of Flanders," and that "there he would make himself all of gold."

If, however, this piece is indeed one of those presented to him by the people of Tournai in gratitude for some of the services that "artful Master Jehan," as Louis XI called him, knew so well how to get paid for, we have here one of the rare works that can be ascribed with certainty to Tournai (see Nos. 7-11 for some others); despite the abundance of this city's output, we can in most cases only "attribute" surviving tapestries to it. We also learn that different pieces in the same set could be woven by different ateliers. And we get — this is fairly rare — an exact date. It was in 1477, a little before the capture of Arras, that the Lord of Lude moved to the Tournai region. Before this, the town had been neutral, but Olivier le Daim, the famous barber to the King, had just entered it with his troops. In 1479, Jean de Daillon was bailiff and Governor of the province of Tours. Thus it must have been between these two dates that the people of Tournai decided to give him a set of tapestries, and weaving was probably started then. After he left, the work must have got delayed a little, which would explain why he did not receive the pieces before his death. And lastly, we should have a reliable example of the Tournai millefleurs style; here we may note that the plants, though similar to those in classical millefleurs pieces, are set more closely together and drawn more finely.

It remains to identify the letters I-E. Such letters could have been, at the end of the Middle Ages, the initials of the first names of a married couple, those of a person's first and surname, or an emblem (see Nos. 18-24 and 49). Here the I could be for Jehan de Daillon, but the E does not fit either of his two wives, Renée de Fontaines and Marie de Laval. Perhaps it was for his second given name. It is not likely, in any case, that this is the second letter of the name Jehan. We must resign ourselves to not knowing.

Lent from 1916 to 1919 to the Metropolitan Museum. Bought from Sir Edgar Speyer in 1935. Bequeathed to the National Trust by Sir Malcolm Stewart in 1960.

BIBLIOGRAPHY. Philippe de Commynes, *Mémoires, passim.* — Eugène Soil, *Les tapisseries de Tournai, les tapissiers et les hautelisseurs de cette ville...,* Tournai, Vasseur-Delmée, Lille, L. Quarré, 1892, p. 384-385. — *The Connoisseur,* June 1946, p. 71. — P. Kjellberg, *La tapisserie gothique, sujet de constantes recherches : nouveaux trésors divulgués,* in *Connaissance des Arts,* nº 142, Dec. 1963, p. 168, fig. p. 169. — J.B. de Vaivre, *La tapisserie de Jean de Daillon,* in *Archivum Heraldicum,* 1973, nº 2-3, p., fig.

48
Millefleurs Tapestry with Arms of John Dynham

Wool and silk
12-15 warp threads to the inch

The Metropolitan Museum of Art,
The Cloisters Collection

As in the tapestry of Philip the Good at Berne and that of Jacqueline of Luxemburg at Langeais (No. 49), we have here a large coat of arms in the center of a millefleurs tapestry. But in this one the background is scattered with the owner's emblem : the upper part of a mast with a streamer bearing a St. George's cross and five arrows in the top. The coat was also cantoned with four smaller ones; but the tapestry has been cut off at the bottom and a similar band of flowers has been sewn on, above which appears a piece of a standard and one of the emblems.

Surrounded by the garter with its device : "Honi soit qui male y pense," and supported by two stags, this coat is *gules, four fusils ermine, fesswise, crested : a chapeau de maintenance surmounted by an ermine between two candles, mantlings : gules and ermines;* it is repeated top left, smaller, and simply surrounded by the garter, which is also repeated on the right surrounding *arms party, dexter,* the same as before, and *sinister, gules, three arches argent (2 and 1).*

12 ft. 8 in. × 12 ft. 1 in. (3,86 m × 3,68 m)

The central coat of arms is that of John Dynham, an English knight, who was born in 1433 in Devon and died in 1501 after having served five kings. After having offered his fee to Henry VI of Lancaster in 1458, he changed over to the service of Edward of York. He helped the latter to cross the Channel after his defeat at Ludlow and rendered him sufficient other services to be raised to the peerage after the Duke of York had become king. He was placed in command of a fleet, and later was Governor of Calais, where he stayed throughout the short reign of Edward IV and that of Richard III. He must have come to the help of Henry Tudor in his conquest of England, since in 1486 the new king appointed him Lord Treasurer of England, which he remained until his death.

Since the arms of the part *sinister* of the shield at the top right are those of the Arches family — his father married an Arches — this shield is certainly that of John Dynham's mother, who had also helped the future Edward IV. The shield on the left, accordingly, must be that of John Dynham's father. Clearly, the son must have wished to associate his parents with his fame.

John Dynham was made a knight of the garter, probably in 1487, certainly by 1488, and he may have ordered this tapestry to commemorate the honor. The work was done between 1488 and 1501 in any case. It was probably one of a set in the great hall of his home at Lambeth, Surrey, which he bequeathed to his second wife. The piece has been attributed to the Tournai ateliers from which Henry Tudor (Henry VII) bought a number of sets, especially one of the *Trojan War* (see Nos. 7-11). This provenance could be correct, even though the Tournai works usually have a more brilliant color range, and this tapestry is different from the millefleurs tapestry of Jean de Daillon (No. 47), which in all probability comes from Tournai. Nevertheless, the difference in colors between the only two sets that we know for certain come from Tournai — the *Trojan War* and the Bourges *Life of St. Ursin* — shows that the production of this center was not always the same. But merchants like the Greniers, who were not artisans but contractors, supplied the cartoons they owned to weavers whose output they then sold, and they could have commissioned work from weavers outside Tournai. There were such in other towns — Ghent, Lille, Enghien — of whose production we know little. Audenarde, for example, also comes to mind; in 1473, a weaver was condemned there for having used threads dyed a color that was "false and forbidden." Later works from this center were rather dull in color. However this may be, it is clear that it was wrong to go on thinking of millefleurs tapestries as a homogeneous group; distinctions must be made among them, and this will help to solve the problem of their origin.

This work was in 1876 and again in 1914 in Appleby Castle, Westmoreland. In 1929 it was in the collection of Myron C. Taylor, New York; when this collection was sold in 1960 it was bought for The Cloisters.

BIBLIOGRAPHY. Bonnie Young, *John Dynham and his Tapestry*, in The *Metropolitan Museum of Art Bulletin*, t. XX, June 1962, p. 309, 316, fig. — J.-P. Asselberghs, *Tapisseries héraldiques et de la vie quotidienne*, Tournai, 1970, n° 6, fig. 1.

49
Millefleurs Tapestry with Arms of Jacqueline of Luxemburg

Wool and silk
12-14 warp threads to the inch

the Château, Langeais

Of the same type as the celebrated Berne millefleurs tapestry with the arms of Philip the Good, this piece has been cut on all four sides, and especially the bottom; it has a field of closely set bouquets, medallions in the four corners formed of a thorny branch surrounding two back-to-back e's, linked by a girdle, and in the center a lozenge-shaped shield, *per pale, dexter, quarterly, argent, three fesses gules* (Croÿ) *and argent, three axes gules, two addorsed, the third turned dexter* (Renty); *sinister, quarterly in the first and fourth argent, a lion gules, with tail forked saltirewise, crowned, armed and tongued or* (Luxembourg); *in the second and third, grand quarterly, azure, semé with crosses crusily, fitchy or, a fleur de lys or in chief, two addorsed fish* [bars] *or* (Duchy of Bar), *and azure, semé with fleurs de lys or* (France); *in the escutcheon, per pale, fessy, vair and gules* (Coucy), *and gules, three leopards or* (England).

8 ft. 11 in. × 12 ft. 6 in. (2,71 m × 3,80 m)

This precise blazon gives a certain identification. These are the arms of a woman of noble family, Jacqueline of Luxemburg, who married on February 28, 1455 not, as has been said, Philip of Croÿ (son of Jean), Count of Chimay and knight of the Golden Fleece (died 1483), but his cousin, also named Philip, the son of Antony, one of the most powerful noblemen of the court of Burgundy (died 1475). He himself was lord of Croÿ, Arschot, and Renty, and he died in 1511 after giving Jacqueline three sons. The last, William, was known as the lord of Chièvres; he was to be tutor to the future Holy Roman Emperor Charles V, and was destined to play such an important part alongside the latter that he was called "the director of Continental policy."

However if we believe Commynes, Jacqueline of

Luxemburg's father came to disapprove of this marriage in 1464, at the time that he was conducting the affairs of Charles the Bold, who had just exiled the Croÿs, whom he held to blame for his father's having returned the Somme towns to Louis XI. The Croÿs had to flee the lands of the Duke of Burgundy "and lost much furniture." Antony recovered his land in 1473, but his son Philip was persuaded by his father-in-law to go over to the King of France and had his possessions confiscated once more. He repented, and obtained the pardon of Charles the Bold and the return of his property the day before Louis XI had his wife's father beheaded, the latter being the famous Louis of Luxemburg, Count of Saint-Pol and Constable of France.

This individual, who had alienated all and sundry with his succession of treasons, had married Jeanne de Bar, daughter and heiress of Robert de Bar, himself son of Henri de Bar and Marie de Coucy. Now, Henri de Bar was descended from the French royal family by his mother, the daughter of John the Good, and Marie de Coucy was the granddaughter of the English King Edward III; Jeanne de Bar's mother was also a descendant of the Coucys. Thus is explained the complexity of Jacqueline of Luxemburg's arms, and in particular the presence of the fleurs de lys of France and the leopards of England, which were proof of her illustrious forbears.

The two e's are certainly a sign of the Luxemburg family, since in the furniture inventory of the Constable of Saint-Pol, Jacqueline's father, were mentioned several tapestries sprinkled with "tufts and EE's." What do these two letters mean? They cannot be initials of names, as is often the case with linked letters, and probably with the AE's of the *Unicorn Hunt* (see Nos. 18-24). Are they short for a motto whose meaning escapes us? We know that Philip the Good, Duke of Burgundy, had used as a device similar tiny e's, linked, at the end of his reign; but these were facing, instead of back to back as here. The Treasurer of France and confidential adviser to Charles VII and Louis XI, Etienne Chevalier, also had the famous *Hours,* painted for him by Jean Fouquet around the middle of the century, decorated with two linked e's; these were disposed normally and are not, as has been wrongly stated, ec's, the initials of his name, or of his first name and that of his wife. Do such letters, like the y's on the Angers *Apocalypse,* the AE's of Charles of France, brother of Louis XI, or the two S's of Charles VIII and Anne of Brittany, have any meaning? Have they any connection with the "Saracen letters" mentioned in the 15th century and in particular in 1453, on a chain enameled with the colors of King Charles VIII? The mystery has not yet been explained.

We are no more certain about where the tapestry was woven. Note however that the flowered field here is not that of the "classical" millefleurs tapestry's; the plants are much more closely packed and do not have the marvelous freedom and refined naturalism of those in the *Lady with the Unicorn* (Nos. 37-42) or the *Narcissus* (No. 33). Neither do they have the quality of the flowers (which are different from those in the earlier works) of the tapestry of Philip the Good in Berne, which we know was woven in Brussels. The Langeais piece thus probably came from other ateliers. There were plenty of these in the second half of the 15th century, and as we have already discussed above (see No. 38), millefleurs pieces were fashionable in the last third of this century and were made in a number of different places, though with the exception of the Berne tapestry we have no means of knowing to which centers to assign the various different types that have survived.

However, since she was by her marriage a subject of the Dukes of Burgundy, Jacqueline of Luxemburg must have gone for it to some town in the southern Netherlands. As well as those already mentioned, we may suggest Malines, Enghien, Audenarde, Ghent, or Middelburg, or again Louvain, which has been put forward because her husband had property there.

The date is also unsure. It must be between Jacqueline of Luxemburg's marriage (1455) and her death, probably on June 29, 1513. However, the tapestry was probably woven after 1475, firstly because Philip of Croÿ's return to favor must have ushered in a period of greater prosperity than the years preceding it, and secondly because until his death in that year only his father was entitled to bear full arms, and he himself would have had to bear an heir's difference that does not appear here. Nevertheless, there is considerable margin for doubt.

This work was bought on May 29, 1889, from the Lannoy dealers by M. Siegfried. He bequeathed it to the Institut de France with the Langeais château.

BIBLIOGRAPHY. Philippe de Commynes, *Mémoires,* book I. ch. II — Jean Scohier, *La généalogie et descente de la très illustre maison de Croÿ,* Douay, 1589, p. 16-17, fig. — Jules Gauthier, *Inventaire du mobilier du connétable de Saint-Pol en 1476,* in *Bulletin archéologique,* 1885, p. 24-57. — G. Dansaert, *Guillaume de Croÿ-Chièvres dit le Sage (1458-1521)...,* Paris-Courtrai-Bruxelles, J. Vermaut, undated, p. 17. — *La Toison d'Or, Cinq siècles d'art et d'histoire, Exposition... 1962,* Bruges (1962), n° 45, p. 127. — Sophie Schneebalg-Perelman, *Les sources de l'histoire de la tapisserie bruxelloise et la tapisserie en tant que source,* in *Annales de la Société Royale d'Archéologie de Bruxelles,* t. LI, 1966, p. 313 and fig. 14. — R. Van Uytven, *Nieuwe bijdrage tot de studie der Leuvense tapij-twevers XIVe-XVIIe eeuw,* in *Arca Lovaniensis. Artes atque historiae reserans documenta,* 1972, p. 19-25 and 34, fig.

50
Tapestry with Arms of Louise of Savoy-Angoulême

Wool and silk
15 warp threads
to the inch

Museum of Fine Arts,
Boston

Composed of pieces that clearly come from the same work, this heraldic tapestry, when compared with Nos. 49 and 51-52, shows the extraordinary diversity of form that could be taken by the arms, emblems, and ciphers that nobleman and princes used to give distinction to their families and persons.

Here, the arms are all grouped in the central stripe of the top border. We

see alternately the shield of France, *a label with three lappets argent* (Orléans), surrounded by the collar of the Order of St. Michael, and with a count's coronet as crest, and another *per pale, dexter* with the preceding arms, and *sinister* with those of Savoy, *gules, a cross argent,* also crested with a coronet; these are the arms of Louise de Savoy, wife of Charles of Angoulême and mother of the future Francis I.

The knots in the vertical girdles that separate the motifs, and which do not imply widowhood any more than they do in No. 46, recall the knot of Savoy. There is a play on words (they were much appreciated at the time) discernible in the two horizontal lines of wings in joined pairs on either side of the central stripes : they suggest both Louise's initial and one of her devices : "Pennas dedisti, volabo et requiscam" (Thou gavest me wings, I will fly and find rest).

The principal elements in the work are portrayed alternately in a festoon of medallions : they are the salamander and a cipher composed of several interlaced letters. The salamander, together with the motto "Nutrisco et extingo" (I nourish and extinguish), an allusion to this creature's supposed ability to live in fire, had been used from his childhood by Francis of

Angoulême; he had no doubt borrowed it from his grandfather, who was the youngest son of Louis of Orleans (brother of Charles VI). The cipher was read by Gustave Dupont-Ferrier as C (Charles), K (Karolus), F (François), L (Louise), A (Angoulême), S (Savoie); for the last three letters, this interpretation has since been generally accepted. But Gertrude Townsend, while accepting the C (Charles), saw also in it an O for Orléans and an R for Romorantin. A. Brandenburg rejects the C, but returns to the original F; he agrees on the O and R, but suggests an E for Epernay, since Louise of Savoy was Dame of Epernay and Romorantin. Perhaps there are in fact eight letters, and we should retain the C for Charles of Angoulême since it appears next to the L of his wife in tiny scrolls near the top of the pilasters, with vases and small children, that alternate with the stripes of salamanders and ciphers.

11 ft. 4 in. $\times$ 15 ft. 5 in. (3,50 m $\times$ 4,70 m)

The dating of this tapestry, though accepted to be between 1488, the year of Charles of Angoulême's marriage to Louise of Savoy, and 1515, when Francis I raised his mother to the rank of Duchess, has posed problems. For the Angoulême family differenced the arms of Orléans (of France, a label argent) with a crescent gules on the lappets of the label; no such crescents appear here. For Brandenburg, the reason is that the male arms are not those of Charles, but of his son, which Louise often associated with her own at the beginning of the 16th century. It seems that the young Count of Angoulême did not difference his arms after 1498 and up to his accession to the throne in 1515; and before 1496, in any case, the Savoy part of his mother's arms included a two-color border, for Philip of Bresse, Louise's father, acceded to the ducal throne only in that year. Now Charles of Angoulême had died on January 1, 1496; and furthermore, between 1499 and 1508, Louise of Savoy parted her arms with the serpent of Milan. Therefore the tapestry dates between 1508 and 1515. Brandenburg believes it to be earlier than the marriage of Francis to Claude of France, daughter of Louis XII and Anne of Brittany, which took place on May 14, 1514; he thinks that after this date he would have taken the cipher of his wife.

The tapestry in any case is only a little earlier than 1515. It shows a taste for a new style introduced by Fouquet in the middle of the 15th century. It did not catch on immediately and only began to be accepted at the end of the reign of Charles VIII (died 1498), after his Italian expedition. The motifs — vases, cornucopias, acanthuses — are pure Renaissance; and this piece, which contrasts strikingly with contemporary production, seems to have been one of the earliest manifestations in France of an art transplanted there by that country's princes. It was an art that was soon to replace the Gothic style, despite its resistance, and despite the fact that it had never ceased to flourish and develop.

This work is said to have been found about 1925 in the attic of the château of La Bellière, at La-Vicomté-sur-Rance, Ille-et-Villaine. It was bought from the Raphael Stora Gallery (Paris and New York) on February 6, 1936, by the Museum of Fine Arts.

BIBLIOGRAPHY. Gustave Dupont-Ferrier, *Origine et signification de la salamandre ornementale dite de François I*, Lecture to the Institut de France, Académie des Inscriptions et Belles-Lettres, 1935. — Gertrude Townsend, *A French Armorial Tapestry*, in *Bulletin of the Museum of Fine Arts, Boston*, t. XXXXIX, n° 235, Oct. 1941, p. 67-73, fig. — Adolph S. Cavallo, *Tapestries of Europe and of Colonial Peru in the Museum of Fine Arts, Boston*, Boston, Museum of Fine Arts (1967), n° 14, t. I, p. 66-68, t. II, pl. 14 (b/w) et 14a (color). — Alain Erlande-Brandenburg, to appear shorty in *Bulletin Monumental*, 1973.

51-52
Tapestries with Arms of Dinteville-Pontailler and Vienne-Dinteville

Wool
15 warp threads
to the inch

Château of Commarin,
Côte-d'Or

These extraordinarily decorative pieces are entirely different in composition from the other heraldic tapestries in the exhibition. One bears the arms, emblems, and devices of Jacques de Dinteville and his wife Alix de Pontailler; the other, those of their daughter Bénigne de Dinteville and her husband Gérard de Vienne.

51
Arms of Dinteville-Pontailler

This tapestry, which is mutilated, is built up from a pattern of three kinds of square.

On one, the collar of the Order of St. Michael appears against a red background around a quarterly shield : *in the first and fourth, sable, two leopards or* (Dinteville-Jaucourt); *in the second and third, azure, a cross or accompanied by eighteen billets of the same (5, 5, 4, 4)* (Choiseul); with two mermaids as supporters, surrounded by a banderole with the motto "Tant le desire," and surmounted by a helmet bearing a pair of wings as a crest issuing from a wreath of the mantling.

The second kind of square has a white background; it bears a fissured globe from which issue multicolored flames that send out sparks in all directions, while the motto "Tant le désire" is repeated in scrolls at the four corners.

The third kind of square bears, on blue ground, a lozenge-shaped shield, *per pale, dexter, arms of Dinteville-Jaucourt and Choiseul; sinister, gules, a lion or, crowned, armed and tongued azure* (Pontailler). In the corners are four banderoles with the motto "D'aultre jamais."

8ft. 8in. × 10ft. 2in. (2,65 m × 3,10 m)

The château of Commarin contains a second tapestry with the arms of the Dinteville-Pontailler family, on which there are also three kinds of square, but the design is different. The flaming globe is replaced by a cluster of arrows, and the sides have Renaissance borders.

There are also in the château two tapestries with the arms of the Vienne-Dinteville family; the larger is exhibited here.

52
Arms of Vienne-Dinteville

There is a pattern of four sorts of square.
One bears the arms of Vienne : *gules, an eagle or.*
In the second is a fountain, framed with rose branches, against a blue

background. Touching the sides are two banderoles with the motto "Plus fresche que rose."

On the third kind of square, against a white background, is a lozenge-shaped shield, *per pale, dexter, the eagle of Vienne; sinister, arms of Dinteville and Choiseul.* In the four corners are scrolls with the motto "A moy ne tient."

The fourth kind of square has a blue background, and bears a different fountain from that in the second; above it is a seated woman, and on each side are fruit trees, while all around is a banderole with the motto "Aigrez et doulcez."

The lateral borders have Renaissance motifs. On the top border, the eagle shield alternates with the lozenge-shaped shield, separated by banderoles with "Aigres et doulcez," on a background decorated with fruit.

The tapestry has been mutilated, and has been resewn in the center.

8 ft. 8 in. × 20 ft. 1 in. (2,65 m × 6,35 m)

Here again (see Nos. 48 and 49), the heraldry tells us whom these tapestries were made for.

The Dintevilles were one of the most important families in Burgundy. Its two best-known members in the early 16th century were Gaucher de Dinteville, Master of the King's Household, lieutenant at Siena, then Bailiff of Troyes, Knight of the Order of St. Michael in 1517, and Governor of the Dauphin, the eldest son of Francis I; and Gaucher's brother Jacques de Dinteville, lord of Dampnartin and Master of Louis of Orleans' Hunt, who after the duke's accession to the throne became Master of the Royal Hunt from 1498 to his death in 1506. However, it was not for these that the Commarin tapestries were woven, but for one of their elder brothers, also named Jacques, the third child of Claude de Dinteville, lord of Eschannay (or Eschanetz), and of Jeanne de la Baume; he was to become lord of Commarin, Eschannay, and Bar-sur-Seine, as the two elder sons took orders. It was he who married, in 1478, a Pontailler, a descendant of the former viscounts of Dijon, named Alix, the daughter of Guillaume de Pontailler, lord of Talmey, who died before 1476, and Guillemette de Vergy.

Jacques bore arms quartered of those of Dinteville — which in fact were those of Jaucourt, as in the 14th century one of his ancestors, Pierre de Jaucourt, took the name of Dinteville while retaining the Jaucourt arms — and of those of Choiseul, a family of which his great-grandfather, Gérard, lord of Eschannay, had married a member, Alix. The estates at Commarin came from Jacques' paternal grandmother, Agnès de Courtiamble, the first wife of Jean de Dinteville, who was the son of Gérard and the father of Claude. Jacques also owned from his ancestors the estate of Eschannay, and from his wife that of Villeneuve, and Louis XI had given him the seat of Bar-sur-Seine. His influence was in fact sufficiently important for the King, who had seized Burgundy in 1477 and was trying to woo the population away from the inheritors of the former dukes, to think of obtaining his loyalty in this way. No doubt for the same reason he was appointed by Charles VIII, on December 20, 1491, captain and governor of the city and château of Beaune, at a salary of about 100 livres a year, without counting gratuities. He was to be responsible for the building of much of this town, but it nearly brought about his downfall. For in 1501, while he was Master of the King's Hunt in Burgundy, he was, with other local noblemen, liberally pensioned by Louis XII, who wanted to be sure of peace and quiet in the former duchy before launching his crusade against the Turks and the reconquest of Naples. He was given the income from Villiers and Maisy-le-Duc (400 livres) plus a gift of 1,320 livres; but he then found himself accused of promoting the escape of two Beaune merchants who had plotted to hand over the city to Maximilian of Austria. He managed to clear himself, and received the collar of the Order of St. Michael, apparently during the reign of Louis XII. In 1508 he gave to the collegiate church of Notre-Dame in Beaune a sepulcher with his portrait, that of his wife, and also that of his dog, who had saved him from drowning. Later he was to be buried in the church. At about this time he purchased the estate of Lusigny, and in 1515 he endowed a daily mass in Notre-Dame of Beaune. He was still living in 1519; he probably died in 1522, since his successor as captain of Beaune

was appointed on December 19 of that year. The motto "Tant le désire" that goes with arms must certainly have been his, as well as the two emblems of the flaming globe and the cluster of arrows; "D'autre jamais" seems to have been the device of his wife.

Their only daughter and heiress, Bénigne, with whom we may associate the motto "A moy ne tient," brought Commarin in her dowry to Gérard de Vienne, whom she married in 1501, or so it seems; at any rate, the first daughter of this match, Claude, was born on July 5, 1504. The Viennes were one of the oldest and most famous families in Burgundy, and Gérard, eldest son of Louis de Vienne and Isabeau de Neufchâtel, was lord of Pymont, Antigny, and Ruffey, knight of the Order of St. Michael, knight in the Dijon Parlement (1515), and gentleman in waiting to Queen Eleonora of Austria, the second wife of Francis I. He was appointed in 1516 to command the ban and arrière-ban of the Duchy of Burgundy, and negotiated for the King the treaty of neutrality signed with the Swiss in 1522. He provided for his interment with his wife in the chapel he had built within the Sainte-Chapelle in Dijon; he had his parents, who had buried in Brussels, reinterred there. "Aigres et doulces" is probably his motto and the fountain his emblem, together with the device "Plus fresche que rose," which may be an allusion to the quality of the water.

What is the date of these tapestries?

For No. 51 the time of the Dinteville-Pontailler marriage, around 1478, has been suggested. But the shield supported by mermaids is surrounded by the new collar of the Order of St. Michael, in which a form of S, from 1516 onward, replaced the knots that earlier separated the shells. The tapestry is thus after this date. It is probably also earlier than Jacques's death, in 1522.

No. 52 is probably contemporary with No. 51, for it seems that one of the side borders, the style of which is pure Renaissance, is woven on the original warp and not added. An earlier date would have explained why the leopards and lion are much more beautifully worked than on the other piece, and why there is a different emblem; Jacques de Dinteville might have abandoned the arrows for the globe in the intervening period. But he probably had two emblems, just as his son-in-law had two kinds of fountain, and the unequal quality of the drawing may have been due to the employment of two different cartoon makers of varying skill, or to restorations.

The Vienne-Dinteville tapestries must have been woven between the dates of the marriage (1501) and the deaths of Gérard and Bénigne; they are contemporary with the previous work if, once more, one of the side borders of the latter is original. For these borders are the same. The two pieces would thus be dated, like the two Dinteville-Pontaillers, between 1516 and 1522, which corresponds to the style of the borders and of the fountain emblems. All four would be just a little later than the Louise of Savoy tapestry (No. 50), the style of which is so new.

Thus the problems of identification and dating can be solved. The same cannot, however, be said of that of the man who did the cartoons and of where the works were woven. All we can say is that the painter was influenced by Italian art, that out of the simplest square design he was able to create compositions of an eminently mural nature, and that these transcend fashion with authority and unsurpassed brillance.

The tapestries have been in the château of Commarin since the 16th century.

BIBLIOGRAPHY. Père Anselme, *Histoire généalogique et chronologique...* t. VIII, 1733, p. 714-719, and t. VII, 1733, p. 793-794 and 802. — C. Bigarne, *Notice sur Jacques de Dinteville, capitaine du château de Beaune,* in *Société d'histoire, d'archéologie et de littérature de l'arrondissement de Beaune, Mémoires,* 1883, p. 203-214. — *Chroniques de Louis XII par Jean d'Auton,* publ. by R. de Maulde La Clavière, Paris, H. Laurens, t. II, 1891, p. 6-11. — *Les plus belles œuvres des collections de la Côte-d'Or, Musée de Dijon, Palais des Etats de Bourgogne,* 1958 (introd. by Pierre Quarré), (Dijon, Imprimerie de Darantière) undated, nᵒˢ 84-85, p. 39-40, cov. — Pierre Kjellberg, *La tapisserie gothique, sujet de constantes recherches : nouveaux trésors divulgués,* in *Connaissance des Arts,* Dec. 1963, p. 168 and fig. — Louis de Vogüe, *Le château de Commarin (Côte-d'Or),* in *Vieilles Maisons françaises,* n° 56, April 1973, p. 7 and 10.

53-54
Two Rabbit-Hunting Scenes

53
Rabbit-Hunting with Ferrets

Wool and silk
13-16 warp threads
to the inch

M. H. de Young
Memorial Museum
San Francisco

Before a growth of primarily oak and holly, seven peasant men and three peasant women are engaged in trapping rabbits that have been driven from their holes by ferrets. At the lower left a peasant kneels to introduce a ferret into one of the holes; this he probably has just removed from the carrying basket held by the woman directly behind him. Above, to the right, a net trap has been put in place over another hole, while in the center a rabbit is just making his exit from a hole covered by a trap. In the center a rabbit has just sprung into a trap, and from three other traps the peasant men are removing rabbits caught in the nets. To the left a woman stands ready with dogs on a leash, in case any of the rabbits should escape.

10 ft. × 11 ft. 11 in. (3,05 m × 3,63 m)

This tapestry so undeniably resembles two others, No. 54 and one in the Burrel Collection, Glasgow, that it must represent the main event in a series of related scenes. The Glasgow piece shows the preparation for the hunt, while No. 54, little known till now, show the repast after the hunt.

54
A Peasants' Picnic

Wool and silk
10-18 warp threads
to the inch

Private collection

In a forest, composed mainly of oaks and hazels, eight men and five women have gathered for a picnic. Two of the women are sitting, with a large loaf and a knife on their knees, and there are pears, a slice of tart, and a gourd on the ground by a man who is drinking from a bottle. All are just back from the hunt : the peasant at the top is putting a rabbit into a bag held out to him by one of the women; several more rabbits hang from sticks, top right and in the foreground. Two men on the right are carrying, tied to the ends of their sticks, the nets that in the Glasgow piece they are placing in front of the rabbit-holes, and in No. 53 have just caught some

rabbits. The basket in the foreground with its little central opening is identical with the one held by a woman in No. 53, and by another woman in the Glasgow piece. Other details recur in the three pieces, notably the dog, seen here in right foreground, the sickles tucked into belts, and the rolled-up nets.

9 ft. 2 in. × 11 ft. 6 in. (2,80 m × 3,50 m)

The three tapestries are so closely related that we are entitled to conclude they were done from the same set of cartoons. The composition, the scale, and the weaving all match. The treatment of the figures is the same : some superimposed, some partly concealed, in a forest with the foreground planted with bouquets against green or blue, in such a way that all the greenery shades in together. The vigorously drawn figures, with powerful heads and strong faces, and with simple clothes boldly catching the light and shade, are in a very personal style. Their expressions are direct, but there is nevertheless a certain delicacy, for instance in the pink modeling on the faces. The costumes are the same in the three pieces : the fur hat and red robe of the man who is here top right appear again on the hunter in the bottom left-hand corner of the Glasgow tapestry, and the dress of the woman who here is preparing to eat a piece of bread is worn in the Glasgow work by the woman who holds the ferret basket, while the man who is drinking comes up again in the center of No. 53, taking a rabbit out of the net. The colors of No. 53 overall differ a little from the others, so this piece may perhaps belong to an earlier or later weaving of the cartoons : the other two pieces have the identical clear tones, with a typical bright red.

William Wells has suggested the name of Rogier van der Weyden for the designer, and he compares the Glasgow and San Francisco pieces with the well-known *Seven Sacraments* set, that has been tentatively attributed to the Tournai merchant Pasquier Grenier. These suggestions are debatable. It is not improbable that the *Ferret Hunt* was woven in Tournai, but its style seems different from that of the *Seven Sacraments,* and even more so from the tortured, serious art of Rogier van der Weyden. It seems safer to say that the designer was a painter of whom we know nothing, but who certainly understood the tapestry medium. His sense of gesture was extraordinarily good; it enables us to understand perfectly how this kind of hunting was done.

No. 53 and the Glasgow piece have been dated in the third quarter of the 15th century. We may pinpoint them more closely at 1460-1470.

BIBLIOGRAPHY. Hitherto unpublished. The two other pieces in the same series have been published, that in Glasgow by William Wells, *Two Burrell Hunting Tapestries,* in *The Scottish Art Review,* vol. XIV, n° 1, 1973, p. 10-12, fig. col. and b/w; that in San Francisco by Jean-Paul Asselberghs, *Tapisseries héraldiques et de la vie quotidienne.* Tournai, 1970, n° 19 and fig.

55-56
The Wine Harvest

Wool and silk
12-15 warp threads to the inch

The Toledo Museum of Art,
Toledo, Ohio

After hunting, wine making was one of the most popular homely subjects for tapestry in the Middle Ages. In these two pieces we see several stages of the process. The fabric has probably been cut, since the Burrell Collection in Glasgow has two much larger pieces with other scenes to the right of these. Some of the characters on the right-hand side of the Glasgow pieces recur in a tapestry in the Musée des Arts Décoratifs in Paris; this piece, incomplete on the left, may have formed part of No. 56.

55
Casking

At the top, two figures watch closely as a man who is making wine pours some into a bowl, while another couple pays little attention to the scene. In the center two men, one with breaches partly unfastened, are carrying a vat; in the foreground, the new wine is being run into one of a row of casks.

12 ft. 2 in. × 6 ft. (3,10 m × 1,85 m)

56

Transporting Grapes and Selling Wine

Below a group of men who are busy with wine casks, a woman leads a donkey laden with baskets full of grapes. At the bottom a couple receives payment from a customer.

10 ft. × 12 ft. 7 in. (3,05 m × 1,70 m)

These vigorously drawn tapestries have been considered similar in style to the *Trojan War* (Nos. 7-11), and in color to typical Tournai work. When we consider their date, it is interesting to note that while the two Glasgow pieces can be said to be of the time of Louis XI (1461-1483), a comparison shows that here, particularly in No. 56, the costumes have been modified; this proves that the cartoon was reused. The present pieces and the one in Paris, in which the fashion is also later, may thus be placed around 1480. This updating of the figures tells us something about how the way the Tournai weavers worked : they were able to avoid continually having to call on the services of artists by reusing their models, with modifications of detail, for a considerable period.

From the Dupont-Auberville and François de Montrémy collections, Paris. Sold by Parke-Bernet in the Joseph Brummer sale (1st part, lot No. 773, April 20-23, 1949); bought by the Toledo Museum of Art.

BIBLIOGRAPHY. William Wells, *The earliest Flemish tapestries in the Burrell Collection, Glasgow (1380-1475)*, in *L'Age d'or de la tapisserie flamande*, Brussels, 1969, p. 439. — J.-P. Asselberghs, *Tapisseries héraldiques et de la vie quotidienne*, Tournai, 1970, introd. and n° 35.

57

Gypsies at a Château Gate

Wool and silk

The Currier Gallery of Art,
Manchester, New Hampshire

The finest of a group of which others are in the château of Gaasbeck (Belgium) and the Cranbrook Academy of Art (Bloomfield Hills, Michigan), this shows a landscape with a stag hunt in progress, and gypsies in the foreground. Carrying children, most of them naked, these exotic people approach a château. In front of its gates, on the right, is an aristocratic couple, to whom two hunters offer a haunch of venison and a hare. In the center is a second couple; a child is in the act of stealing the woman's purse. Behind her, an old gypsy woman has taken hold of a lady's hand to tell her fortune. On the left, a younger gypsy is feeding a child from a bowl held out to her by a little girl.

9 ft. 11 in. × 16 ft. 6 in. (3 m × 5,03 m)

The inventory of one of the greatest Tournai tapestry weavers of the early 16th century, Arnould Poissonier, mentions a large number of pieces of the "Histoire de Carrabara dit des Egiptiens." For this reason, the weaving of this type of work has been attributed to Tournai. We do not know the painter who did the cartoons, but the style is quite different from that practiced in Brussels at the time. As we have no knowledge of any painted pictures resembling these pieces, we may surmise that there were artists that specialized in making working drawings like Baudouin de Bailleul a few decades earlier, who supplied the weaving ateliers with the countless "bergeries" and "scènes de genre" that were so much in demand at the time. They give us a clear and fresh picture of this pleasant period when France, with the horrors of war behind her, was emerging from the Middle Ages, and could devote herself in peace and quiet to the pleasures of the countryside.

In the 17th century, this work was, together with two other pieces, in the château of Effiat in Auvergne. Probably at this time *a member of the family, Antoine Coeffier (died 1632), Marquis of Effiat and Marshal of France, the father of the famous favorite of Louis XIII known as "Cinq-Mars," added the arms at the top. Acquired in the middle of the 19th century by the tapestry historian Achille Jubinal, the piece was later in the collection of Mrs. Genevieve Garvan Brady of Long Island. Sold in 1937, it was bought by the Currier Art Gallery of Manchester, New Hampshire, through French and Co., New York.*

BIBLIOGRAPHY. George Leland Hunter, *The practical Book of Tapestries*, Philadelphia. — London, J.-B. Lippincott, 1925, p. 102-103, pl. VI m. — Helen Comstock, *A Tournai tapestry for the Currier Gallery*, in *The Connoisseur*, vol. 100, n° 434, Oct. 1937, p. 208-209, fig. — A.E. Hamill, *A fifteenth-century Tapestry*, in *Journal of the Gypsy Lore Society*, 3e series, vol. XXVIII, 1949, p. 81-82. — François de Vaux de Foletier, *Iconographie des "Egyptiens", précisions sur le costume ancien des tsiganes*, in *Gazette des Beaux-Arts*, n° 1172, September 1966, p. 165-172, fig.

58
Picking Oranges

Wool and silk
12-15 warp threads
to the inch

The Rijksmuseum,
Amsterdam

Are they oranges or apples? The fruit the young man up the tree is picking is a rather dull ocher, and in temperate Europe oranges do not grow in open orchards. But this tree is one of the few that bear flowers and fruit at the same time, as is the case here, and we find in 15th-century inventories or account books that some princes did own tapestries with orange trees pictured in them. The Duke of Berry (died 1416) had no less

than "six green tappiz strewn with oriengiers, of Arras workmanship," plus "two other green and three red ones, of Paris workmanship, with an orange tree in the middle," to say nothing of embroideries with the same motif and "six pieces of white tapestry, scattered with pine cones and oranges." And in 1466, Philip the Good, Duke of Burgundy, bought from the Tournai merchant Pasquier Grenier a room set of orange-tree tapestry, comprising a bedcover, four wall tapestries, and a benchcover, as a gift for his sister Agnes, widow of Charles I, Duke of Bourbon.

9 ft. 11 in. × 5 ft. 7 in. (3 m × 1,70 m)

Thus it is to Tournai, where many tapestries of the kind known in France as "de genre," which we may best describe as "documentary," were woven at the end of the 15th and in the early 16th centuries, that this work should be attributed. It has been correctly dated in the years 1490-1500.

From its style, it belongs to a large group of tapestries that have long been considered French, but which Sophie Schneebalg has recently attributed to the Netherlands, and in particular to Brussels (see Nos. 37-42). Here again, however, the figures are not those of Flemish painting at this period; the prototype for the boy in the tree is to be found in the borders of French Books of Hours at the end of the 15th century. In these, two fruit-picking scenes occur frequently :

one shows three superimposed figures above a woman who is gathering flowers; the other, less finely drawn, shows only three upper figures, and in reverse order.

In 1927 the work was in the collection of the antiquary Schutz. In 1953 it was bought by the Rijksmuseum from a London dealer.

BIBLIOGRAPHY. A.M. Louise Erkelens, *Wandtapijten I, Late Gotiek en vroege Renaissance*, Amsterdam, Rijksmuseum, 1962, front., p. 6, fig. 12-14. — Sophie Schneebalg-Perelman, *Les sources de l'histoire de la tapisserie bruxelloise et la tapisserie en tant que source*, dans *Annales de la Société royale d'archéologie de Bruxelles*, t. LI, 1966, p. 305 et fig. 11. — Jean-Paul Asselberghs, *Tapisseries héraldiques et de la vie quotidienne*, Tournai, 1970, n° 14, fig. 14.

59-62
Four Bird Hunting Scenes

Wool
12-15 warp threads
to the inch

Private collection

"We do not think that [in these four pieces] one should attempt to see more than a series of isolated unconnected scenes"; so wrote Achille Jubinal, the first historian of tapestry, nearly a century and a half ago. "They do not set out, either, to portray any particular method of hunting. In our opinion they are just episodes generally connected with this kind of activity."

Here we have indeed various stages in a pleasant day's sport. A party of gentlemen and ladies rides horseback in a country valley, accompanied by servants who collect the game taken by the falcons. Interspersed are scenes of a picnic, a musical interlude, and other entertainments.

59
Hunting with Crossbow and Falcon

On the left, a hunter prepares to shoot a bolt at one of the birds swimming in the stream in the foreground. On the right, two people turn toward a servant, in the center, who kneels over two dead herons. Other servants, in the middle distance to the left and to the right, turn the lure : bait to which are attached birds' wings and which is waved about to tempt the falcon back to the gloved left wrist. For it has to be prevented from devouring the bird it has caught; other characters also hold out to it pieces of raw meat to assuage its hunger.

There exists a copy of this piece, with certain differences, such as more space between the servant who is waving the lure on the left and the horseman next to him.

10ft. 8in. × 11ft. 8in. (3,25 m × 3,56 m)

60
The Picnic

While two hunters try to recall the falcons that are attacking a heron (top left), and in the foreground a gentleman helps a lady to dismount, a

couple is already at table; food is piled there in abundance, and they are being served by a young woman. Behind is a group of people who are looking at another couple, still on horseback; these two are leaning down toward a fountain, while a clown waves his bauble in their direction. Nearby is a young man who is preparing to jump down from a pomegranate tree. Besides being a simple scene of noble life at the time, this is clearly an allegory of the madness of love.

10 ft. 9 in. × 15 ft. 4 in. (3,30 m × 4,66 m)

61
Musical Interlude

In the background hunters are still trying to recall their falcons, in the foreground a group listens to a gentleman who plays the flute. On his knees sits a young woman who unrolls the music for him.

10 ft. 4 in. × 15 ft. 5 in. (3,33 m × 4,70 m)

62
Return from the Hunt

Watched by two shepherds, guarding their sheep, the hunters return to the château with their dogs on the leash and laden with game : herons and a hare. Some of the falcons already have their heads hooded.

11 ft. 1 in. × 14 ft. 11 in. (3,37 m × 4,55 m)

Once more, these scenes evoke the life of the aristocracy at the beginning of the reign of Francis I. The costumes, with their slashed sleeves and wide square décolletés, suggest a date around 1520. They are characteristic, in subject matter, style, and technique, of Tournai work at a time when this center was beginning its decline. The drawing is not badly done, especially in the horses, but the figures and groups, some of which seem as if they may have been reused from previous works, are sometimes juxtaposed, as in the mille-fleurs pieces, without much concern for composition.

These pieces were in the château of Haroué, Meurthe-et-Moselle, in 1838 and in that of Thoisy-la-Berchère, Côte-d'Or, until 1970. On March 5 of that year they were sold to a collector who retains a life interest in them but has given them to the French National Museums.

BIBLIOGRAPHY. Achille Jubinal, *Les anciennes tapisseries historiées*, Paris, éd. de la galerie d'armes de Madrid, 1838, p. 42, 4 pl. — *Les plus belles œuvres des collections de la Côte-d'Or, musée de Dijon, Palais des Etats de Bourgogne, 1958*, nos 86-90, 2 pl. — *Vente... 5 mars 1970, Palais Galliéra... Paris*, nos 125-128, 1 pl. col., 3 b/w.

63
Hunting with Crossbow and Falcon

Wool
12-15 threads
to the inch

Private collection

Here we show the second version mentioned in No. 59. One sees that the figures, which are of identical silhouettes, are spaced a little differently in both directions, that elements have been added (a dead bird, for example, between the legs of the man with the crossbow), or changed (the shape of the lure), that the landscape is different, and finally, that the clothes are of a more common cloth.

From this one appreciates precisely how weavers reused cartoons for principal figures, playing with them fairly freely in the composition of the picture. The landscape, on the other hand, shows too many differences not to have been redesigned. The variations in the clothes and their accessories lead us to believe that these particular cartoons were "dressed" — covered over by another cartoon with the same outline but of a different design and colors.

10ft. 10in. × 11ft. 10in. (3,30 m × 3,60 m)

64-67
Allegory of the Ephemeral

Wool and silk
About 12-14 warp threads
to the inch

"Plus ne serez ainsi qu'aurez esté / Dont plourerz, et moult vous poisera / Voir votre cours par vieillesee arresté." (No more will you be as you have been; of this will you weep and it will hang heavy over you to see your course arrested by old age.) So lamented Jean Lemaire de Belges, the greatest poet of this period. But never has the eternal complaint over the passage of time been so attractively presented as in these four tapestries that came from Chaumont. In contrast to the macabre dances of death in 15th-century art, everything here seems to be smiling and happy. Before a background of green hills in which châteaux nestle, and in the midst of meadows bright with flowers through which flow streams with swimming ducks, we see figures radiant with joie de vivre; one has to look closely to see that death awaits them in the midst of their pleasures.

Stanzas woven at the top of each piece explain, and sometimes distort, the meaning of the scenes. Two of them seems to be gatherings of pleasant-looking young men and elegant ladies, with children playing around their feet. *Youth, Eternity* and even more so *Love* suggest the theme of Petrarch's *Triumphs,* which were so popular at this period, especially in Italy; an admirable tapestry set of these, roughly contemporary and from the same art circles as the Chaumont tapestries, is today in Vienna.

64
Time

The Cleveland Museum of Art

"On voit le temps atourné de verdure
aucunes foiz aussi plaisant que ung ange
puis tout soudain change et fort estrange
jamais le temps en ung estat ne dure."

(Sometimes we see Time adorned with green foliage, as pleasant as an angel; and then suddenly he changes and becomes very strange. Never does Time persist in one state.)

A figure of Time, of extraordinary attractiveness, stands in the center; he offers a bunch of flowers to a group of people sitting in front of a musician. Nearby is a clown who no doubt symbolizes the vanity of this carefree happiness. It is probably also Time, here less kindly, who on the right points his staff at a bearded old man, in company of an anxious-looking woman, while children play on the bank of the stream in the foreground. Such is Time's inconstancy! But the symbolism of this tapestry is not only in the characters. The central palisade, for example, not only separates the two groups, but also two worlds : on the left, that of youth, which is also — according to a tradition originating no doubt in *The Romance of the Rose* (one of the best-known works of the Middle Ages) — that of the pleasant and easy life — a theme expressed not only by the ladies and gentleman handing out flowers and fruit to Time, but also by the splendid château in the background, with its lake on which a swan is swimming and in which a villager fishes; and on the right, the world of old age and misfortune, with its craggy hills, its piles of rocks that look like ruins, its path up which climbs a miller bent under his load. The theme of this work is the inconstancy of

happiness; playing on the passing of the seasons and of man's life-span, its symbolism is less religious than in most Brussels work. But beneath its apparent grace, it is no less charged with a profound sense of the impermanence of material things.

11 ft. 1 in. × 14 ft. 5 in. (3,39 m × 4,39 m)

65
Love

Only the central figure of this piece has survived, and the stanza is mutilated. It reads :
"Je frape tout a tort et a...
de ars et de dars les chastes...
mais à la fin quelque iousse [?]...
la mort survient qui tout m..."
(With my art and my arrows I strike the chastë... all around... but finally [?]... it is death that comes and... all...) Here again, under the outward appearance of the triumph of Love over kings (who, if we compare a contemporary French manuscript illustrating Petrarch's *Triumphs*, must be the gods Jupiter, Neptune, and Pluto), we have the final triumph of death, as predicted in the inscription and probably illustrated by some figure that has disappeared.

9 ft. 6 in. × 3 ft. 6 in. (2,90 m × 1,07 m)

66
Youth

"Jennesse bruit tant que elle a le queur sain.
et lui semble que tout tienne en sa main;
maiz ce triumphe est sans eternite.
icy voiés l'exemple tout a plain.
tel est joieux qui a la mort au sain.
per jeunes gens ce doit estre noté."

(Youth makes sounds as long as its heart is healthy, and thinks that it holds all in its hand. But this triumph is not eternal. Here you see clearly an example : he that is happy has death in his breast. Of this young people should take note.)

A tragic figure in the midst of this concert of musicians, young men, fair ladies, and children — one of whom is blowing soap bubbles — a young man falls, struck by death whose head appears from inside the folds of his robe, as is stated in the poem. The young woman standing behind him seems to be pushing back with her raised hands the merry fiddler, who half conceals another death's-head under his coat, thus showing that it is he who is leading the dance of death.

10 ft. 11 in. × 15 ft. 2 in. (3,33 m × 4,62 m)

67
Eternity

The Cleveland Museum of Art

"Rien triumphant par droicte auctorité
Se permanent ne est perdurablement.
Rien permanent dessoubz le firmament.
Maïs audessus triunphe eternité."

(Nothing triumphing by due authority remains permanent and durable. Nothing is permanent under the heavens. But above, eternity trimphs.)

Here, the subject is as religious as those of the other pieces are secular. Yet the scene is not at all like that in the *Triumphs* of Petrarch, in which it is the Trinity, in a chariot drawn by the evangelical animals, that symbolizes the victory of eternity over death. Here we have juxtaposed the themes of the Madonna sitting in the garden of Paradise and that of Mary Queen of Heaven, both very popular in the International Gothic art of the 1400s; and it is the inscription that links this portrayal of the Virgin's coronation by two angels, surrounded by other musical angels, with the preceding illustrations of the inconstancy of Time and the impermanence of life.

10 ft. 8 in. × 12 ft. (3,29 m × 3,92 m)

Even from a stylistic point of view there are differences, as Dorothy Shepherd had already noticed, between the angels and the Virgin of the last piece, who have small heads, elongated faces, and graceful gestures despite their ample robes with heavy broken folds (in the Flemish style), and the fuller figures of *Time* and *Youth*. Those in *Love* have been compared by William Wixom with the nudes of Villard de Honnecourt, and Adèle Weiberg and Charles Sterling have thought that their inspiration is Italian, and more especially from Mantegna. Sterling also compares this piece with the Christ in the altarpiece of Boulbon, of about 1457.

But the drawing in this tapestry is somewhat awkward, and throughout the set, as Dorothy Shepherd has rightly noticed, the figures are placed against the background without really belonging to it; nor do they relate completely one with another. This links these tapestries with the millefleurs example, with which they have also many other points in common : the bunches of flowers against the dark blue or green foregrounds, the stream running all along the lower border of the tapestry, the style of the figures, the differences in scale between the characters, (the small ones are not all children), the nature of the cloths and costumes, and the weaving technique — to say nothing of the colors, which are richer and more intense than in any of the classical millefleurs pieces. Those in the Chaumont set are just as bright, though in a different range of tones, as those in the *Hunt of the Unicorn*. Shepherd has also compared the landscape treatment of these works with the *Story of St. Stephen* from Auxerre Cathedral, now in the Cluny Museum, in Paris; she links them without hesitation with the group of tapestries that were long said to be from the banks of the Loire, though despite their many points in common she excludes the two *Unicorn* series (Nos. 18-24 and 37-42) from these.

Time and *Youth* are indeed similar to a number of millefleurs tapestries, the Gobelins *Concert,* for instance, or at least to the character on the right of this work. And it is typical of the classical millefleurs pieces to associate together figures of different styles in a series quite homogeneous in all other respects : those of *Time* and *Youth,* firstly, and secondly those we see in *Eternity*. Those of *Love* are in quite a different vein, though we find that in an exceptionally fine version of Petrarch's *Triumphs* — pen drawings illustrating an early 16th-century adaptation in French, in which the successive victors stamp their adversaries underfoot instead of crushing them with their chariot wheels — Eternity is represented by the entirely unexpected figure of the Virgin, and Love by a young man with blindfold eyes, large wings, an arrow and a bow, and clad only in a chain-mail skirt that leaves his abdomen exposed as in the Detroit *Eros*. The cartoon maker could have used this manuscript or another like it as a model, but he has given a somewhat style to his *Love*. For *Eternity,* he has kept only the theme of Mary, omitting the figure of Time over which she has triumphed; perhaps he considered it sufficient to link an image of the Virgin surrounded by angels, which he had borrowed from a different drawing, with the series by means of the woven verses only. It seems indeed probable that the ateliers, whatever size they were — and the large group of millefleurs tapestries to which the Chaumont series belongs must have come from a center of repute — must have had in their service a painter whose job it was to enlarge to full size drawings that he borrowed from whatever source he felt suitable.

We may thus explain why there are, side by side in the Chaumont tapestries, scenes that even if they are all more or less concerned with the idea of the impermanence of mortal things, derive from themes of a fundamentally different visual nature: the Life of Pleasure (*Time* and *Youth*), Triumph (*Love*), and the Image of Devotion (*Eternity*). Together, they form a poetical series that, despite certain weaknesses — for example in the angels' faces — remains one of the most charming works of the first years of the 16th century.

This is indeed the most likely date for these pieces; it corresponds to the crowning point in the life of the person who is believed, on very tenuous grounds, to have ordered the set. The tapestries are known to have been hanging in the room known as that of Catherine de Médicis in the château of Chaumont, Loir-et-Cher, in 1851; they were probably there earlier, and perhaps from the beginning. There are similarities between the two letters that appear back-to-back between the tops of the château towers over the fiddler's head in *Youth* and the two interlaced C's of Charles of Amboise and his wife Catherine of Chauvigny that decorate the east and south wings at Chaumont, and also between Chaumont itself and the château shown on the tapestries. It is perfectly possible that Charles II of Amboise (died 1511), who was a powerful figure in the court of Louis XII, Lieutenant General of the Duchy of Milan in the early years of the 16th century, and Grand Master, Marshal and Admiral of France, may have ordered tapestries from the same center as many other great noblemen of his time, such as Pierre and Charles de Rohan (see Nos. 43-45 and 47). At all events, these tapestries give us a superlative picture of the idyllic but disillusioned life of the nobility in the early 16th century.

The tapestries were at Chaumont at least until 1907 and probably until the time of the sale of the château after World War I. They were at Duveen's in New York in 1925, and the three complete pieces entered the collection of Clarence H. Mackay, and became dispersed in 1939. In 1960 they were bought by The Cleveland Museum of Art. Love, in the Marezell von Nemes collection, was sold in 1931; it was bought from A. S. Drey in 1935 by The Detroit Institute of Arts.

BIBLIOGRAPHY. Adèle Coulin Weibel, *Eros triomphant*, in *Bulletin of The Detroit Institute of Arts...* vol. XIV, n° 6, March 1935, p. 76-81, fig. 8. Dorothy G. Shepherd, *Three Tapestries from Chaumont*, in *The Bulletin of the Cleveland Museum of Art*, vol. 48, n° 7, Sept. 1961, p. 158-177, fig.; Rémy G. Saisselin, *Literary Background of the Chaumont Tapestries*, ibid., p. 178-181; William D. Wixom, *Traditions in the Chaumont Tapestries*, ibid., p. 181-190, fig. — Charles Sterling, *Commentaires au catalogue des peintures françaises du XVᵉ siècle, la Pieta de Tarascon et les peintres Dombet*, in *La Revue du Louvre et des Musées de France*, t. XVI, 1966, n° 1, p. 23-24 and fig. — William D. Wixom, *Treasures from medieval France*, The Cleveland Museum of Art (1967), n°ˢ VII-22 to VII-25, p. 336-341 and 386, fig. b/W and col.

68
Rhetoric

Wool and silk
About 12 warp threads to the inch

Musée des Arts Décoratifs, Paris

The ancients divided the knowledge that raised humanity above the level of manual labor into seven "arts," which they grouped in two categories: the *trivium*, composed of Grammar, Rhetoric, and Dialectic, and the *quadrivium*, composed of Arithmetic, Geometry, Astronomy, and Music. Thanks to Boethius and Martianus Capella, who summarized the knowledge of their time and so permitted it to survive the barbaric invasions, this division was still current in the Middle Ages. Study of the arts was then considered to lead up to that of philosophy — the supreme effort of human intelligence — over which only theology, the divine science, took precedence.

Martianus Capella, an African teacher of rhetoric in the 5th century, set out to soften the austerity of his subject. In his treatise *On the Marriage of*

Mercury and Philology, he supposed that this god of antiquity had married, and that his betrothed had appeared on her wedding day accompanied by seven maidens, each one armed with attributes and flanked by the great men who had distinguished her science, lecturing on one of the liberal arts. Rhetoric, for example, appears with weapons and in a coat on which are embroidered a thousand figures.

This conception met with enormous success. For centuries the seven arts were represented by young girls, accompanied by one or more wise men. Among many examples we may cite sculptures in the cathedrals at Chartres, Laon, and Auxerre, the Borgia apartments painted by Pinturicchio in the Vatican, and the fresco at Le Puy.

In our tapestry "Damme Rethoricque" is seated on a throne, surrounded by serious figures including, probably, Cicero in the first row; she seems to be examining a figure on the left, who is reading from an unrolled scroll. Perhaps if he is successful she will give him one of the crowns she is holding.

The tapestry has been shortened on the left, at the top, and at the bottom. At the time of the Germeau sale in 1905 a mutilated inscription on the bottom was removed. It probably did not belong originally to the piece, since it was in French and much longer than those in Latin of the two other tapestries that we associate with this one.

8 ft. 6 in. × 9 ft. 6 in. (2,55 m × 2,90 m)

This *Rhetoric* was certainly made after the same series of cartons that produced the *Arithmetic* in the Cluny Museum. The scale, the style, and the costumes are the same; and the composition is very similar, with men surrounding a woman in a paved interior, a Renaissance pillar to the left, an opening in the foreground to a flowered terrace (of which only vestiges remain here). The walls are built of the same stones, and have the same windows with small panes and wooden shutters through which an identical view appears. The dog with a lion's mane appears on both pieces, as does the lady's scalloped décolleté, and also the festoon at the top. The coloring and weaving technique are similar. The pieces must have belonged to the same set. We know that the same cartoons were often woven several times, though frequently with modifications; a *Music* in the Museum of Fine Arts, Boston, is very close to this tapestry in style, but its figures are placed in a landscape, a variation that may place it in another series.

The Cluny *Arithmetic* shows prominently on the pillar to the right the letters DAVI. F. Alphonse Wauters, the historian of Brussels tapestries, concluded from this that the painter was Gérard David, who died in 1523 at Bruges, of which town the inverted B at the top of the tapestry may be the mark. Though there are certain similar traits in the *Justice of Cambyse,* one of this artist's principal works, the resemblances are however not strong enough, in so far as the drawing appears through its transposition into tapestry, for us to accept David as the original designer for this work. However the DAVI placed where it is suggests that it is a painter's rather than a weaver's name, so it is probably that of one of the many other artists of the time.

We have similar difficulties with regard to the place of

weaving. The style does not seeem to be that of Brussels. If the inverted B of *Arithmetic* does not stand for Bruges (the silk here seems restored) we may well suggest Tournai. This is quite possible since town marks were not frequent at this time, and letters were often woven in for purely ornamental reasons. However the possibility of Bruges, where sets of the *Liberal Arts* were to be woven in the 17th century, would be strengthened if the man responsible for the original drawing was indeed Gérard David, for he made his career in this city.

For the dating of this piece, an indication is once more given by *Arithmetic,* in which the number 1520 appears twice on the book. This may indicate the year when the set was woven, though the style seems a little earlier.

In the Louis Germeau sale, February, 1905. Donated March 14, 1906, by J. Maciet to the Musée des Arts Décoratifs.

69
Astronomy

Wool and silk
12 warp threads to the inch

Röhsska Konstslöjdmuseet, Gothenburg

Astronomy was the third science of the *quadrivium* (see No. 68). Generally accompanied by Pythagoras and Ptolemy, she is described by Martianus Capella as having golden wings with crystal feathers, a crown of stars, a measuring instrument, and a book made of several metals. Here she holds in one hand a banner on which is inscribed her name; with the other she points out the moon and the stars to a man carrying an armillary sphere; he has been said to be the 15th-century scholar Regiomontanus. On the left is another man, seated before a desk on which is an astrolabe, who seems to be preparing to write down what is said in the large volume open on his lap. Behind him two shepherds also contemplate the heavenly bodies.

7 ft. 10 in. × 11 ft. 1 in. (2,40 m × 3,40 m)

We know of still other pieces that illustrate the very popular subject of the *Liberal Arts* : an *Astronomy Seated Next to Arithmetic*, in the Memorial Art Gallery of the University of Rochester, New York, and a *Geometry* in the Freemasons' Hall, London. It is clear that this *Astronomy* does not belong to the same set as No. 68 and the Cluny Museum's *Arithmetic*, since the surrounding columns are different, the scene takes place in the open air (as in *Music*, in the Museum of Fine Arts, Boston) and the weaving is cruder; the style, which Elizabeth Strömberg thinks is French, is not quite the same either.

Most probably woven in the same center as No. 68, *Astronomy* is roughly contemporary with it and may be dated around 1510-1515.

From the Homberg collection, in Paris, this work was with M. G. Martini, New York, in 1964. It was acquired with the help of the Friends of the Röhss Museum association.

BIBLIOGRAPHY. Elisabeth Strömberg, *"Astronomie,"* en fransk medeltids-gobeläng, in *Röhsska Konstslöjdmussets, Arsbok 1963-1964,* Gothenburg, 1965, p. 15-28 and 46-47, fig.

70-73
Four Hunting Scenes

70
Boar Hunt

Wool and silk
12-15 warp threads to the inch

Private collection

Horsemen and hunters follow a wild sow, which, with its young, heads toward a frightened young man who has taken refuge in a tree. In the background, a hunter pierces with his lance a boar risen on its hind legs; on the right, another hunter attacks a hind. In the foreground, to the left, is a group of gentlemen and ladies; separated from them are two dog-handlers, one of whom wears a sword with the words IAN VAN ANVERP back to front on the scabbard.

9 ft. 10 in. × 15 ft. (3 m × 6,10 m) approx.

71
Death of the Stag

A stag at bay defends itself against dogs, while a servant pierces its side with his spear. Hunters surround them; one, on horseback, prepares to finish off the stag with his sword. Foot servants sound the horn. Two figures have taken refuge up trees; others hide in the undergrowth.

16 ft. 9 in. × 17 ft. 3 in. (2,95 m × 5,25 m) approx.

72
Preparations for a Falcon Hunt

We see here various stages in the hunt, with a number of men and women in different parts of a wooded glade with flowing streams. At top left falcons are being transported on their perches; at lower center one drinks from a basin (similar scenes appear in Nos. 25-26), and in the right middle distance a servant has removed his robe and appears only in doublet and hose, according to the fashion that was just beginning to spread. In the foreground to the right a woman, sitting on an X-shaped chair, caresses her pet parakeet.

73
Falcon Hunt

On both sides of a river teeming with fowl, gentlemen and ladies are occupied in the pleasures of falcon hunting. To the right is a young man who waves the lure, which serves to call back the bird and prevent it from devouring its prey. Notice here, as in the first and third pieces, the way the ladies of this period rode horseback — sidesaddle, with both feet placed on a plank supported by stirrup-leathers.

The Middle Ages come to life again in these scenes filled with vivid detail; they show why tapestries have been called a "mirror of civilization."

This set is of interest also in that it probably shows us what a Brussels "hunting and hawking" series was like. Most of the works we know from this city present religious, mythological, or romantic subjects, even though "bergeries" and country scenes are mentioned in the documents. The Jean of Antwerp whose name appears on a scabbard in the *Boar Hunt*, and whom we might have taken for a painter (who could have forgotten the reversing effect of low-warp weaving — the hunter with the spear and the horseman in No. 71 hold their arms in their left hands) — seems, however, to be identifiable with the weaver Jan de Clerck, known as van Antwerpen, a Brussels burgher who signed an agreement on May 14, 1521, with the merchant Pieter van Aelst for the sale of tapestries; he brought with him as guarantor another Brussels weaver, Willem de Kempeneer. The de Clercks were an important weaving family and this Jan is probably the one who owned an atelier in 1499. The names woven into tapestries at this time seem indeed to be the signatures of weavers rather than cartoon makers (see Nos. 78 and 80). The placing of this set as Brussels work is important in that it enables us to judge the differences, in colors particularly, against the scenes of daily life that are probably from Tournai (see Nos. 55-56 and 57), and especially with the millefleurs pieces.

The dates of Jan van Antwerpen seem to correspond with the period of the dresses with slashed sleeves seen in this set.

BIBLIOGRAPHY. Hitherto unpublished. For Jan van Antwerpen, see H. Göbel, *Niederlande*, t. 1, p. 324, 373 and 375, and S. Schneebalg, *Un grand tapissier bruxellois : Pierre d'Enghien dit Pierre van Aelst*, in *L'âge d'or de la tapisserie flamande*, Brussels, 1969, p. 279, 306-307 and 313.

74
Adoration of the Magi

Wool, silk, gold, and silver
22-25 warp threads to the inch

Cathedral of Sens

This was a subject often chosen by artists of the Middle Ages. The recognition of the divinity of the child Jesus by the representatives of the three parts of the world then known was then a theme of deep significance, and interpretations of that event gave scope for exotic fantasy. In the 15th century, one often saw the Virgin and Child on one side of the work, receiving the procession of the three kings with their presents. Here, however, we have another formula : the Virgin is seated full face front in the center, holding the naked Child; on either side kneel magi, who according to tradition symbolized both old age and the prime of life, and Europe and Asia. The third king, an elegant young man standing to the left, accompanied by a black servant, represents Africa. The scene is balanced by a group to the right, composed of an ecclesiastic and two soldiers standing near St. Joseph; the scene takes place under an arcade opening onto a Western European landscape.

The picture is framed by a border scattered with sparks, at the four corners of which is a shield *azure, semé with fleurs de lys or, in bend a baston gules,* surmounted by a cardinal's hat and a Metropolitan cross. In the middle of the short sides is a banner with the words N'ESPOIR, NE. PEUR rolled around an arm issuing from a cloud and holding a flaming sword; the latter's point has on either side the monogram "Che." The device and monogram are repeated on the long side.

4ft. 6in. × 10ft. 10in. (1,38 m × 3,31 m)

This device and monogram identify the original owner, Charles II of Bourbon (1434-1488), son of Duke Charles I and Agnes of Burgundy, archbishop of Lyon in 1447, Papal legate in 1465, member of the king's council in the following year, chosen by Louis XI in 1470 as godfather to the future Charles VIII, and made cardinal in 1476.

The presence of the cardinal's hat in the tapestry has led to the conclusion that it was woven between 1476 and 1488. However, the costumes suggest a slightly earlier date; the long, pointed shoes, especially, went out of fashion around 1475. If the border has been sewn on, this may suggest that Charles of Bourbon, after his elevation to the purple, had these emblems of his dignity added to a work that had been finished some years earlier; if not, the tapestry must date from the first years of his new title and cannot be much later than 1476.

Charles de Bourbon was fond of tapestries and acquired a large number, especially from Bruges and Arras. Being first cousin and brother-in-law to Charles the Bold, he was in a position to obtain them also from other cities in Burgundian

territory, such as Brussels. The present tapestry is thought to have been woven in Brussels, and the cartoon was probably the work of the artist known as the Master of the View of St. Gudule, who seems to have worked there around 1470-1490. The Virgin is of the same type as one in a picture attributed to that master by various authors, especially Max Friedländer. In this work, in the Diocesan Museum of Liège, a benefactress introduced by Mary Magdalene is shown in prayer before a puny child who has many points in common with the one in the tapestry, in the leg movement, for example. There are other similarities : the lion decorating a seat upright occurs in both works, though in the Liège painting it is wrestling with Samson; the fine hands, with precious gestures; the mannered drawing of the young king, typical of this disciple of Rogier van der Weyden. If the design of our tapestry is indeed by him, it is certainly with its extraordinary individualization of the characters, the poetry of its background, and the richness of its colors, one of his major works. The name by which he is known is due incidentally, to the presence in the backgrounds of his pictures of views of the cathedral of St. Gudule, Brussels.

Beyond the quality of the cartoon, the excellence of this work is in large measure due to the weaving and the materials used. The richness and fineness of its execution are quite unusual, probably because the work was intended as an altar frontal. But in addition, the weaver had the virtuosity to interpret every tiny detail of the cartoon's intention, whether in the faces, the splendid cloths, or in the shimmering reflections on the armor of the soldier on the right. The attribution of this masterpiece to Brussels is probably correct. The output of this city, though very considerable from the end of the 15th century on, is little known before this period; yet there were nearly five hundred weavers already there between 1417 and 1446. The fact that there were many weavers there in the second half of the 15th century, and that the work of the man who painted the model seems to be connected with this city, are not the only reasons for assigning it to Brussels (cartoons, after all, could travel.) Two technical aspects of the work carry more weight. First, the extreme precision of the interpretation, as in the *Hunt of the Unicorn* (Nos. 18-24), could have been achieved only on a low-warp loom, where the weaver worked from a detailed cartoon placed under the warp. Second, the weaving technique of the plain areas, such as the Virgin's mantle and St. Joseph's robe, on which light and shade are interpreted by vertical "beating", is found again in later Brussels tapestries.

The Adoration of the Magi *is mentioned in a 1561 inventory in the Cathedral of Sens. In another, of 1595, it is described thus, along with the* Three Coronations *(No. 75) : "The decorations that Monsieur de Borbon has given, the one for the top of the altar, on*

165

which is shown the Assumption; the second is the Adoration of the three kings." As the cardinal Louis de Bourbon-Vendôme was archbishop of Sens from 1536 to 1557, it has been assumed up to now that he had probably inherited the two pieces from his "uncle" Charles de Bourbon and then given them to his cathedral. However, his relationship to the archbishop of Lyon was remote, and it is necessary to go back to the 14th century to find a common ancestor for them, in the person of Louis I of Bourbon (1279-1341) eldest son of Robert de Clermont. It seems more likely either that Louis de Bourbon-Vendôme bought the two tapestries from,

or was given them, by his distant cousin, or that Charles de Bourbon himself gave them to Sens Cathedral.

BIBLIOGRAPHY. Marquet de Vasselot and Weigert, *op. cit.*, p. 180-181. — Max Friedländer, *Der Meister von Sainte Gudule, Nachträgliches,* in *Annuaire des musées royaux des Beaux-Arts de Belgique,* t. II, 1939, p. 23-31. *fiamands. Exposition... Bruges..., musée communal des Beaux-Arts...,* 26 juin-11 septembre 1960, Bruges, Presses Saint Augustin (1960), n° 54, p. 139-140, pl. — Georges Costa, *Une note de Prosper Mérimée sur les tapisseries de la cathédrale de Sens,* in *Revue de l'art,* n° 13, 1971, p. 72-75, fig.

75
The Three Coronations

Wool, silk, gold, and silver
27 warp threads to the inch

Cathedral of Sens

This exceptionally fine work, with harmonious design, splendid colors, and luxurious yet delicate weaving, honors the Virgin Mary, whose coronation by the Holy Trinity, a theme dear to the Gothic period, is shown flanked by two scenes taken from the stories of Solomon and Esther, following the medieval tradition of searching in the Old Testament for analogies to events that occurred after Christ's incarnation.

On the left, "Solomon" crowns his mother, "Bathsheba" — stretching a little too far the text of the First Book of Kings. According to this, after the young man had succeeded David, his half-brother Adonijah, who had tried to get himself recognized as king before the death of their father, came to Bathsheba to ask her to intercede on his behalf for the hand of Abishag the Shunammite. The new king got up to meet his mother and "bowed himself unto her, and sat down on his throne, and caused a seat to be set for the king's mother; and she sat on his right hand..." To her request for a favor, he answered, "Askon, my mother, for I will not say thee nay." But it displeased him greatly ("Ask for him the kingdom also!"), and he rejected it and put Adonijah to death. As there are few scenes in the Old Testament that could serve as a re-enactment of the Coronation of the Virgin, the triumphant arrival of Bathsheba was chosen, despite the unfortunate sequel to her behavior.

As for the scene on the right, this is not in fact a coronation (the traditional title of the tapestry is incorrect). Yet the Book of Esther, from which it is taken, has one available: after having repudiated Vashti, Ahasuerus assembled all the "fair young virgins" of the kingdom to choose from, but he "loved Esther above all the women... and he set the royal crown on her head." The scene chosen here, which is better known, took place later. After Mordecai had asked his niece to intercede in favor of the Jews who were threatened with extermination by the king's minister Haman, "Hester" went to see "Assuerre" without having been summoned, and so at the peril of her life; but the king touched her with his golden scepter and told her that the terrible order was only to concern common subjects; she invited him, together with Haman, to a banquet at which she obtained pardon for all her people.

This work was composed as an altar hanging and decorated the top of the altar; when Louis XV gave orders in 1759 for church plate to be melted down, it was recut to replace the "table of gold." It was them transformed into a rectangular frontal, with the Virgin's Coronation scene brought down to the level of the two others and shortened at either side. This meant that a part of the two circles of angels had to be removed,

and the celestial concert at the bottom of the central part was also cut off; fortunately, it was preserved, and after the first World War the work was restored to its original shape. It is difficult to say, however, where the cardinal's arms, which are those of Charles de Bourbon, as in No. 74, were placed originally.

5 ft. 5 in. × 10 ft. 5 in. (1,65 m × 3,18 m)

The chances are that this shield is original and that the *Three Coronations* is the second decoration mentioned in the Sens Cathedral inventory of 1595 as a gift of "Monsieur de Bordon"; the Virgin surrounded by angels might easily have been inventoried as an "Assumption" by a careless writer. Moreover, in the inventory made in 1653 the work is listed more accurately, alongside the *Adoration of the Magi*: "Two large altar decorations in high-warp tapestry picked out in gold and silk, on the larger of which is shown the Adoration of Jesus Christ by the three kings, and in the upper part of the other the Coronation of the Virgin."

The style of the work is of the years around 1480, and this fits perfectly with the suggestion that Charles de Bourbon was its first owner. He could have ordered it after his elevation to the cardinalate in 1476; it does in fact seem a little later than the *Adoration of the Magi*.

Apparently it is not from the same cartoon maker. H. Bramsen has compared it to the polyptych of St. Vincent in Lisbon, attributed to Nuño Gonçalves; he finds in both

works "the same attributes, the same ceremonious, formal sumptuousness, the sad faces, the weak modeling of the bodies, the tapering fingers." This comparison, however, is not convincing; the tapestry has a rather mannered gentleness that is quite absent from the St. Vincent altar piece, whose figures are vigorously drawn. The artist of the tapestry was more likely one of the numerous Brussels painters who followed Rogier van der Weyden's sad style.

Same historical account as the Adoration of the Magi *(see No. 74).*

BIBLIOGRAPHY. Marquet de Vasselot and Weigert, *op. cit.*, p. 180-181. — H. Bramsen, *Attributions à Niño Gonçalves. Le polyptyque de saint Vincent à Lisbonne et les tapisseries de l'époque*, in *Gazette des Beaux-Arts*, 6th series, t. L, Dec. 1957, p. 311-318. — *Les Trésors des églises de France, Musée des Arts Décoratifs; Paris, 1965*, 2nd ed. (Paris), Caisse Nationale des Monuments Historiques (1965), n° 826, p. 438. — Georges Costa, *Une note de Prosper Mérimée sur les tapisseries de la cathédrale de Sens*, in *Revue de l'art*, n° 13, 1971, p. 72-75, fig.

76-77
Annunciation and Adoration of the Magi

Wool, silk, silver, and gold
About 20 warp threads
to the inch

These two pieces are no doubt the remains of a larger sequence. They differ in the architecture under which the scenes take place, the number of prophets, and the presence, in No. 76 of "precursors" — the Old Testament figures in which medieval art so frequently saw analogies with characters of the New Testament; precursors are absent in No. 77. Nevertheless the size, the general composition, the style, and the workmanship are the same, as well as the drawing of the two prophets on either side of the main scene at the bottom.

76
Annunciation

Musée de la Manufacture
des Gobelins,
Paris

In the center, the Virgin turns away from her book to listen to Gabriel, who bears a scroll with the first words of the Hail Mary : Ave Maria g[ratia] pl[en]a d[omi]n[u]s tecu[m]. The scene takes place in a comfortable 15th-century interior, with God the Father, surrounded by angels, looking on and sending to Mary the Dove of the Holy Ghost.

On either side, beneath arches, at the top and at the bottom, stands one of the prophets announcing the virginal conception.

At bettom left, we have Isaiah, with the inscription : "Ecce virgo concipiet et pariet filium et voca/bitur nomen eius emmanuel. Ysae 7o Capitulo" ("Behold a virgin shall conceive and bear a son, and shall call his name Immanuel." Isa. 7 : 14). On the right, David, whose scroll reads : "Descendet dominus sicut pluvia in vellus et sicut / stillicidia stillancia super terram. David. Psalmo 71°" ("The Lord shall come down like rain on a fleece, and like drops of water landing on the ground.") This sentence matches the episode of Gideon represented above.

In the top left-hand corner, Ezekiel says : "Porta haec clausa est, haud aperi[e]/tur in eternum. Ezechiel. XXº Capitulo" ("This gate has been closed, and shall never be opened again." Ezek. 44 : 2). On the right-hand side, Jeremiah's banner reads : "Dominus novum faciet super terram mulier / circumdabit virum. Jeremie. 3º capitulo" ("The Lord shall create a new thing in the earth, a woman shall compass a man." Jer. 31 : 22).

There are two scenes outside the architectural frame. On the left, with God looking on disapprovingly, Eve, tempted by the serpent, has plucked the apple, thus making the Redemption of Man necessary. The beginning of the Redemption is expressed by the Annunciation to Mary of the central scene (see Nos. 92-93). On the right, Gideon kneels before an angel who bears the inscription : "Descendet dominus sicut pluvia." This refers to the request made by the judge of Israel to the Lord, that he should give him a sign of his mission; and God had covered with dew the fleece of wool that we can see here spread before him, whereas the surrounding ground remained dry.

7 ft. 8 in. × 8 ft. 7 in. (2,34 m × 2,62 m)

77
Adoration of the Magi

Musée du Louvre
(Dépôt du Musée de la
Manufacture des Gobelins)

The Magi surround the Virgin and Child in the center. Just as in No. 74, it is not the youngest king who is black, but his servant.

At the left, Balaam prophesies : "Orietur stella ex Iacob et consurget / virga de Ierusalem. Balaam. NUMERI. 24." ("There shall come a star out of Jacob, and a scepter shall rise out of Jerusalem." Num. 24 : 17).

On the right, David announces : "Reges tharsis et insule munera offerent / reges arabum et saba dona adducent. David Psalmo 71" ("The Kings of Tarshish and of the isles shall bring presents, the kings of the Arabs and of Seba shall offer gifts." Ps. Vulg. 72 : 10). At the top, smaller than the precursors of the Annunciation, the Magi join up on the left, each following the star; on the right, they arrive in a procession.

7 ft. 8 in. × 9 ft. 8 in. (2,34 m × 2,95 m)

The origin of these two works is not known. Although they have become a little dull with age, they are of very high quality, and their workmanship is sophisticated. Note the "crapautage" of the silver threads on the robe of the young king on the right (weft threads crossing more than one warp thread) to bring the motifs up in relief.

The pieces may well have been woven in Brussels, in which case they would be among the oldest we can reasonably attribute to this city. For few Brussels works dating from the 15th century have been preserved, although we know that the production was abundant and that there were large numbers of low-warp weavers there.

felt that the *Annunciation* derived from a composition by Rogier van der Weyden, and that the cartoons of the two works could have been by Vranke van der Stockt, his successor as painter of the town of Brussels. This artist happens to be one of those who signed the well-known agreement between the weavers and the painters of Brussels, after the latter had complained that the tapestry makers were having cartoons made without employing their services; the tapestry makers were authorized to design the plants and animals of their verdures, and to have already-existing cartoons enlarged, but the painters were to do the rest. Thus, while the mille-fleurs ateliers continued to draw from their repertoire of patterns (see Nos. 35 and 37-42), the Brussels tapestry makers turned their attention to weaving works designed by painters, and hence composed like paintings. We have, in these two tapestries, an example of this phenomen; they must have been made not long after the agreement. There is another example in the *Nativity*, the oldest tapestry in the Patrimonio Nacional of Madrid, which is in many respects similar to the present works. Other examples are Nos. 74-75, and the *Virgin in Glory* in the Louvre, dated 1485; this might also explain why tapestries produced in Brussels should become so particularly precious.

Bequeathed in 1885 by Albert Goupil to the Musée de la Manufacture des Gobelins.

The style is typical of Brussels. In it, the influence of sculpted and painted altarpieces is obvious and, as early as the beginning of this century, Joseph Destrée pointed to the altarpiece of Hugo van der Goes, comparing its St. Joseph with the one in No. 74 and its Everlasting Father with the old king of the same tapestry. Hulin de Loo, on the other hand,

BIBLIOGRAPHY. Joseph Destrée, *Tapisseries et sculptures bruxelloises à l'exposition d'art ancien bruxellois... Bruxelles... juillet à octobre 1905*, Brussels, G. van Oest, 1906, nos 1-11, p. 15-17, pl. I and II. — *Exposition universelle internationale de Bruxelles, 1935, Cinq siècles d'art, t. II, Dessins et tapisseries, 24 mai-13 octobre, Catalogue* (introd. by Marthe Crick-Kuntziger), Brussels, Nouvelle Société d'Editions (1935), nos 601-602, p. 55-56. — Marthe Crick-Kuntziger; *La tapisserie bruxelloise au XVe siècle*, in *Bruxelles au XVe siècle*, Brussels, Ed. de la Librairie Encyclopédique, 1953, p. 95-96, fig.

78
The Redemption of Man

Wool, silk, silver, and gold
18 warp threads to the inch

The Metropolitan Museum of Art

The original richness and brilliance of this exceptionally delicate piece have suffered from the oxidation of the many metal threads it contains. The subtle subject matter illustrates the system of concordance between the Old and New Testaments that was in favor in the Middle Ages : this "typology" established a symbolic link between the principal episodes of the life of Christ *(sub gratia)*, events prior to the law of Moses *(ante legem)*, and others occurring between the pronouncement of the Decalogue and the Annunciation

(sub lege). The scenes are separated by jeweled moldings forming five lobes, which divide the background into ten compartments.

In the center, the Nativity and the Crucifixion are curiously juxtaposed; a symbolic foreshortening places the infant Jesus at the foot of the Cross, only separated from it by the skull of Adam; according to tradition, he was buried on Golgotha and Christ came to atone for his sin. It is this sin that is depicted in the two upper lobes; they show Adam and Eve standing in shame in front of God the Father surrounded by angels. In the bottom right-hand lobe, Moses has received the Tablets of the Law from Jehovah and is presenting them to the people, who kneel in prayer. This must be the second set of Tablets that Moses brought back from Mount Sinai, since he broke the first in his wrath at the sight of the Israelites worshiping the Golden Calf.

The scene on the left is difficult to interpret. Joseph Breck saw in it a Visitation, but this would hardly conform with traditional iconography. Since the two top lobes refer to the same event in Genesis, it would seem plausible that this is another episode in the life of Moses, linked perhaps with the

preceding one. The only one that might fit is Moses telling the Israelites to provide everything needed for building the house of Jehovah, and "all the women who were able spun with their hands and brought their work : violet purple, scarlet purple, crimson and fine linen." However, this explanation is not altogether satisfactory, especially in view of the two men on the left who appear to be commenting the scene. Carmen Gómez-Moreno may be right in suggesting that this scene may be of Mary in the temple before her marriage being visited by her family, and holding a closed box, which would be a symbol of virginity. The Virgin was fairly often depicted at this period of her life with a basket, though normally she is weaving the veil of the Holy of Holies. Behind her, here, is a stag, an animal held to be symbolic of Christ in the medieval bestiaries; is it actually a stag, somehow connected with this episode, or is it the ass of the forthcoming Nativity, next to the ox, drawn with antlers by mistake ?

The animals in the bottom corners refer undoubtedly to the Resurrection — the pelican because it killed its offspring in anger, and three days later pierced its side with its beak and brought it back to life with its blood, and the lion because its cubs were supposedly born dead and brought to life on the third day when it breathed on them.

In the top corners, the prophet Zechariah and "Salomon" bear scrolls announcing the divine sacrifice to come. On the left is "vinea dabit fructum suum, Zach. VIIº" ("the vine shall give her fruit," Zech. 8º, 12), and on the right," De fractu [fructu] manuum suarum plantivi [t] vinea [m]. Prov. XXXº" ("with the fruit of her hands she planted a vineyard," Prov. 31 : 16). At the bottom, center, is St. Paul, seated on a vine branch, who seems to be reading from a banner on which is written a passage from his Epistle to the Galatians : "Misit Deus filium suum ut eos qui sub lege erant redimeret, Gal. 4" ("God sent forth his son to redeem them that were under the law," Gal. 4 : 4-5).

10ft. 2in. × 13ft. 3in. (3,10 m × 3,99 m)

This combination of subjects appears to identify this tapestry as one that Isabel the Catholic, Queen of Spain, received at Alcalá de Henares on April 2, 1498. There were in fact two — so similar both in subject matter, despite its complexity, and in dimensions that we may wonder whether the same one was not described twice by mistake, though the writer of the inventory would have forgotten to mention, in one case, the two subjects at the bottom, and in the other case the left-hand one only, perhaps because its meaning was already obscure. There seems to have been only one when the Queen's collections were dispersed in 1505, after her death. Moreover, in the first mention the piece is said to be worn and very yellowed, and it is stated that it was given by the bishop of Palencia; this information is not given in the second entry. No. 147 in the inventory is described as "a rich panel of devotional tapestry, large, with silver and gold, in which there is Our Lord on the cross and on one side God the Father with angels around and on the other Adam and Eve, and at the foot of the cross the birth of Our Lord with many other figures, measuring four and three quarter varas in length and three and a third varas in height" (13 ft. × 10 ft. 2 in.); No. 172 is noted as "a large panel of tapestry, rich, with gold, in which is Our Lord on the cross between two robbers, and at the top, on one side Adam and Eve and on the other God the Father with two angels, and at the bottom the birth of Our Lord and on the other Moses with the tablets of the law, measuring five varas wide and three and a half varas high" (13 ft. 9 in. × 9 ft. 7 in.). The differences in measurement are small and may be the result of mistakes, or of deformations in the course of the centuries. At all events, the bishop of Malaga bought one of these tapestries for one hundred ducats at the sale in 1505 — a "paño de ras" as they were described, "rich, with gold, in which there is Our Lord on the cross between two robbers and at the top God the Father and Adam and Eve and at the bottom the birth of Our Lord."

If it was indeed in 1498 that Isabel the Catholic received this work, which was most probably woven at Brussels, it appears from its style that it must have been woven some ten or fifteen years earlier.

From the letters ROEM that have been deciphered on the bottom of the robe of the angel standing behind Eve, and which recur with others on the decorated border of Zechariah's coat, the cartoon has been attributed to an artist who is today little known but was important in Brabantine art in the first quarter of the 16th century : Jean van Roome or John of Brussels. He worked for Margaret of Austria, daughter of Emperor Maximilian and Marie of Burgundy, and regent of the Netherlands during the minority of her nephew Charles V of Germany and I of Spain. Jean is known to have made designs for stained-glass windows, sculptures—especially those on the tombstones at Brou — and cartoons for tapestries : in 1513 he received payment from the Brotherhood of the Holy Sacrament at St.-Pierre de Louvain for the "petit patron" of the *Miraculous Communion of Herkinbald,* now in the Musée du Cinquantenaire, Brussels. To him have also been attributed the models for a number of large Brussels tapestries of the early 16th century, in which there are numbers of melancholy-looking characters in sumptuous, heavily draped garments crowded into buildings with half-Renaissance, half-Gothic architecture, such as the *Story of David,* in the Cluny Museum, and the *Story of Mestrà* and *Story of Jason* in the Hermitage Museum (Nos. 87 and 88-89). The "paños de oro" in the Madrid Patrimonio Nacional have also been assigned to this artist. The *Redemption of Man,* however, is stylistically different from all these works, even though the characters' faces have the same grave melancholy. Could this difference be due to the painter's artistic develop-ment, the piece apparently being at least ten years earlier than the paños de oro, which themselves antedate the other tapestries by a similar period ? This is possible, if Jean van Roome, whose dates of birth and death we do not know, but who disappeared after 1521 after having first been heard of in 1498 as a member of the Brotherhood of Our Lady of the Seven Sorrows, was at this date around forty, for our tapestry is the work of a man at the peak of his powers. But perhaps the letters ROEM, which are hardly decipherable — the first and last have always been doubtful — have quite a different meaning, if indeed they have one at all. In the *Adultery of David and Bathsheba,* in the Patrimonio Nacional, the letters MOER on the hem of a garment were also interpreted as an anagram of Jean van Roome's name until Marthe Crick-Kuntziger discovered the existence of a weaver named Michel de Moer. Moreover, the St. Joseph in the central Nativity is very reminiscent of that by Rogier van der Weyden in the Granada and Miraflores altarpieces. For the cartoonist of this *Redemption,* we should perhaps go back to one of those Flemish artists who carried on the severe and tragic style of Rogier van der Weyden's art, and who, at a time of rich development in artistic expression, had the inspiration to interpret deeply significant theological themes in forms of great emotive power.

In the Gavet collection toward the end of the 19th century. Bequeathed to the Metropolitan Museum, 1917, by Colonel Oliver H. Payne.

BIBLIOGRAPHY. Joseph Breck, *A tapestry bequeathed by Colonel Oliver H. Payne,* in *Bulletin of the Metropolitan Museum of Art,* vol. XIII, n° 2, Feb. 1918, p. 46-52; fig. — Francisco Xavier Sánchez Cantón, *Libros, tapices y cuadros que coleccionó Isabel la Católica,* Madrid, Consejo Superior de Investigaciones Científicas, 1950, p. 122-123, 128 and 148. — James J. Rorimer, *The Glorification of Charles VIII,* in *The Metropolitan Museum of Art Bulletin,* vol. XII, n° 10, June 1954, p. 295-296 and fig. p. 297.

79
The Triumph of Christ

Wool, silk, silver, and gold.
18-23 warp threads
to the inch

The National Gallery of Art,
Washington

It has been written of this work that it is "the world's most beautiful tapestry," the high point of the art of weaving. Whatever may have been said recently to the contrary, it very likely formed part of the collection of Cardinal Mazarin (1602-1661), hence its familiar name, the Mazarin Tapestry. This cardinal was a sophisticated lover of art and collected some of the finest pieces of "the golden age of Flemish tapestry," including The *Hunting scenes of Maximilian,* today in the Louvre. The present work, like others of its period, has lost some of the brilliance of its abundant metal threads through oxidation; it remains remarkable, however, not only for the delicacy of its design, the perfection of its workmanship, and the exceptional richness of its materials, but for its wealth of symbolic meanings.

The tapestry is a triptych, its scenes separated by arches supported by jeweled columns. Like certain other Brussels tapestries of this period (see Nos. 92-93) it synthesizes the whole story of the salvation of the world. It has been said to signify the triumph of Christ (in the center) and of the new law over the Roman Empire, which is represented (on the left) by the Sibyl of Tibur, who announces to Augustus that a Hebrew child will reign over the world after him; and that the church of Christ will replace all former churches, just as the Roman Empire defeated those that came before it, symbolized by the empire of Persia, which is evoked here, on the right, by the story of Esther and Ahasuerus. But Esther may be meant here, by her frustration of Haman's plans to exterminate the Jews, to anticipate the final victory of Christ; the two scenes at the sides would thus be a pair, symbolizing the announcement of the triumph of Jesus, on the left, over the pagan world, and on the right over the Jewish people. The tapestry is rich in meanings on many levels that are not always easy to interpret.

On the small columns, traditional themes in Christian inconography — Adam, the Church, the Synagogue, and Eve — summarize the story of Salvation.

In the center, the seated Christ raises his right hand in blessing, and holds in his left the open book of the Gospels. Behind him, two angels hold up a ceremonial hanging. On either side of Christ are two more angels, the one on Christ's left holding the Sword of Justice, the one on his right (the position of honor), the Lily of Mercy. Below, in front of a landscape of great delicacy, are two groups of people in adoration : on the left, the ecclesiastical world, with the Pope, cardinals, bishops, monks, and so on, and on the right the laity, with the Emperor, who has laid his sword on the ground, in the front row, and a king.

On the left are three scenes, those at the bottom separated from that at the top by an arch shaped like a basket-handle to which is attached a scroll with an inscription :

regem regum adoravit
augustus imparator
cum sibilla demonstravit
quo patuit salvator
(The Emperor Augustus worshiped the King of Kings when the Sybil showed to him where the Savior appeared).

The small scene to the right of the scroll illustrates its text. It depicts a subject that was common in the art of the very end of the Middle Ages : the legend of Octavius and the Sibyl; it had been known for several centuries, in Rome especially, and there were several different versions. The Emperor

Octavius Augustus was supposed to have asked the Prophetess of Tibur to whom the rule of the world would belong after him; she showed him, in the sky, an altar with the Virgin and Child above it, while a voice said : "Haec est ara coeli" (Behold the altar of the heavens) or "Haec ara filii Dei est" (Behold the altar of the Son of God).

In the foreground a richly dressed woman, with a group of maidens behind her, kneels before a bearded old man who carries a scepter and wears a crown; the inscription "Octavianus" below suggest that this is the Emperor. Joseph Destrée, writing at the beginning of this century, could not imagine that "a mysterious being like a Sybil should have such a numerous following"; he wondered, instead, whether this scene might not depict David receiving Abigail, or perhaps a coronation, perhaps of Bathsheba by Solomon, as in No. 75. But in this group of Brussels tapestries of around 1500 all the characters, pagan or religious, are portrayed sumptuously dressed in contemporary style, and one should not be surprised to see the Sybil of Tibur treated in this manner; no doubt the cartoon had been originally drawn for another purpose and was reused. We may follow the majority of opinions in interpreting this scene as the Emperor Octavius Augustus questioning the prophetess, with the figure behind him, according to George H. McCall, holding the crown destined for his successor. This would be taking place before the appearance of Christ in the sky.

More enigmatic is the small scene at the top in which a peasant pauses in his digging at the edge of a wood to greet a group of figures, while a young man arrives from the right. Destrée saw in this the parable of the kingdom of heaven being likened to a treasure buried in a field (Mat. 13 : 44); George L. Hunter and McCall are probably nearer the truth in suggesting that this is the digging of the foundations for the altar that Augustus was supposed to have set up to the Son of God on the spot where he saw his vision — the site today of the church of Santa Maria in Aracoeli, on the Capitol, Rome. However, this interpretation is not universally accepted, and we may wonder whether this scene does not illustrate a text that is now lost.

To the right of the tapestry are three more scenes, disposed as on the left, with an inscribed scroll on which we can recognize the story of Esther :

"Cum osculata fuerat
Sceptuum [sceptrum] assueri
hester scipho utitur
regis pleio [pleno] meri"

(When she had kissed the scepter of Ahasuerus, Esther drank from the king's cup, which was full of wine.)

The scene in the foreground has usually been interpreted as the marriage of Esther, to whom Ahasuerus, in the presence of a group of men and women, holds out a ring set with a red stone. Above left, she has come at the risk of her life to seek from the king the favor of his presence at a banquet, at which she will ask him to spare her people who are threatened with extermination by the edict issued by his minister, Haman (Esther 5-7). The king signifies his acceptance by holding out to her his golden scepter. W.G. Thomson, however, has seen in the foreground episode the gift of a signet ring to Esther by Ahasuerus and indeed, is it credible that this is a marriage scene, with Esther sitting down, already crowned, and feeding a little squirrel that she holds in her arms? It is more likely to be an illustration of a passage (Esther (8 : 2) in which Ahasuerus, after having taken back from Haman the ring he gave him with his permission to massacre the Jews (Esther 3 : 10), gives it to Mordecai, to whom Esther has revealed she is related and who could be the bearded person on the left. A better explanation still, perhaps, is that this is Ahasuerus giving Esther and Mordecai his ring for them to seal with it a letter "in favor of the Jews" to the chiefs of the one hundred and twenty-seven provinces of his empire, revoking Haman's edict. "For a letter written in the king's name and sealed with the royal ring cannot be revoked" (Esther 8 : 8). Since all this takes place in the Bible after Haman has been hanged it cannot be he who is standing on the king's right; in any case, the same character comes up again in the background of the small scene of Esther introducing herself to Ahasuerus, at which Haman was not present, which makes this hypothesis all the more unlikely.

The scene at the top is even more obscure. Destrée saw in it an illustration of the parable comparing "the kingdom of heaven to a merchant seeking after precious stones," and who, "having found one, goes and sells all that he has to buy it" (Matt. 13 : 45-46). Others, for instance Hunter and McCall, have suggested that it shows Esther choosing requirements for the banquet she is to give for Ahasuerus and Haman. This is not entirely convincing since it does not explain the attitude of the young man on the left who seems to be bringing news. In any case, despite the presence of articles of gold plate, there is no direct illustration here of the end of the text in the inscription (Esther drank from the king's cup). No doubt, like the small scene on the left, this scene is based on a text that has not come down to us.

The composition of this tapestry is repeated, with some important differences, in three other pieces, one at Saragossa, one at Brussels, and one in the Cloisters collection; these three are almost identical, though the third, known as the *Glorification of Charles VIII,* is much larger and includes several other scenes on either side.

11 ft. 3 in. × 14 ft. 2 in. (2,43 m × 4,16 m)

Since the 19th century, the figures of Ahasuerus and Esther have been interpreted as symbolic of King Charles VIII of France and his wife Anne of Brittany, which would date our tapestry immediately after their marriage in December, 1491; but there is no evidence at all for this. Another hypothesis, less unlikely, is that they are Philip the Handsome, ruler of the Netherlands, who in 1496 married Joanna the Mad, daughter and heiress of the Catholic sovereigns Ferdinand of Aragon and Isabelle of Castile; the tapestry was certainly woven at Brussels, and the maker of the cartoon may have wished to symbolize his monarch in a work that was perhaps created for him. But these are only conjectures, and indeed the probable date of the tapestry makes them hazardous; we do not know in which collection it was before it came into Mazarin's possession, though it is said to have come from Spain.

Neither do we know the artist. The names of Memling, Gerard David, and Quentin Metsys have been suggested, but rather than a painter of pictures, he may have been a professional cartoon maker. Probably he was the same one who designed the paños de oro, that is, possibly Jean van Roome (see No. 78); some have thought that the inscription REOON on the thigh of a child to the left of the work known as the *Glorification of Charles VIII* might be his signature, but this is again a conjecture.

Despite their highly individual characterization, the faces in our tapestry do have the dreamy, almost vacant expressions of Jean van Roome's figures. There are nevertheless some differences between this and the only tapestry we know for certain to be by this artist, the *Communion of Herkinbald* in the Royal History and Art Museums, Brussels. Maybe these are due to an evolution in his style, since while *Herkinbald* is dated 1513, the present tapestry can hardly be later than 1490 : the women in it still wear their hair with a ring of dark cloth on a very high forehead, a fashion that had virtually disappeared by the end of the century.

At all events, the extreme delicacy of this work, in which the workmanship is similar to that of the Madrid *Mass of St. Gregory*, which bears the inscription BRUXEL, suggests that it was woven in Brussels — a city that through successes of this nature was to ensure its supremacy for nearly two centuries.

Bequeathed by Cardinal Mazarin to his nephew by marriage, Armand-Charles de la Porte, Marquis of La Meilleraye, Duke of Mazarin, and the husband of Hortense Mancini. After his death, the tapestry was bought by Claude-Louis-Hector, Duke of Villars and Marshal of France, who left it to his son Honoré-Armand, Duke of Villars and Governor of Provence (died 1770). The tapestry was then placed in the château des Aygalades, near Marseilles, which, on the death of the Duke of Villars, went with its contents to Monsieur Mestre d'Aygalades, and then to Monsieur Barras de la Penne; the latter exhibited it in Paris in 1824, where it was sold to a Russian nobleman who took it to St. Petersburg. It was bought back by the Count of Castellane, who also acquired the château des Aygalades, in which he replaced it. His heirs sold it to a London dealer, from whom it was bought by J. Pierpont Morgan, Jr. He lent it to the Victoria and Albert Museum from 1901 to 1910, with the exception of some months during which it was in the Brussels exhibition of ancient art of 1905. In 1910 it crossed the Atlantic and was exhibited in the Metropolitan Museum until 1916. It was then sold it to Joseph Widener, who continued to lend it for some months to the Metropolitan. In 1942, the Widener collection was housed in the National Gallery of Art.

BIBLIOGRAPHY. Joseph Destrée, *Tapisseries et sculptures bruxelloises à l'exposition d'art ancien bruxellois... juillet à octobre 1905*, Brussels, G. van Oest, 1906, n° IV, p. 7-8, 18-20 and 84, pl. IV-VI. — George Leland Hunter, *The Practical Book of Tapestries*, Philadelphia, 1925, p. 111-114 and pl. — W.G. Thomson, *A History of Tapestry from the Earliest times until the Present Day*. London, Hodder and Stoughton, 1930, p. 174-177, pl. col. — George Henry McCall, *The Joseph Widener collection. Tapestries at Lynnewood Hall, Elkins Park, Pennsylvannia, with Historical Introduction and Descriptive Notes*, Philadelphia, 1942, n° 1, p. 7-22 and 41-49, 2 pl. col. and 1 pl. b/w.

detail

80
Deposition from the Cross

Wool, silk, and gold
20-23 warp threads
to the inch

Musée Royaux
d'Art et d'Histoire,
Brussels

Here we see Christ supported by St. John, the Virgin and Mary Magdalene in the midst of a crowd of sorrowing disciples, a young man taking down from the cross the crown of thorns, and a holy woman preparing to wrap the crown in a cloth. A considerable number of religious tapestries were woven in Brussels ateliers at the end of the 15th and beginning of the 16th centuries; this one may be an isolated piece but is more likely the survivor of a series of a *Story of Christ* in view of the scenes at the top : Christ's descent into limbo, at the left, and his entombment, at the right.

9ft. 9in. × 10ft. 9in. (2,98 m × 3,28 m)

"One does not know what to praise most in this work : the grandeur of the concept, the balance of the composition, the way the feelings of all the actors in this sublime scene are expressed, the nobility of the drawing, or the richness of the colors, to which the passage of time has brought new charm" — so wrote the Belgian scholar Joseph Destrée at the beginning of this century. He attributed it to a "master" by the name of Philip, on the basis of the inscription PHILIEP on the edge of the cloak worn by the bearded old man standing behind St. John. He identified this painter with the "Philips den schilder" who in 1513 received payment from the Brotherhood of the Holy Sacrament at St. Pierre de Louvain for making the full-size cartoon of the *Miraculous Communion of Herkinbald,* for which Jan van Brussel, alias Jean van Roome, had done the small patron (see Nos. 78, 79 and 87-89), and pointed to analogies between several figures in this work and others in the *Deposition from the Cross;* this led him to attribute all the series associated with the name of Jean van Roome to this painter. These analogies are indeed undeniable, and the PHILIEP may well be a cartoon-maker's signature. However, though "Philip the painter" was paid more than Jean van Roome for the *Communion of Herkinbald,* this could be because his work took longer, and he is not, like Jean, described as "Master." In any case, this first name was by no means rare and there may have been another Philip. Furthermore, there are differences between this work and the *Herkinbald* tapestry, which is, for instance, a more open composition, without architectural elements and with more importance given to the landscape. This Philip, if it was he who did the cartoon, may have been one of those painters of the years around 1500 who kept the numerous weaving ateliers supplied and whose style, under the influence of current fashion probably, is curiously uniform, judging by the number of tapestries that have been assigned to the "Jean van Roome group"

and by the fact that a piece long attributed to this "school" has been identified by Marthe Crick-Kuntziger as a signed work of the painter Knoest. One should not overlook the possibility that the signature is that of the weaver; at this period they were more common than cartoon-makers' signatures. See that of Jan van Antwerpen on No. 70, and those of Peter van Aerlst and Michael de Moer on several early 16th- century Brussels tapestries (see No. 78).

Destrée's comparison of the four principal figures in the *Deposition from the Cross* with those of the Perugino *Pietà* in the Uffizi Gallery, Florence, is more interesting. They are more or less the same, though inverted. Thus, the cartoon-maker was familiar with Italian painting. Yet the works themselves are quite different. The Perugino group, which includes only two disciples, is set against an austere line of semicircular arches; such a bare treatment would not have suited tapestry technique at all, and so we find here various subsidiary scenes and many figures to fill up the fabric. Many of these may have been borrowed, like the figures of the central group, from other people's work. In any case, the *Deposition from the Cross* illustrates well how these cartoon-makers worked and what an extraordinary capacity for assimilation they had; it demonstrates too how difficult it is to distinguish individual styles in composite works, in which contributions from the most varied sources are blended with consummate skill into compositions of surprising uniformity.

Purchased by the Musées Royaux d'Art et d'Histoire in 1861 at the sale in Brussels of the Madame van Antwerpen collection.

BIBLIOGRAPHY. Joseph Destrée, *Maitre Philippe auteur de cartons de tapisseries : Etude suivie d'une Note à propos de Jean de Bruxelles dit van Room,* Brussels, Vromant, 1904 in 4°, 39 p., fig. — Marthe Crick-Kuntziger, *Maitre Knoest et les tapisseries «signées» des Musées royaux du Cinquantenaire,* Liège, G. Thone, 1927, in-8°, 20 p., fig. and *Musées royaux d'Art et d'Histoire de Bruxelles, Catalogue des Tapisseries (XIVᵉ au XVIIIᵉ siècle),* (1956), in-4°, n° 20, p. 37-38, pl. 26.

81
Scenes from the Story of Esther

Wool and silk
17-20 warp threads
to the inch

Victoria and Albert Museum

After David, few Old Testament characters have figured so frequently in tapestry as Esther (see Nos. 75 and 79). The most popular episode is the one in which, breaking the rule that any person who appeared in his presence without being summoned was put to death, King Ahasuerus touches Esther with his scepter; on the orders of her uncle Mordecai, she had

come to invite him to a banquet in which she would ask him to pardon the Jewish people, condemned to extermination by the king's minister Haman. This is the scene in the center here.

The two smaller subjects at the top are more difficult to identify. The one on the left is probably not the presentation of Esther to Ahasuerus after his repudiation of Queen Vasthi; the woman kneeling is already crowned. Neither is it an episode from the banquet. The king is wearing the same clothes as in the center scene, which shows that these are not characters from another story. Maybe we have here the moment immediately before the central scene. At top right Esther and Ahasuerus would appear to be listening to music played by a woman in their retinue; such scenes, having nothing to do with the main story, are quite usual in early 16th century Brussels tapestries, and help to fill their vast surfaces.

10 ft. × 12 ft. 9 in. (3,04 m × 3,90 m)

For it is indeed to the Brussels of this transition period between the Middle Ages and the Renaissance that this piece should be attributed. Its origin is unknown, but it belongs to the school of Jean van Roome. Compare, especially, the young man standing on the right with the Autolycus in the *Story of Mestra* (No. 87); the style is identical, even if the present tapestry is not one of the great tapestries woven with gold thread. This is a good example of more ordinary production; the same cartoon could in any case serve to make more or less finely woven and luxurious works.

Acquired by the Victoria and Albert Museum in 1866.

BIBLIOGRAPHY. A.F. Kendrick, *Victoria and Albert Museum, Department of Textiles, Catalogue of Tapestries,* London, 1924, n° 22, p. 37-38, pl. XVII.

82
The Head of John the Baptist being Handed to the Emperor Theodosius

Wool, silk, and gold
17-20 warp threads
to the inch
(central strip)

The château, Pau

The *Baptism of Christ,* either separately or as one of a set devoted to the twelve articles of the Creed or the *Life of Jesus,* was a frequent subject for tapestry; there are also a number of series relating the story of John the Baptist. Apart from the four tapestries in the château at Pau, there are two scenes in the Angers Cathedral tapestry museum and admirable early 16th century Brussels sets at Madrid (4 pieces) and at Saragossa (2 pieces).

The tapestries of the Pau series are in the form of a long frieze which carries the figures — they are smaller than usual — framed by pale blue borders with bronze foliage, and two strips, one above and one below, added at a later date. The first piece shows the Jews being baptized by St. John and his penitence, the second, Jesus receiving his envoys and the prophet preaching, and the fourth, the head of the saint being carried in triumph to Constantinople. The exhibited piece is believed to portray the pious women of Cosilaon handing this head to the emperor Theodosius. No doubt it is the episode in the *Golden Legend* according to which the chariot bringing the head of the saint to Constantinople stopped near Chalcedon and could go no further; whereupon Theodosius asked the girl who was guarding the precious relic for permission to take it, which she gave, thinking wrongly that he would get no farther than Valens.

37 ft. 10 in. × 11 ft. 7 in. (11,55 m × 3,63 m)

The Pau set is probably not complete, since essential scenes, such as the *Decapitation of the Saint,* are lacking. If they have disappeared, this happened very early, since the set of four pieces has been recorded since the 16th century.

J. Guiffrey has found under No. 39 of the inventory for the Royal Furniture under Louis XIV the mention : "A set of tapestry in wool and silk, picked out in gold, made in England, showing the *Story of St. John* in small figures, within a border with blue background and foliage in golden bronze color, measuring 13 aunes by 11/3 aunes, in four pieces lined with green canvas."

The notation "made in England" was commonly used by inventory writers of this period to designate works woven in the Netherlands; thus there is here no obstacle to attributing the Pau set to early 16th-century Brussels. Although it does not have the perfection of the Spanish Patrimonio set, which belongs to the stylistic group of Jean van Roome (see Nos. 78, 79 and 87-89), it has much in common with it, as if its cartoon-maker had borrowed various parts. For example,

the drawing of Penitence, a charming young woman, crowned and holding a whip, is the same in both sets. This we see how the cartoon-makers worked : in order to keep the enormous number of weaving ateliers in Brussels busy, they made their own cartoons and reused models of figures in different compositions — not only in the millefleurs tapestry centers but also in Brussels itself.

We do not know how these four pieces got into the royal collections at the time of Louis XIV nor when they left them. They have been in the château at Pau since the middle of the 19th century.

BIBLIOGRAPHY. J. Guiffrey, *L'Histoire de saint Jean et l'Histoire de Psyché, Notice sur des tapisseries du Mobilier national conservées au château de Pau,* extract from *Bulletin archéologique du Comité des travaux historiques et scientifiques.* Paris, E. Leroux, 1888, 14 p. — J. de Laprade, *Musée national du château de Pau, Guide du visiteur.* Paris, Réunion des Musées nationaux, 1950, p. 27-31, pl.

83-84

Nine Scenes from the Life of the Virgin and of Christ

Wool and silk
15 warp threads
to the inch

Cathedral of the Holy Savior,
Aix-en-Provence

One of the types of tapestry most in favor at the end of the 15th century and the beginning of the 16th was the choir tapestry. In the form of a long frieze, it illustrated the life of the patron saint of the church and was hung only on great feast-days or during special seasons. The number of scenes in the tapestry or set of tapestries was probably determined by the total length required for the particular church. Ordinarily, the choir tapestry would be replaced by painted pictures, which were much less expensive. Many churches were dedicated to Christ and especially to the Virgin, and the principal episodes of the New Testament, and also scenes from the Apocrypha, were accordingly illustrated in this way. The Aix set now has no less than twenty-six scenes, starting with the *Birth of Mary* and ending with the *Assumption* and the *Triumph of Christ* (a twenty-seventh scene was mentioned at the beginning of the 19th century). The set has been defaced, which probably explains the absence of such customary scenes as the *Adoration of the Magi* and the *Last Supper*. A tapestry recently sold in Paris shows a *Last Supper* between an *Entry of Christ into Jerusalem* and a *Washing of the Feet;* these scenes were woven to the same cartoons as the Aix set.

The Aix pieces are framed with a border of fruit and flowers among which appear here and there coats of arms surrounded by devices; they are divided by pilasters decorated with Renaissance motifs (except for that between the *Birth of the Virgin* and her *Presentation in the Temple*).

83

The first of the pieces we exhibit shows the Birth of the Virgin, her Presentation in the Temple, the Annunciation, the Visitation, and the Apparition to the Shepherds

In the first scene, St. Anne lies in bed while two women prepare a bath for the infant. The second shows the child Mary, watched over by an angel and received by the High Priest, climbing the steps of the Temple; her parents, who have brought her there, stand on the left. In the border at the top is a coat of arms, *per pale*, probably that of Henry Dean, archbishop of Canterbury from 1500 to 1503 (it recurs in the Pentecost scene); in the bottom border is a monogram with an i over a P, and below this two letters that have been deciphered as T and G. This sign, which is repeated in the *Adoration of the Shepherds*, the *Death of the Virgin*, and the *Assumption*, has been considered by some to be a weaver's mark, but more convincingly by Montague Rhodes James to be the monogram of Thomas Goldstone, prior of Canterbury, one of the two donors of the set (the arms of the priory appear on the scene of the *Entry of Christ into Jerusalem*).

In the *Annunciation*, the Virgin is kneeling with her back to the angel Gabriel, while the dove of the Holy Spirit spreads his wings in a gloriole above her. Unusually, two angels accompany her in her meeting with Elizabeth; at the top is a shield with two animals and the bust of a king; this recurs in the *Calvary* scene (No. 84). Another angel bears a banner with the words in the Gospel according to St. Luke, "Gloria in excelsis deo," and announces the birth of the Savior to three surprised shepherds and a shepherdess.

Birth of the Virgin

Presentation in the Temple

Annunciation

84

The second of the exhibited pieces includes the Flagellation, the Crown of Thorns, Calvary, and the Deposition from the Cross

On the left of the first scene a bearded figure wearing a turban carries a long stick; the same figure appears, seated, in the preceding scene, in which Jesus is brought to him. He has been wrongly identified as Caiaphas; the High Priest did not order the flagellation and was not present at it. This must be Pilate. In the top border is a deer crested with the letter R and kneeling inside a streamer bearing the words "Soli Deo honor et gloria." This deer already figured in the *Sermon on the Mount* scene and is found again at the top of the *Resurrection;* it reappears, without the streamer, in the lower border under Pilate, and also below the Christ in the *Sermon, Calvary,* the *Resurrection,* and the *Pentecost.* We must have here the canting arms (arms containing a visual pun) of the second donor of the set, Richard Dering (Dering = deer). An inscription in the upper border refers to him : "Richa/rdus huius ecclesie / commonachus et / celerarius me

Visitation

Apparition to the Shepherds

fieri / fecit anno domini millesimo quingentesimo / undecimo" (Richard, monk and cellarer of this church, had me made in the year of our Lord fifteen hundred and eleven). Around the Christ of the *Calvary* scene are grouped the Virgin and three holy women, and also two figures who may be Nicodemus and Joseph of Arimathea, since they recur in the *Deposition from the Cross*.

The presence of the arms of Henry Dean and, elsewhere in the set, of two other archbishops of Canterbury — Morton (died 1500) and Warham, Dean's successor — and also, in two places, of the quartered shield with fleur de lys and leopards of the kings of England, has for long been taken to suggest that this *Life of the Virgin and of Christ*, bought in 1656 in Paris by a canon of Aix Cathedral, was made for the metropolis of the Church of England. M. R. James proved this at the beginning of this century when he found the set in the Canterbury inventories. That of April 10, 1540, drawn up after the dissolution of the monastery, laconically mentions a beautiful new set of rich tapestry comprising six pieces of the *Story of Christ and Our Lady*, but a description in 1640 states that a part of this *Life of the Savior* was given by the Prior Thomas Goldstone and the other by Richard Dering

the cellarer in the time of Henry VIII, as witness the "Memorials" in the border. it also mentions two inscriptions : on the south side, "Thomas Goldstone huius ecclesiae Prior sacraeque Theologiae Professor me fieri fecit Anno Dom. Millesimo quingentesimo undecimo"; on the north, "Richardus Dering huius ecclesiae Commonachus et Celerarius me fieri fecit, anno Dom. Millesimo quingentesimo undecimo," which corresponds to the surviving inscription and shows that the set is not complete.

It probably had about five scenes par piece, or some thirty in all; those on the south side, given by Goldstone, probably dealt with the *Life of the Virgin*, while those on the north, donated by Dering, the *Story of Jesus*.

The date 1511 fits the style of this work perfectly; it has been compared to that of Quentin Metsys and also, less

Flagellation   Crown of Thorns

convincingly, to that of Jean van Roome. The simple, uncluttered composition, the firm, full drawing of the figures, which have a robust frankness despite the conventional and sometimes rather affected character of some of the gestures, are a long way from the crowded, suavely precious works of Jean van Roome. No doubt this is a work of Brussels style, probably drawn by a cartoon-maker who was influenced by the painting of the time and especially by Metsys, with certain weaknesses here and there as in the Christ of the *Resurrection.*

It is likely to have been woven, too, in Brussels, with its modeling emphasized by vigorous vertical combing. Such a work, intended for an English cathedral, is very different from most of the choir tapestries that have been preserved in French churches, whose origin thus seems to have been equally different.

The set hung in the choir of Canterbury Cathedral from 1511 to at least 1640. It was bought in Paris in 1656 by Canon de Mimata, for 1200 écus, on behalf of the Cathedral of the Holy Savior at Aix. It was sold at the time of the Revolution, but bought back again by Monseigneur de Cici, archbishop of Aix from 1802 to 1810. Declared a "monument historique" on June 14, 1898.

BIBLIOGRAPHY. Fauris de Saint-Vincent, *Mémoire sur la tapisserie du chœur de l'église cathédrale d'Aix.* Paris, J.B. Sajou, 1812, 29 p. (extract from *Magasin encyclopédique,* December 1812). — Montague Rhodes James, *The tapestries at Aix-en-Provence...* in *Proceedings of the Cambridge Antiquarian Society,* t. XI (new series, vol. V, 1903-1907, p. 506-512. — *Le XVIᵉ siècle européen, Tapisseries, Paris, Mobilier national, octobre 1965 — Janvier 1966* (Paris, Réunion des Musées nationaux, 1965), nº 18, p. 33-34, fig. p. 42-43.

Calvary

Deposition from the Cross

85
Offering of Fruit to the Infant Christ

Wool, silk, and gold
About 17 warp threads
to the inch

Musée des Arts Décoratifs
de Lyon

One wonders what the inner meaning of this charming piece may be, since it is not an ordinary Adoration of the Shepherds, but the offering of a fruit by a grave-looking figure to the infant Jesus. The Virgin, seated on a dais, holds the Infant on her lap; behind are three angels surrounded by a group of men with serious, almost reproving expressions. The tapestry is said to come from the house of Ravenna, and according to tradition the donor was a member of this family, perhaps Ambrose le Camaldule (1378-1439). There are in fact two other versions of this scene, less finely worked and with some variations, one in the City Art Museum in St. Louis, Missouri, the other in the Vatican. Perhaps these are repetitions — made because the cartoon was liked — of a subject that was indeed originally woven to the special order of a family; or perhaps the subject is some episode in the life of a pious figure (he has no halo).

10ft. 8in. × 9ft. 10in. (3,25 m × 3 m)

The whole work has a special blend of grace and austerity that has caused it to be attributed to the creator of the *paños de oro*, the *Mass of St. Gregory* in the Spanish Patrimonio Nacional, and a number of other tapestries, and even to Jean van Roome (see Nos. 78, 79, 80 and 87-89). This last is not impossible, since the style of the characters is the same, even if the vigorous movement of the Child reaching for the fruit and the drape of the donor's coat are not paralleled in the *Communion of Herkinbald*, which is much more static. At all events, both in style and execution — which is of remarkable quality — this piece is clearly from Brussels and of the opening years of the 16th century.

From the collection of Count Laratelli del Corno at Ravenna, this tapestry was bought by the Museum at the sale of the Vaysse collection at Marseilles in May, 1885 (No. 370). Declared a "monument historique" January 10, 1909.

BIBLIOGRAPHY. *Le XVIe siècle européen. Tapisseries. Paris, Mobilier National, octobre 1965 - janvier 1966* (Paris, Réunion des Musées Nationaux, 1965), n° 17, p. 33, fig. p. 40.

86
Nativity with an Allegory of the Redemption

Wool and silk
15 to 18 warp threads
to the inch

Mayer van der Bergh Museum,
Antwerp

Charged with allegoric significance, this piece summarizes the history of humanity from the first human couple up to the resurrection of Christ, the new Adam who, by his incarnation and death, wiped out the sin of the old.

Top left, we see God giving his instructions to Adam and Eve, no doubt forbidding them to eat of the fruit of the tree of knowledge, even though in Genesis this order is given to Adam alone, before the creation of woman. Behind, a pool decorated with a curious shaft is certainly the Spring of Life. To the right is the Tempter, most exceptionally shown here as a horned woman, who offers the forbidden fruit to Eve; on the left of the tree she eats it with Adam.

In the foreground is the Nativity, with two shepherds and two women standing by to the right; it does not take place at the foot of the Cross (compare No. 78), but in front of an angel who bears the labarum of the risen Christ and a small picture showing Jesus leaving the tomb. In an arresting summary of the Passion, three angels surround him, carrying two crosses and the column of the Flagellation. To the left is a man who is probably the symbol of the sinner redeemed; with him are five women, one of whom is probably Mary Magdalene carrying her vase of precious ointment. She and two of the others would then be the holy women who found Christ's tomb empty when they came to anoint his body; the fourth and her neighbor could be the image of the human race. The one on the left carries a broken-off tree, which may be the tree of knowledge; the legend is that Adam took from it a branch that was later used by Christ's executioners to make the cross. However, these five women may be Virtues equally well as they are in most *Redemption* pieces.

11 ft. 4 in. × 11 ft. 4 in. (3,45 m × 3,45 m)

detail

This piece is typical Brussels work, both from its style and subject matter. Marthe Crick-Kuntziger sees it as of the school of Jean van Roome (see Nos. 78 and 80); yet in some of the figures there is a movement that seems a little out of keeping with the static art of this painter, and there is no element of architecture to recall the way the creator of the *Communion of Herkinbald* liked to plan his composition. But in these years 1500-1510 there were too many different painters imbued with the same artistic spirit to permit a name to be suggested for the exhibited work.

Probably bought in Paris in 1899 from Touzain the elder.

BIBLIOGRAPHY. Marthe Crick-Kuntziger, in *Trésor de l'art flamand du Moyen Age au XVIIIe siècle*, Brussels, 1932, t. II, p. 55, 61-62, 66 and pl. LXXII.

87
The Story of Mestra

Wool and silk
15-20 warp threads
to the inch

The Hermitage Museum,
Leningrad

Without the inscription (top right) it would not be easy to identify the subject matter of this work, since, as is the case with many tapestries from Brussels in the early 16th century, the maker of the cartoon reduced it to the common denominator of the court scene, in which the characters consist of little more than their costumes. These are contemporary, in the style of Margaret of Austria, Regent of the Netherlands, whether the subject is an episode from the Bible, as in the *Story of David* in the Cluny Museum, or ancient mythology, as here.

Ovid tells the story, in Book VII of his *Metamorphoses,* of Eresichton of Thessaly, who was condemned to insatiable hunger for his profanation of a forest sacred to Ceres. Having squandered all his belongings in his efforts to appease it, he sold his daughter, Mestra. But she appealed to Neptune, who had been her lover, and he changed her into a fisherman and so enabled her to escape from her master. Once more back in her original form, she was sold again by her father; under the successive guises of a mare, a bird, and an ox, she escaped from several masters. In the end, Eresichton ate himself, and Mestra married Autolycus, the son of Mercury, well known for stealing herds.

The tapestry apparently depicts the marriage of Mestra and Autolycus, if we consider it with one of the two parts of another *Story of Mestra,* in the Royal Fine Art Museums, Brussels. In this set, after a first tapestry devoted to Eresichton's sacrilege and the girl's entreaties to her father not to sell her, a second shows, as here, a couple moving among a group of gentlemen and ladies, with figures in the gallery above and (top left) a woman kneeling in front of a bearded old man. The cartoon is almost identical, but the Brussels tapestry is a good third longer, and it has a group of musicians on the right behind some bystanders, who are different from the two seated women near the side of the present tapestry. Above all there is, at the top,

a scene of the rape of Mestra by Neptune, announced in the Leningrad tapestry by an inscription: IN DIE DEDICATIONIS DI NE NEPTUNUS MESTRAM RECIPUIT, DEINDE EAM DEFLORUIT; but here, the scene is not shown, probably either because it was decided not to include the right-hand portion when the part with the inscription had already been woven, or because the weavers forgot to modify the inscription before weaving a shorter piece, which would therefore be without the rape scene. What is particularly strange is that the inscription in the Brussels tapestry, in which the episode does figure, is different from that in the Leningrad version; it makes no reference to it and merely lists the names: DEANA, NEPTUNUS, MESTRAM. Contrary to what Anne van Ypersele de Strihou has written on this subject, the inscriptions thus indicate that the queen standing in the middle of the gallery is not Venus, but Diana, and the little scene at top left is not Mestra and Autolycus thanking Neptune for his help, but a much earlier episode : Neptune receiving Mestra (whose expression is incidentally more one of grief than of gratitude). Thus there are elements that are not found in Ovid, and, as elsewhere, we must assume that the maker of the cartoon derived inspiration from another source; if we knew which, we should perhaps be able to explain the main scene more satisfactorily. However, the identification of the young man on the right as Autolycus is supported by the presence of the figure sitting behind Mestra, who has one foot bare; this could well be Jason, who had been Autolycus' companion in arms (see Nos. 88-89). According to the legend, Jason lost a shoe while crossing a river carrying on his back an old woman whom no one else had been willing to help across, and whose ever-growing weight was crushing him; this was Juno, who afterward took him under her protection.

11 ft. 4 in. × 12 ft. 11 in. (3,45 m × 3,95 m)

Most of the figures shown here are probably no one in particular, and are present only to fill primarily decorative surface with their sumptuous garments. In spite of the Renaissance elements in this work, especially in the architecture of the gallery, the work is a far cry from the pictorial conception of tapestry introduced by Raphael's *Acts of the Apostles* a few years later. The design remains faithful to medieval composition ideas, with its scenes, one above another, filling the whole area.

It was certainly woven in Brussels, probably around 1510, and has been attributed to Jean Van Roome, a cartoon maker who seems to have played a large part in the history of tapestry at this time (see Nos 78-80 and 85); indeed, there are a number of resemblances with the *Miraculous Communion of Herkinbald*, for whose "petit patron" the Brotherhood of the Holy Sacrament at St. Pierre de Louvain paid him in 1513 : the composition is similar with its scenes and figures one above another, its analogous architectural elements, and

its identical characters with vacant expressions, calm movements, and rich clothes falling in heavy folds. The same style is seen in many other tapestries including the Cluny Museum's *Story of David*, the *Story of David* in the Patrimonio Nacional, Spain, the story of *Jason* (Nos. 88-89) and the *Story of Oriens and Beatrice* in the Hermitage. This style is admirably suited to tapestry, and to it the art of low-warp weaving in early 16th-century Brussels owes its finest pieces.

Formerly in the Stieglitz Museum, this work has been in the Hermitage Museum since 1923.

BIBLIOGRAPHY. Anne van Ypersele de Strihou, *Deux tapisseries bruxelloises de l'Histoire de Mestra*, in Bulletin de l'Institut royal du Patrimoine artistique, t. III, 1960, p. 103-110, fig. — Nina Birioukova, *Old tapestries from the Hermitage Museum, a collection of German, French and Flemish Wall hangings of the 15th and 16th centuries*, Prague, Artia. — Leningrad, The Soviet Artist (1965), p. 25-26 and pl. 49-60.

88-89
The Story of Jason

Wool and silk
16-20 warp threads to the inch

The Hermitage Museum, Leningrad

Here again we have a display of gorgeous costumes, but, unlike No. 87, without inscriptions to clinch the identification of the subject. The second of the pieces, No. 89, is in some ways so like No. 87 that it has long been considered part of it : Mestra giving presents to her father. However, Ovid's story does not include such an episode, the old man with a beard receiving the casket does not look like Eresichton, and the border of the tapestry is different.

In view of the similar borders and similar colorings, Nina Birioukova suggests that Nos. 88 and 89 represent the *Story of Jason.* Son of Eson, Jason was sent by his uncle Pelias to Colchis to win the Golden Fleece : he succeeded with the help of the king's daughter, Medea, priestess of Hecate, who had fallen in love with him and whom he married and brought back to Greece after his victory.

88
Jason and Medea

Jason, recognizable by his bare foot — he only had one sandal when he went to see his uncle Pelias, who had usurped Eson's throne — appears at

the top left swearing fidelity to Medea. He appears again on the right in the scene in which Medea, surrounded by Argonauts, seems to be promising to help him. The winged female figure at the bottom, taking Medea by the arm, is probably Hecate.

11 ft. 4 in. × 10 ft. 11 in. (3,46 m × 3,32 m)

89
Handing over the Casket

Medea, rejected by Jason, who is about to marry Creusa, daughter of Creon, King of Corinth, seems to be giving him the casket containing the poisonous robe and crown that will cause her rival to perish in agony. The figure at the top is probably Creon making a sacrifice.

10 ft. 8 in. × 11 ft. 2 in. (3,25 m × 3,42 m)

This is another of the sumptuous sets made in Brussels around 1510, and in it we can recognize the style of Margaret of Austria's painter, Jean van Roome, or Jean of Brussels. He certainly had his own atelier — in which it is believed the great painter and cartoon- maker Bernard van Orley began his career — and he succeeded in giving considerable unity of style to works on which other artists probably collaborated with him (this has been proved in the case of the *Communion of Herkinbald,* for which a sketch by the master was enlarged to full size by the painter Philip). However, he did not hesitate to introduce elements of a different style into these vast areas, in which figures are crowded more for decorative reasons than because the composition needs them. This is obviously what was done in one of the pieces of the *Story of David, Nathan Admonishes David* (No. 97); a

cupbearer, on the left, has manifestly been borrowed from a 15th-century work. This may be the case with the winged figure of No. 88, whose flying movement is in sharp contrast to the style of the rest of the work, and especially to the static nature of Jean van Roome's characters. it is not impossible that this one figure is the work of the young Bernard van Orley, who later gave such verve to the figures in his *Maximilian's Hunting Scenes* in the Louvre and his *Story of Jacob* in the Royal Art and History Museums, Brussels.

Formerly in the Stieglitz Museum, this work has been in the Hermitage Museum since 1923.

BIBLIOGRAPHY. Nina Birioukova, *Old tapestries from the Hermitage Museum...,* Prague, Artia - Leningrad, The Soviet Artist (1965), p. 26-27 and pl. 61-72.

90-91
The Legend of Notre-Dame du Sablon

Wool and silk
15-18 warp threads to the inch

The sets of tapestries with which the exhibition ends are rich in history and legend. Despite their Renaissance elements, they express the quintessence of mediaeval thought. At a time when the Protestant movement was beginning to encroach on the worship of the Virgin and the saints, they show us that the forms and beliefs inherited from the preceding period were still dominant.

The present set was woven only once, and illustrated a specific event : it related in four tapestries the transfer in 1348 of a small statue of the Virgin and Child from a church in Antwerp to that of Notre-Dame du Sablon in Brussels. The set is now dispersed and incomplete.

It is said that in that year the Virgin appeared to a pious old spinster of Antwerp, Beatrix Soetkens, in her sleep; this vision was illustrated in the left-hand scene of the first tapestry, the upper part of which (the Virgin surrounded by angels) was in the Kaiser Friedrich Museum, Berlin, in 1918 but apparently disappeared during World War II, and the lower part (Beatrix in her bed), is in the Burrell collection, Glasgow. The Virgin told Beatrix to take a statuette known as Notre-Dame à la Branche out of the church where it was kept and have it cleaned, which she did; the central panel of the first tapestry (formerly in the Astor collection, London, bought in 1963 by the Royal Art and History Museums, Brussels) shows her taking the statue off the side altar of a church and asking the churchwardens' permission to remove it. The upper right-hand part of this work (also once in the Kaiser Friedrich Museum, now missing) showed Beatrix in the workshop of an artist to whom she had brought the statue to be restored; in the lower part (in the Ile-de-France Villa-Museum at St.-Jean-Cap-Ferrat) she is seen replacing the statue in the church.

90
The Virgin Orders the Statue Transferred

The Hermitage
Museum, Leningrad

The second tapestry, which has been preserved intact, has the traditional composition : three scenes that take place under flattened arches supported by four small columns, with winged putti above holding coats of arms (left to right : Aragon, Castile, Léon, Aragon-Sicily).

On the left, the Virgin appears a second time to Beatrix Soetkens to tell her to take the statue to the church of Notre-Dame du Sablon.

In the center, the old woman is kneeling in the church near the statue, which is placed under a dais bearing the inscription "Maria." She asks permission to transfer it, but this is refused.

202

On the right, the Virgin appears for the third time and insists that Beatrix carry out her mission.

These events are commented upon in inscriptions on five banners that are deployed in the beautiful border that surrounds the tapestry, two at the top and three at the bottom; each is preceded by a letter of the alphabet that indicates their order. The inscriptions are in hexameter / pentameter couplets :
— Top left : "F. Illa quiescebat rursus sub nocte silenti / Delabri superis visa Maria polis" ("Once more she was resting in the silent night. Mary seemed to come down from the upper spheres").
— Bottom left : "G. Effatur nostram referas ex aede figuram / Hac Sabulina decet preside templa frui" ("She said : take my image out of the church; the shrine of le Sablon should have its protection").
— Bottom center : "H. Hec sacrata movet properos ad limina gressus / Sed negat optatam dura repulsa deam" ("She moves with rapid steps toward the holy threshold, but a stern prohibition denies her the desired [image of] the deity").
— Bottom right : "I. Nox ruit. En vultu dive redeuntis eodem / Forma soporanti talia visa loqui" ("Night falls. To the sleeping woman, the vision of the goddess who returns with the same appearance seems to say as follows").
— Top right : "K. Eia age pone metum statuam volo sub lege nostra / Ipsa ego presenti patrocinabor ope" ("Come now; be not afraid. I want the statue under our law. I shall personally protect thee with effective aid").

The rest of the border is decorated with heraldic or ornamental motifs. In each corner is the bust of a warrior, in profile, surrounded by a wreath. At the top, between the two banners, are two of a kind of cornucopia accosted to a shield; despite anomalies due to restorations, this is the shield of Philip the Handsome, son of Maximilian of Austria and Mary of Burgundy, King of Castile from 1504 to 1506 (by his marriage with Joanna the Mad), and later the shield of his eldest son, Charles I of Spain, the future Holy Roman Emperor Charles V. At the sides are Renaissance motifs around two banners, between which is a shield attached to a winged mask. The lefthand shield bore, before a faulty restoration, the arms of the powerful family of Taxis : *per fess, in the first : or, an eagle issuant sable, crowned or; in the second : azure, a badger argent.* On the banners is the device "Habeo quod dedi" (I have what I have given). On the right is the shield of the Magnasco family : *argent, an uprooted tree vert, supported by two lions gules facing each other;* on the banners a second device is repeated : "Dum vixit bene bene vixit" (While he lived a good life, he lived well).

The third tapestry, after having been cut into three pieces, is now restored, and is in the Musée Communal at Brussels. It illustrates the removal of the statue by Beatrix, who takes it to Brussels in a boat, while the sacristan who tries to prevent her is struck motionless. The magistrate of Antwerp then sends a letter to John, Duke of Brabant, which permits an allusion in the tapestry to the imperial postal service and a first portrait of its director, François de Taxis, who appears three times in the fourth piece; he was the son of Paxius (or Pasino de) Taxis and Tolona Magnasco (or Monasco), and the arms in the side borders are his. De Taxis is shown in the third tapestry with his two imperial protectors, Frederick III and his son Maximillian I. The features of the latter suggest the Duke of Brabant, who appears again in the fourth piece in the features of Philip the Handsome and his son Charles.

91
The Statue is Taken to Notre-Dame du Sablon

This fourth tapestry, preserved intact like the second, is particularly interesting in that it is a veritable portrait gallery.

The shields supported by the putti above the small columns bear the arms of Portenau, Burgau, Kyborg, and Ortenburg.

On the left, while clergy watch the scene from a bridge, Beatrix hands the statue to a prince with a crown, in sumptuous clothes and wearing the collar of the Golden Fleece, who has been said to be Philip the Handsome (1478-1506); heir to the Netherlands and especially the province of Brabant through his mother, Mary of Burgundy, he appointed François de Taxis as Captain and Master of the Posts there. This would explain the presence in the foreground — taking no part in the scene, and holding a sealed envelope, as in the two other pieces in the set — of the man who on March 1, 1500, established the basis of the European postal organization, with headquarters in Brussels.

In the center, under a dais supported by angels and bearing the inscription : "Ave. Regina. Celorum" (Hail Queen of Heaven), the statue is borne on a litter, in the midst of a throng, on the shoulders of two perfectly recognizable young men : the one at the back is none other than the then reigning Duke of Brabant, Charles of Austria, born in 1500, eldest son of Philip the Handsome and Joanna the Mad, declared king of Spain on March 14, 1516, elected Holy Roman Emperor in 1519, on the death of his grandfather Maximilian, under the name of Charles-Quint; the

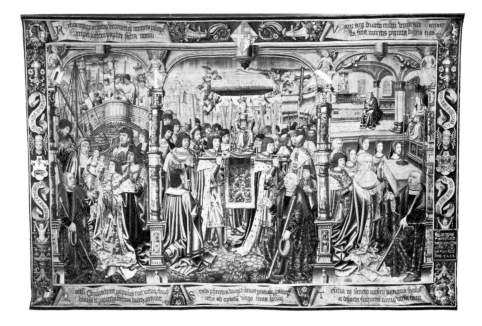

one in front is his younger brother, Ferdinand, who was to succeed him as Emperor in 1556. On the right we have François de Taxis again, while the kneeling young man on the left must be his nephew and heir Jean-Baptiste de Taxis, who on November 12, 1516, had signed jointly with him and King Charles an important contract including Rome, Naples, and Verona in the postal domain of the Taxis family. Marthe Crick-Kuntziger thinks that it may be this contract that François de Taxis is holding in the three scenes of this tapestry.

For we find him once more in the right-hand panel in which the statue of the Virgin is placed on an altar and is worshiped by seven persons, in the front row of whom we recognize Margaret of Austria, daughter of Maximilian and Mary of Burgundy, sister of Philip the Handsome and Regent of the Low Countries during the minority of her nephew Charles. She also signed a contract with François de Taxis, in 1507; the document that the latter shows in each of the scenes may thus be the charter he has obtained from each of the rulers portrayed there. Here Margaret takes the form of the wife of the Duke John, who is said to have followed the statue on foot, with all his court, until it was set up in Notre-Dame du Sablon. Behind her kneel the second son of Philip and Joanna the Mad, Ferdinand, who appeared in the preceding scene, and his four sisters, who all were to become queens : Eleonora, wife of Manoel of Portugal, and later of Francis I, Isabel, who married Christian II of Denmark, Mary of Hungary, and Catherine, who married Joao III of Portugal, Manoel's successor. On the left is a woman of lesser rank, perhaps the wife of François de Taxis, Dorothy Luytvoldi or Leytboldi. Above, a second scene shows Beatrix Soetkens sitting in the church; she spent the rest of her life in Brussels in the service of the miraculous Virgin.

Inscriptions :

— Bottom left : "Q. Portum cymba tenet populus ruit undique clerus /obvius it proceres littora duxque petunt" ("The boat arrives in the port, the people throng from all sides, the clergy come to meet it, the notables and the duke himself head for the shore").

Top left : "R. Celica magnanimus veneratus munera princeps / Excipit inflexo poplite sacra manu" ("The noble-minded prince, having venerated this gift from heaven, receives the sacred object, kneeling, in his hand").

Bottom center : "S. Grata pheretra duces subeunt natusque paterque / Fertur ad optatum virgo serena locum" ("The dukes, father and son, place themselves under the precious litter. The serene Virgin is carried toward the place she longs for").

Bottom right : "T. Sistitur in sancto miseris patrona sacello / Nec despecta frequens concio vota facit" ("She is placed in the holy shrine as patron to the poor; the people coming together address to her prayers that are not despised").

Top right : "V. Hanc age devoto cultu venerare Mariam / Illa feret meritis premia digna tuis" ("Come, worship this image of Mary in devoted veneration. She will send thee recompense in accordance with thy merits").

The border carries the same motifs as that of the preceding piece, except for the shield at the top, which is here that of Margaret of Austria; also, a scroll which seems to be contemporary with the tapestries is sewn on the right. It is inscribed : "Egregius / franciscus de / Taxis pie memorie / postarum magister / hec fieri fecit / anno 1.5.1.8.". ("The noble François de Taxis, of pious memory, Master of the Posts, caused these to be made in the year 1518").

11 ft. 9 in. × 17 ft. 10 in. (3,55 m × 5,45 m)

detail

The inscriptions complete and confirm the information supplied by the tapestries themselves. It was thus indeed François de Taxis who, to the glory of the miraculous Virgin of Brussels, his Hapsburg protectors, and indeed his own glory, ordered the Sablon set. This need not surprise us, for he owned a house near this shrine. However, he did not live to see the work completed, for he died between November 30 and December 20, 1517. Though the suggestion has been made that 1518 was the date of the order — in which case it would have been placed by Jean-Baptiste de Taxis in accordance with his uncle's wishes — it is more likely that 1518 is the date of completion; the design and weaving would thus have taken place between the date of the contract (November 12, 1516), to which reference is clearly made in the fourth tapestry, or at all events in the central scene, and 1518, which is long enough if each piece was produced on a different loom.

The set is thus a precious landmark for the study of stylistic development in Brussels tapestry weaving; for it is clear from the type of weaving and the colors that this evocation of a local legend is a product of this city — possibly the only place capable, at this date, of making such a work.

After the crowded composition of the sumptuous works attributed to Jean van Roome, and at a time when weaving was going on in the same city, to the Pope's order, for Raphael's *Acts of the Apostles*, which was to introduce the revolution of Italian perspective into the art of tapestry, the Sablon set is evidence of a new spirit, even if it retains, like its predecessors, a full background and the traditional composition subdivided by columns. Renaissance elements appear in the architecture, and the border is quite different from borders of the beginning of the century, in which flowering stems frame the tapestries. The Sablon border is very similar to a border designed a little later by the great Brussels painter Bernard van Orley for a genealogical tapestry of the House of Nassau. Now this artist, who was to be one the most talented cartoon makers of his age, had painted in 1515 the portraits of the six children of Philip the Handsome, and in the following year, those of Charles, Eleanor, and Isabel. Furthermore, about 1512 he had painted a triptych for the Sablon church. He was thus well placed to attract the attention of François de Taxis, who founded a chapel in this shrine shortly before his death. There are certainly aspects of van Orley's style in this tapestry, even if there are also characteristics of what has been called "the school of Jean van Roome," and the treatment is rather different from works like *Maximilian's Hunting Scenes* in the Louvre and the *Story of Jacob* in the Musée du Cinquantenaire, Brussels, where less crowded figures move with vigor against a background that is frankly pictorial. However, the taste for true detail — for instance, in the socks and candlestick near Beatrix's bed or the rich drapery of the Virgin's litter — and the expressive energy in the faces, especially in that of François de Taxis, which is heavy with age and suggestive of imminent death, suggest that the Sablon tapestries may be attributable to Bernard van Orley; he was young at the time, and may not yet have thrown off earlier traditions of composition. However, given the facts that there were ateliers of cartoon makers and that Bernard van Orley may have begun his career in Jean van Roome's, we should not exclude the possibility that several persons were involved in designing these tapestries.

Where was the set to be hung? Not in the house of François de Taxis, it would seem, but in the church itself; Marthe Crick-Kuntziger has found, in the account of Philip II's journey to the Netherlands in 1549, a mention of "an ancient and rich tapestry" in this building, "retracing the miraculous episodes" of the removal of the statue, "with explicatory verses." However, the 18th-century documents make no mention of the set, and we know nothing of its later history until it appeared in Paris, complete in the 19th century.

Emile Peyre exhibited three of the four pieces in 1874. Frédéric Spitzer then acquired the set, and cut the first and third pieces into three sections each. The eight pieces were dispersed when the Spitzer collection was sold, June 16, 1893. The second piece was acquired from the Paris dealer Loewengard by the Stieglitz collection, and then entered the Leningrad Hermitage Museum in 1923. The fourth piece was bought for the Royal Art and History Museums at the Spitzer sale.

BIBLIOGRAPHY. Marthe Crick-Kuntziger, *La tenture de la légende de Notre-Dame du Sablon*, Antwerp, de Sikkel, 1942, 36 p., XX, pl. *Musées royaux d'art et d'histoire de Bruxelles, Catalogue des tapisseries (XIVᵉ au XVIIIᵉ siècle)*, (1956), n° 15, p. 31-34 and pl. 20-21. — Roger-A. d'Hulst, *Tapisseries flamandes du XIVᵉ au XVIIIᵉ siècle*, Brussels, l'Arcade, 1960, n° 17, p. 139-146 and 299, fig. b/w and color. — Nina Birioukova, *Old tapestries from the Hermitage Museum...*, Prague, Artia, Leningrad, The Soviet Artist (1965), p. 31-32 and pl. 119-128.

92-93
The Redemption of Man

Wool and silk
metal threads
in the *Creation*
About 17 warp threads
to the inch

This enormous series, known also as the *Combat of Vice and Virtue* and the *Seven Deadly Sins,* is in the purest tradition of medieval iconography. It probably marks the zenith of a form of allegorical thought that had left its imprint on innumerable generations, but which the Renaissance and Reformation were shortly to alienate from the centuries to come. Few compositions have interpreted in so grand a manner the entire history of the Christian world, from the Creation to the Last Judgment. We do not know who planned this set for the painter, but the influence of the religious theater (the "Mysteries") is obvious; theological thought here finds artistic expression with an inspiration seldom equaled, and on a scale that required not less than ten pieces to unfold its majestic story. Two pieces of the set, which was woven several times and of which most of the elements are known in several examples, are shown here : the first and the last.

92
The Creation of the World

The Cathedral of St. Just,
Narbonne

Surrounded by a thin border with flowers and grapes, scattered with a few birds, this tapestry exists in two other versions, one in the castle of Haar, Holland, the other in the M. H. de Young Memorial Museum, San

Francisco. It is the only one the ten tapestries that does not have prophets in the lower corners.

The members of the Trinity appear seven times — the sacred number — not in their usual form of bearded old man, young Christ, and dove, but in the much rarer one of three identical figures, each with a scepter and closed imperial crown.

At top left, amid a magnificent cloud of drapery, we see the Trinity bathed in light emerging from clouds; this is no doubt the creation of Light and also the division of the waters with the firmament. Below, the Trinity is on earth, which was created on the third day and is shown covered with plants. To one side, the three persons raise their hands toward the "lights" : the sun, the moon, and the stars, in the firmament of-heaven; this is the fourth day. Next, to the right of a stream crowded with the creatures of the waters and with birds by its edge, we have the creation of the fifth day; on the far right is the sixth, with the beasts of the earth and the first human couple. Above, in the center, in front of musical angels, the Trinity rests for the seventh day, with, on either side, two Virtues who dispute for its favors : Mercy, in the place of honor, and Justice, brandishing a sword. On the right, Eve, tempted by the serpent, holds out the apple to Adam; an angel drives the guilty pair out of Paradise, while the second person of the Trinity, in a movement of great beauty, asks God the Father for permission to sacrifice himself to redeem mankind.

13 ft. 10 in. × 24 ft. 1 in. (4,20 m × 7,85 m)

The redemption is unfolded on eight tapestries in which Virtues and Vices follow the steps of Man, for whose soul they strive, and Christ, who has come to save sinners.

2nd piece : Man is assailed by the Tempter (three examples : in the cathedrals of Palencia and Saragossa, and in the M. H. de Young Memorial Museum, San Francisco).

3rd piece : the Virtues intercede for Man (two examples : one in the Metropolitan Museum, which came from Burgos Cathedral; one in Hampton Court, England. Three shortened versions : in the Victoria and Albert Museum; in the Burrell collection, Glasgow; and formerly in the Schutz collection, Paris).

4th piece : Scenes from the life of the Virgin up to the Nativity (a single example, in The Cloisters Collection, from Burgos cathedral).

5th piece : Scenes from the childhood of Christ from the Circumcision up to the discussion in the Temple with the Doctors (two examples : one in Palencia Cathedral; the other, which has been cut, in the Fogg Art Museum, Cambridge, Mass;).

6th piece : Scenes from the public life of Jesus, from the preaching of St. John the Baptist up to the Resurrection of Lazarus, and preparations for the combat of the Virtues and Vices (two complete examples : one in Palencia Cathedral and one in the Museum of Fine Arts, Boston; plus the right-hand side in Hampton Court).

7th piece : The combat of the Vices and Virtues (four examples : Burgos Cathedral; Haar castle; the Vatican; the M. H. de Young Museum).

8th piece : The descent into limbo, the Resurrection and Apparitions of Christ (three complete examples : Burgos Cathedral, the Vatican, and the M. H. de Young Museum, plus a shortened version in the Chicago Art Institute).

9th piece : The Ascension of Christ; the Grace of God presenting Man to the Trinity, while the Vices are driven out (two examples : Palencia Cathedral, Haar castle).

93
The Last Judgment

The Louvre, Paris

In a powerful vision, the dead rise as the angels sound the trumpets, at the feet of Christ who is sitting in heaven flanked by the Virgin, St. John the Baptist, and the Apostles; to the left, angels carry away the souls of the elect or crown those who kneel behind Mercy; on the right, they drive the damned away to Hell, aided by Justice who raises his sword over a group of seven young women who probably symbolize the Vices. At bottom left, a prophet holds a quotation from Isaiah : "Judicabit gentes, arguit [arguet]

populos multos. Ysaie II" ("And he shall judge among the nations, and shall rebuke many people." Isa. 2 : 4); to the right is another prophet with a quotation from Isaiah : "Dominus ad judicandum veniet. Ysaie III" ("The Lord standeth up to·plead." Isa. 3 : 13).

Another example of this tapestry, without border, is in the Worcester Art Museum, Mass.

13 ft. 3 in. × 26 ft. 11 in. (4,09 m × 8,20 m)

Though the subject matter of this set is still completely medieval in spirit, from the point of view of style it is transitional between the great tapestries of the 15th century, in which the crowding of the characters is often echoed in the architectural elements, and the vast Renaissance pieces, in which a small number of characters appear against an unencumbered landscape. Here, except for the seventh and tenth pieces, in which crowds of figures are arranged in masterful compositions, the characters are harmoniously disposed in independent groups over two registers, with little depth. By analogy from the "mansions" of the theater of the time, these scenes take place in a vernal landscape, in which, as here, there need be no buildings at all.

In the 19th century it was thought that the painter of this set was Jean Gossaert, but this is untenable. More recently, Francis Henry Taylor has suggested that a model for the series could have been made by Hugo van de Goes to celebrate the marriage of Charles the Bold and Margaret of York in 1468; he dated the Louvre's *Last Judgment* twenty or thirty years later, and the Worcester version around 1470. But this hypothesis is no longer acceptable, since Hugo van der Goes died in 1482, while the whole set is in the style of the 1500s. Nevertheless, certain motifs, such as the serpent in the temptation of Eve, do derive from Hugo van der Goes' art; they may have been borrowed from him as stock-in-trades in the atelier. Marthe Crick-Kuntziger thought that this work was of the school of Jean van Roome, like No. 86.

But perhaps it is too much to attribute all the great tapestries of the early 16th century to this artist. Though some features here — the serious faces, the restrained gestures, the garments falling in heavy, broken folds — are also found in the work of Jean van Roome (Nos. 78 and 87-89), they are after all of the art of the period. On the other hand, elements borrowed from the great Flemish painting of the 15th century can be discerned here and there. Apart from the serpent, traceable to Hugo van der Goes, three characters in the *Last Judgment* — the Virgin, St. John the Baptist, and Christ — show inspiration from the polyptych of Rogier van der Weyden at Beaune, though the draping of Jesus' robe is reversed. There are also differences between one tapestry and another. Possibly, then, this is the work of a clever painter who has borrowed from the traditions of the 15th century, blending them together in a profusion of figures with measured gestures and melancholy faces, draped in heavy robes, according to the fashion of the period; or else of an atelier that pieced elements of differing styles into the vast ensembles that current taste demanded, in order to keep the enormous industry of Brussels low-warp weaving supplied with cartoons.

The *Redemption of Man* was certainly woven in Brussels in the first years of the 16th century, or perhaps even at the very end of the 15th (the architecture of the pieces not exhibited here is still Gothic); in any case, it is typical of a period that treated all the scriptural stories in the same lavish way.

We do not know in which atelier this set of tapestries was woven. Some have attributed it, but only as a guess, to the weaver Pieter van Aelst, who had probably just finished the *paños de oro* and was soon to make Raphael's *Act of the Apostles*. Strangely, Taylor has suggested the name of Philip de Mol, even though Phyllis Ackerman, whom he cites, thought this individual was a maker of cartoons, the famous "philiep" of the Brussels *Deposition from the Cross* (No. 80), who was cited in a suit brought in 1527 against Bernard von Orley, and to whom "all the Jean van Roome group" has sometimes been attributed; she thought she could read his name on several tapestries of the *Triumphs*. Unfortunately, Taylor based this theory on some letters he deciphered as MOL on the hem of the Virgin's cloak in the Worcester *Last Judgment;* but these letters in fact are NOV, a group that probably has no significance, like most of the letters that decorate such borders.

So, after all, we do not know who wove this set. Nor do we know for whom it was made, or if it was ordered by any particular person. Maximilian has been suggested because of the two-headed eagle in the fourth piece over the scene of Joseph and Mary paying the Roman tax-

detail

collector, but this eagle could just as easily symbolize Augustus' empire. It has also been said that the set could have been given by Maximilian to his son, Philip the Handsome, for the occasion of his marriage to Joanna the Mad in 1496. However, these enormous Brussels sets seem often to have been made in advance, without any particular client in view — further evidence of the power of the tapestry industry of the time. Some of the arms the Brussels pieces bear are indeed additions. This is the case with the four pieces in the Cathedral of Palencia, Spain, on which the arms are those of Don Juan Rodriguez de Fonseca, who was bishop in that city from 1504 to 1514, after which he held the see of Burgos until his death in 1524.

The Creation of the World *is the only surviving piece of the ten that the archbishop of Narbonne, François Fouquet, gave to the chapter of St. Just on February 19, 1673, at a time when he was* *in exile at Alençon after the disgrace of his brother, the Superintendant of Finance to Louis XIV. The* Last Judgment *was sold with the collection of the Duke of Berwick and Alba in 1877, with five other pieces of the series; it was exhibited in Brussels in 1880 by Baron d'Erlanger and given to the Louvre by its Association of Friends in 1901.*

BIBLIOGRAPHY. D.T.B. Wood, *Tapestries of the Seven Deadly Sins*, in *The Burlington Magazine*, t. XX, 1912, p. 210-222 and 277-289, fig. — Francis H. Taylor, *A piece of Arras of the Judgment*, in *Worcester Art Museum Annual*, t. I, 1935-1936, p. 1-15, fig. — *Le seizième siècle européen, Tapisseries, Paris, Mobilier national, octobre 1965-janvier 1966* (Paris, Réunion des Musées Nationaux, 1965), n° 19, p. 34 and fig. p. 43. — Roger-A. d'Hulst, *Tapisseries flamandes du XVᵉ au XVIIIᵉ siècle*, Brussels, l'Arcade, 1960, n° 15, p. 121-128 and 298-299, fig. b/w and col. — Adolph S. Cavallo, *Tapestries of Europe and of Colonial Peru in the Museum of Fine Arts, Boston*, Boston, Museum of Fine Arts (1967), n° 24, p. 91-95 and pl. — Anna Bennett, *Tapestries of the "Redemption of Man" series*, typescript., 1969, 38 p., fig.

94-97
The Story of David

Wool, silk, silver, and gold
15-20 warp threads
to the inch

Musée de Cluny, Paris

Probably no Old Testament character was illustrated so frequently in tapestry at the end of the Middle Ages as David. Apart from isolated pieces like the one in the National Museum in Stockholm (late 15th century), or the early 16th-century *Bathsheba at the Fountain* in the Brussels Hôtel de Ville, there is a beautiful set in the Madrid Patrimonio Nacional illustrating the story of David's love for Bathsheba, similar in style to the Cluny tapestries, but nevertheless woven to different cartoons; and there is another set in Sigmaringen Castle, from the loom of one of the greatest Brussels weavers of this time, Pieter van Aelst. The inventories record a great many more : Anne of Brittany owned a *Story of David* as early as 1494, and Henry VIII of England, who was a great collector — the inventory made after his death mentioned more than two thousand tapestries — had no less than seven sets of this subject, each of five to fifteen pieces, to say nothing of isolated works. This popularity has been explained as reflecting the current doctrine of the divine right of kings, suggesting that the rulers of the time saw in David an example of a king imposed by God, in the place of Saul. But maybe it is simply due to the influence of the books of Hours; the use of these prayer collections spread considerably during the 15th century, and in them the psalms devoted to the penitence of their author, David, played an important part. For David, though a model sovereign, was guilty of a serious crime : instigating the murder of Uriah, one of the officers of his army, whose wife he had seduced.

This is the story told in the ten sumptuous pieces of this set in the Cluny Museum, four of which are exhibited here.

However, they are not all concerned with the guilty passion of David for Bathsheba, and the siege of Rabbah. The first illustrates a much earlier incident : the *Bringing of the Ark to Jerusalem.* This seems at first sight to have no connection with the others. Yet it nevertheless quite definitely forms part of the set. The style, execution and border are identical, and furthermore the left part of this piece is occupied by a figure seated in front of a book who is obviously either the author or the reader of the story related in the ten pieces; below him is an inscription, embroidered in silver, that summarizes the early episodes. The same figure recurs to the right of the tenth piece above a similar quatrain that summarizes the end of the story. The first tapestry, which illustrates Chapter VI of the second Book of Samuel, is thus perhaps intended to explain David's conduct by his estrangement from his wife, Michal. Apart from this "author," it includes two scenes : a small one in which Uzzah falls dead for having laid his hand on the Ark of the Lord, which David wanted to bring to the city of Jerusalem, which he had captured; and a large one, showing the procession entering the town and David dancing barefoot and clapping his hands before the Ark, while Michal watches disapprovingly. She was later to reproach him severely for this behavior, and he was displeased; and "Michal the daughter of Saul had no child unto the day of her death."

Next we come to the linked stories of David's adultery with Bathsheba and the campaign against the city of the children of Ammon, who had insulted David's messengers. The king sent his army under the command of Joab to lay siege to Rabbah, but he himself stayed in Jerusalem. Walking one day on the roof of his palace, he caught sight of a very beautiful woman bathing; after making enquiries and finding that she was Bathsheba, wife of Uriah, he sent sent servants to fetch her. This action is the subject of one of the tapestries; the famous bath scene is not shown.

94
Preparing to Attack Rabbah

This piece shows only one scene : soldiers assembling in the middle of a wide landscape to attack the town of Rabbah, which is visible in the distance. On the left, "Urias," identified by an embroidered inscription, is putting on his armor. He is beardless, in contrast to the way he appears thoughout the rest of the story (cf. No. 95). There are three possible explanations for this difference : carelessness on the cartoonist's part; or the exigencies of military life, which may have caused Uriah to let his beard grow — an explanation that fits well with his ascetic refusal to go into his house when King David sent for him to come to Jerusalem; or a later addition of the inscriptions identifying principal characters. This latest hypothesis is quite plausible, since Francis Salet has noticed in the scrolls of the 1st and 10th pieces, which were clearly intended

to take inscriptions, that there are letters woven in gold under the embroidery. Similar letters are not visible under the names embroidered here and there on some of the figures, and maybe there are none there. If these embroidered inscriptions were added later without the aid of preexisting letters in gold, the characters may have been wrongly named, and the figure on the left labeled "Urias" may not have been Uriah in the cartoonist's intention. In this case, Uriah would not appear on the tapestry at all, and the tapestry's chronological position in the set may be entirely different from that previously assigned to it; this piece may in fact show preparations for the final storming of Rabbah, which took place long after Uriah's death, rather than the army's first assault on the town.

The fact that no other piece in this series shows the city of the children of Ammon being attacked, which is strange, given that the last two pieces illustrate David receiving the insignia of the defeated king and the city being pillaged, further supports this theory. Notice also that the standard-bearer in the center of this tapestry, whose horse has a splendid caparison decorated with the letter A, reappears in the piece showing the handing over of the insignia. Should it be objected that David ought to appear in the final assault against Rabbah, since Joab wrote to him to come, having himself previously taken "the city of the waters," one could reply either that this tapestry shows the assault on this latter city of the waters, or that David might not have been present at the assembly of the troops (he is also not present in the last piece of the set, even though, according to the Bible, he presided over the pillage and the massacre that followed the taking of the city) or again that the figure in a helmet with lowered vizor in the middle distance on the left may be David, since all the army is converging on him and he has with him a standard-bearer and a bearded figure on a richly caparisoned horse, who is the Joab of the 10th piece.

15 ft. × 26 ft. 7 in. (4,58 m × 8,11 m)

95
David Sends Uriah to His Death

After seducing Bathsheba (the scene at top left) and later learning that she is pregnant, David calls Uriah back (the scene shown below). But Uriah refuses to go into his house while Joab and the army "are encamped in the open fields." In order to rid himself of the problem of Bathsheba's husband, the king gives him (in the center of the tapestry) a sealed letter to Joab, telling Joab to "set... Uriah in the fore front of the hottest battle, and retire... from him, that he may be smitten, and die."

On the right, Uriah is saying farewell to Bathsheba, an episode not in the biblical story. At the top we see Uriah's death beneath the walls of Rabbah.

14 ft. 9 1/2 in. × 26 ft. 10 in. (4,51 m × 8,18 m)

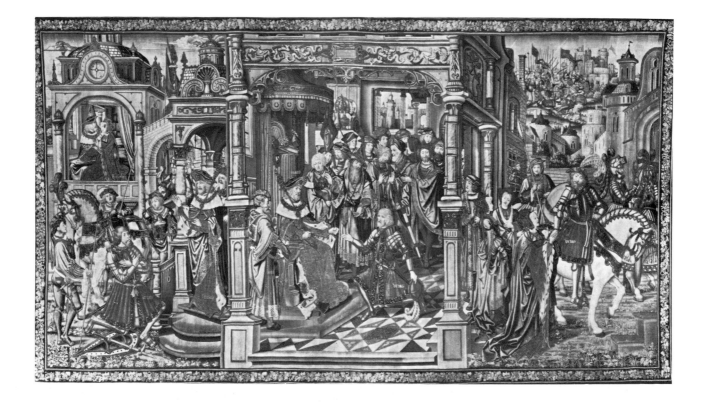

96
Bathsheba Comes to David for the Second Time

When he heard of Uriah's death, "and when the mourning was past, David sent and fetched [Bathsheba] to his house, and she became his wife, and bare him a son." It is this second arrival of Bathsheba, in state, which is magnificently portrayed here.

However, Francis Salet finds it surprising "that this occasion, which would call for discretion, should be interpreted with such ceremony." He suggests that this piece may in fact represent the proclamation of Solomon as heir to the throne, with Bathsheba present as a supplicant to

remind David of the promise he had made to choose her son. But, quite apart from the fact that David is not shown as an old man on the point of death, the author closing the book on the right of the tenth piece clearly indicates that the story ends with the capture of Rabbah, while the other episode took place many years later. Furthermore, Bathsheba's first arrival in the palace, which one really might have expected to be clandestine, is itself shown with the Court present. And if, in the present tapestry, the figure to the right of the central register surveying the scene disapprovingly were taken to be Nathan, his presence would be amply explained by the last sentence of 2 Samuel, chapter XI : "But the thing that David had done displeased the Lord."

15 ft. × 23 ft. 11 in. (4,57 m × 7,27 m)

97
Nathan Admonishes David

In this piece, we see God (top left) sending Nathan to David. The prophet appears before the king, who is seated next to Bathsheba, surrounded by his Court. Nathan tells him the famous parable of the rich man who had many flocks and herds, but who sacrificed the poor man's only ewe lamb. When the rich man's action arouses David's anger, Nathan says : "Thou art the man"; and he threatens him with the direst punishment. But the king repents, as is shown both by his expression and the inscription held by the figure in the bottom left-hand corner : *David a Deo per Natam correptus penitet.* So he is pardoned, but the child of his sinful union dies, as is shown in the next piece, together with David's departure for Rabbah; the ninth and tenth pieces illustrate his victory there.

No. 97 is unique in this set in that its sky is filled with beautifully drawn figures with large wings, personifying; from left to right, Contribution, the Wrath of God, Mercy, Justice, Wisdom, and finally Penitence driving away a charming representation of Lechery.

14 ft. 11 in. × 27 ft. 5 in. (4,56 m × 8,31 m)

We do not know who ordered this work, in which it is hard to decide what to praise most. In every respect it is one of the finest examples of Brussels low-warp weaving at the beginning of the 16th century : in the unity and variety of its scenes, the virtuosity of its composition — the crowds of figures majestically disposed around the principal subject always accompany rather than dominate it — the elegant attitudes, the quiet beauty of the faces, the sumptuous costumes, the rich colors, and the incomparable quality of the weaving with its lavish use of metal threads. Above all, the work is pervaded by a kind of noble solemnity that makes this set a masterpiece of courtly art, created at a time when this art was in the service of the most elegant courts the world has ever known.

Tapestries so perfect could only have been woven for a prince. When they were sold to the Cluny Museum they were said "to have been created for the Court of France," but we have no proof of this. They have also been linked with an order made in 1517 from the great Brussels weaver Pieter de Pannemaker by the Emperor Maximilian of Austria, who wanted to own the same set as the Duke of Juliers and Berg; but this order was only for four pieces. The name of Margaret of Austria, regent of the Netherlands during the minority of her nephew the future Holy Roman Emperor Charles V, has also been suggested for the origin of the commission; but once more, there is no proof that she was the person for whom this set was made, as it does not appear in her inventories. The fact that in the tapestry of *Bathsheba's First Arrival in the Palace* there is a screen similar to one that was being erected in the old ducal palace at Brussels does not imply that it was she who ordered these pieces, this is a much more forceful argument for attributing the cartoons to Jean van Roome, who in 1509-1510 was commissioned to design this screen, as he was the one person best in a position to be familiar with it. Another candidate as patron for this set is King Henry VIII of England; amongst other series, he owned a *Story of David* in ten pieces and another in eleven (there is nothing to prove that the Cluny set is complete, and that it did not, for example, consist of eleven pieces). His possible ownership is supported by the tradition that this series belonged to a Duke of York.

In any case, the cartoons were woven at least twice, and possibly three times, because there are repeats of two of the pieces : one, the *Bringing of the Ark,* is in the Museo de

Santa Cruz at Toledo, and the other, *Preparing to Attack Rabbah,* which bears the arms of the Grompo family, is in the Museo Civico at Padua.

The set was certainly woven at Brussels. At the date suggested by its style, only this city, whose supremacy had by then been established for more than century, was capable of producing such a work. The man responsible for the cartoons of the *David* series was very probably Jean van Roome, the court painter to Margaret of Austria whose role as "eminence grise" of Brabantine art in the first quarter of the 16th century has already been described (see No. 78-80, 85, 87-89). He most likely got help in producing such enormous cartoons, and he also included extraneous elements in his compositions, apparently borrowed from earlier works (e.g. the cup-bearer in the left foreground of No. 97) as well as touches of Italian influence, as in the Wrath of God at the top of the same piece. But he was in all probability the conductor for this vast symphony. Quite apart from the evidence in *Bathsheba's First Arrival in the Palace* that the cartoonist was familiar with the statued screen in the Balienhof at Brussels (never completed and today totally destroyed — at the time it was hardly past the drawing stage); we find here the same kind of elements as in the *Communion of Herkinbald.* There are closely packed figures disposed with a sure sense of mural composition, a very high horizon, heavy draperies falling in deep folds, expressions of dreamy, serene sadness, and in several of the pieces, the same rhythm created by a mixture of Renaissance and Gothic architecture. We may thus assume that the *David and Bathsheba* set is roughly contemporary with *Herkinbald,* for which Jean van Roome made the small

pattern to the order of the Brotherhood of Louvain, and we may date it around 1510-1515.

In its crowded figural composition and its juxtaposition of several scenes in some of the pieces it is still a medieval work; but there are already signs of a new spirit, not only in the composite nature of the architecture, but also in a more open layout, a certain attempt at perspective, and the presence of wide landscapes in some of the pieces (e.g. No. 94). Dating from the time just before Raphael set the art of tapestry off on a new direction, on that of the woven picture, with his *Arts of the Apostles* which were woven at Brussels for the Sistine Chapel in the Vatican, the *David* series is thus a link between two worlds — one of the most brilliant manifestations of an art that was at the summit of its technique, playing for the Northern countries the part of the fresco in Italy, and one of the world's great masterpieces.

The David *set is believed to have belonged to a Duke of York and the marquesses of Spinola before coming into the collection of the Serra family of Genoa; it was bought by the Cluny Museum in 1847.*

BIBLIOGRAPHY. Elisabeth Dhanens, *The David and Bathsheba drawing,* in *Gazette des Beaux-Arts,* April 1959, p. 215-224, fig. — Ministère des Affaires Culturelles, *Le XVIe siècle européen. Tapisseries, Paris, Mobilier national, octobre 1965-janvier 1966.* (Paris, Réunion des Musées nationaux, 1965), no 20, p. 34-35 and pl. 41 *(Preparing to attack Rabbah).* — Geneviève Souchal, *La tenture* de David *et la Bible,* in *Gazette des Beaux-Arts,* Jan. 1968, p. 17-32, 10 fig.; idem, *Expositions, Galeries nationales du Grand Palais,* La tenture de David *du musée de Cluny,* in *Revue du Louvre,* 22nd year, no 1, 1972, p. 43-50, 6 fig., 1 pl. col. — F. Salet, *Au Grand Palais,* La tenture de David *du musée de Cluny,* in *Archaeologia,* no 45, March-April 1972, p. 34-43, 5 fig., 1 pl. col.